CROCKETT'S INDOOR GARDEN

PHOTOGRAPHY BY
RUSSELL MORASH

LITTLE, BROWN
AND COMPANY
BOSTON/TORONTO

CROCKETT'S INDOOR GARDEN

BY JAMES UNDERWOOD CROCKETT

WITH THE ASSISTANCE OF **MARJORIE WATERS**

First Edition
T 10/78

Designed by
Dianne Smith/Designworks

Botanical Drawings by
Robin Brickman

Instructional Drawings by
George Ulrich

Published simultaneously in
Canada
by Little, Brown & Company
(Canada) Limited

Printed in the United States of
America

Library of Congress Cataloging in Publication Data
Crockett, James Underwood.
    Crockett's indoor garden.

    Includes index.
    1.   Indoor gardening.   2.   House plants.
3.   Greenhouse plants.   I.   Title.
SB419.C67   635.9′65   78-8939
ISBN 0-316-16124-1
ISBN 0-316-16126-8 pbk.

Acknowledgments When my wife, Margaret, encouraged me to write my first book more than twenty years ago, I'm sure she didn't realize how seriously I would take her suggestion. Nor could she have known how grateful I was and continue to be for the love and support without which each book would have been a labor rather than an adventure.

Every author owes debts to countless individuals whose teachings, reassurances, and plain hard work help to bring his book into being. I have but to recall that this book would not have been written were it not for a chain of circumstances that led Russell Morash, the producer-director of *Crockett's Victory Garden*, to ask me to host a television gardening program. One of his many talents appears on nearly every page of this book, for he photographed all the plants you see in such vivid color. As for my editor, William D. Phillips, Senior Editor at Little, Brown and Company, I can only say, "He did it again," pulling off a minor miracle in getting this book to the printer on time. His method combines coaxing and coercion, tugging here, pushing there, always available for questions, always affable even under stress; without him this book would still be just an idea. Marjorie Waters was responsible for getting much of this book on paper; she and I talked for endless hours into a tape recorder, she translated television scripts into the written word; I am deeply mindful of and thankful for her assistance. Dianne Smith of Designworks brought a combination of beauty, order, and practicality to the design of the book. She was assisted by Mary Reilly. George Ulrich made the easy-to-understand how-to sketches; Robin Brickman is the artist who created more than 130 line drawings of plants, so beautiful you'll want to frame them. Little, Brown's Mike Mattil is the copy editor, a man very clever with words; Peter Carr is the General Manager of Manufacturing for Little, Brown who supervised the production of the book, and Donna Baxter and Rachel Bunker were Peter's production assistants.

Donald R. Cutler, my literary agent, provided invaluable help with the business arrangements for this project. My daughter Jean, a journalism student, was the person behind the scenes who typed letter-perfect manuscripts practically overnight. Each of us who worked on this book is profoundly appreciative of her cooperation. Finally, I would like to thank Wilson's Farms, Lexington Gardens, Michael Kartuz of Kartuz Greenhouses, Inc., and John Pelrine, our marvelous gardener who helps keep Crockett's Victory Garden in shape, for their assistance and cooperation.

To Margaret, with whom I've shared my life and indoor garden for more than 35 years, this book is affectionately dedicated.

CONTENTS

TWELVE MONTHS IN THE INDOOR GARDEN

On a north-facing windowsill beside my desk, half-hidden among the African violets, sits a Neapolitan cyclamen, a cloud of pink violet-sized blossoms rising above it as they have each autumn for the last decade. It's a very special plant to me because I started it from a seed more than ten years ago, one I obtained in a seed-distribution program from The Royal Horticultural Society of London. It's an old and dependable friend and, like other friends, has been my companion through days of joy and triumph, of tragedy and grief.

It's that way with houseplants. Beyond their present beauty lie the deeper realms of love and memory. If you're an indoor gardener I'm sure you have at least one plant, given to you in love or inherited from a friend or relative, whose very sight evokes pleasant recollections. I understand these emotions well because I have plants that my mother once cherished and each time I see them she comes alive again in my mind, full of laughter and the love of family and flowers.

All my life I've loved plants, every kind of plant — growing in gardens, living wild in nature, nurtured in flowerpots. It's been a lifetime adventure: I recall at age three planting a dried bean, one my mother was getting ready to bake for Saturday night supper, in an old china teacup, using soil from around the morning glory vines that climbed the trellis beside the porch, in those days called the veranda or piazza. By the time I was in school I was a devoted gardener, happier tending to my flowers than playing baseball, although that was part of the fun of childhood too. My hero was an ancient gentleman named Mr. Barnes, the owner of an equally venerable greenhouse in which he raised some of the most beautiful flowers I had ever seen. To a child he seemed ageless — I suppose he was in his seventies or early eighties when I first knew him. Slow-moving, with bent back, his face wrinkling in a smile each time I went to see him, he was an inspiration to me long before my tenth year. While my friends rewrote their futures weekly — policeman, doctor, rodeo star — my sights were unchanged. I wanted nothing more than to spend my life with plants and that's exactly what I've done. I'm a very fortunate man.

This book is a logical extension of *Crockett's Victory Garden*, the book about vegetables that grew out of my experiences as a television gardener in the PBS series of the same name. Even that book had a sprinkling of flower and houseplant culture along with the vegetables, for I have never grown an all-vegetable garden, nor neglected my indoor garden. In fact, as I read viewers' mail I sense that most gardeners think of me as a family plant doctor — some even ask me to make house calls — who understands African violets and birds-of-paradise as well as asparagus, beets, and broccoli. So apparent is my love of all growing things that one of the most frequently asked questions is, "Jim, what is your favorite plant?"

Although I have no one favorite, that question figured prominently in my selection of plants for this book: first, I had to like each plant myself. It also had to be one that indoor gardeners could find readily and it had to be one whose culture was possible for most of my readers. To make

this last point clear, I have keyed each plant, over 130 of them, according to its ease of culture. Those that require simple care are noted with this symbol: ⊟; more demanding plants that need special attention are marked ♟; and for those lucky people who have a greenhouse I have a category designated ⬠ to indicate those plants that can only be grown successfully under greenhouse conditions.

It may come as a surprise to you that a book about houseplants should be written on a calendar basis: it surprises me that so few other authors follow the natural pattern of the seasons. Even indoors, growing conditions vary from month to month and every experienced gardener knows it. Geraniums that sit and sulk in the short, dreary days of November begin to perk up and send out bright blossoms in response to the lengthening days of the new year. It's true that some tropical plants fit as well into one month as another, especially foliage plants; these are interspersed among the months on a space-available basis. But most flowering plants answer the call of nature's ageless rhythm, the cycle of the seasons. Such plants will be found in the month of their greatest beauty, along with a full explanation of their needs throughout the year.

The plant entries themselves are quite detailed because there is no shorthand for good houseplant care. I cannot tolerate ambiguity; what is more, I realize that many of my readers are beginning gardeners and I cannot assume much depth to their horticultural experience. You will find this book easy to understand. To reinforce this thought in your mind I must tell you another story about myself. Many persons know me because they watch my television program each week; others recognize me as the author of about twenty books on gardening, but neither of these endeavors is my bread-and-butter living. Instead, my livelihood is derived from *Flowery Talks*, a monthly booklet on houseplant care that I have been writing for over thirty years. Retail florists and garden centers all over the United States use *Flowery Talks* as educational advertising, distributing copies to their customers so that they will have sound, down-to-earth advice on the culture of the plants they purchase. It is my practical experience in writing about houseplant care for all parts of the country that permits me to say with confidence that the cultural advice you find in this book will be useful to you.

When writing about houseplants, one always has to face the issue of how to identify them. The scholarly community relies entirely on botanical names, but average gardeners don't understand or use them. They use common names: African violet, jade plant, weeping fig tree. Common names

aren't precise, and some plants are saddled with dozens of them; but they are the familiar language. In some cases, as with a cyclamen or coleus, the botanical and common names are the same. In cases where the common and botanical names are different, I've used the one I think most people will recognize. There are regional differences in plant names, though, and the one I've picked may not be the one you know. All the common names appear in the entries, if not in the headlines, and are listed in the index as well. You should be able to find any plant listed in the book, no matter what you call it. (For more information about the language of botany, see the Appendix, page 313). Just in case you don't know a plant's name, you can still find it by scanning the botanical drawings that accompany each plant-care entry. These show the shape and structure of each plant for easy identification.

As in *Crockett's Victory Garden*, I have attempted to answer at the end of each chapter a selection of the thousands of questions we received at the WGBH Victory Garden from our viewers. You will also find monthly features on general aspects of houseplant care and culture that should be useful to you no matter what kind of plant you grow.

Let me conclude with a few words concerning the blessings that houseplants bestow upon the gardener in return for loving care. If you are already an indoor gardener, you are aware that the growing of houseplants opens up a whole new world of natural beauty. Indoor gardening is an intimate experience because the plants themselves are close at hand, often at eye level. Indeed, the discoveries we make as we undertake indoor gardening are analogous to the mysteries that unfold as we peer through a microscope. A field of flowers excites us by its blaze of color, but indoor blossoms invite us to examine the architectural perfection of leaf and flower and to marvel at the combination of strength and grace, the diversity of design from one plant to another.

I have said that I feel as though I'm among friends when I'm with my plants, but I am not alone here, for this sensation is common to all those who love plants. Plants are like friends who take us as we are, happy or sad; who sit quietly with us when words would be out of place, who soothe our anxious minds and help us put our cares aside.

I urge you to become a gardener, especially an indoor gardener. Start with a few plants or even seeds, anticipate their germination and growth, nurture their adolescence, thrill to the loveliness of their maturity. Remember that a gardener's year is a never-ending cycle of seedtime and harvest, of planning ahead, of constant guidance, of confident expectancy, of unknown joys still to come.

JAN

Feature: Sowing and Growing from Seed

Hybrid cattleya orchid

JAN

Throughout all but the warmest sections of the country the outdoor world is frozen and still in January, but next month will bring the first early days of spring, the time of the year when the gardener is busiest, pruning and repotting to prepare plants for their warm-weather growth. I'd suggest taking advantage of the January lull to organize and stock your work area so you'll be ready when the plants are.

First of all you'll need a working surface that can take some abuse, either an old table or a sheet of plywood set over another table or counter top. The spring gardening jobs often call for new containers, so collect several sizes and types, including small pots and flats for cuttings and seeds and a variety of larger ones for repotting. Buy a bottle of mild liquid houseplant fertilizer and a bag each of general-purpose potting soil and African violet soil. You'll need drainage stones, ½ inch or less in diameter, when you repot large plants. For rooting cuttings, get a bag of coarse sand (available, like crushed pebbles useful for drainage, from lumber companies as well as garden centers) along with a bag each of perlite and vermiculite, as well as a package of powdered rooting hormone. A bag of peat moss is essential, as it is often a recommended ingredient in rooting and potting mediums. For the sake of tidiness, you might want to transfer these loose, bagged materials into covered glass or plastic containers. (Small trash containers with clip-on tops are very useful for this purpose.) Finally, treat yourself to a truly fine pair of pruning shears and a sharp, strong-bladed knife for tough root divisions. You will never regret buying the finest quality shears and knife you can afford.

Now you can consider yourself very well-stocked indeed, and move on to some of the earliest of the spring chores. If you want flowering kalanchoes, ornamental peppers, and Jerusalem cherries to be at their peak in December, this is the month to start their seeds. And if you're thinking ahead to bedding and window box plants, start your seeds of wax begonias, browallias, and impatiens this month, so you'll have healthy young seedlings by early summer. Golden trumpets, flowering maples, passionflowers, and calamondin oranges will all appreciate a pruning this month to get them into shape for spring.

African Violet *(Saintpaulia)* Most beginning gardeners approach African violets with fear in their hearts, but they needn't. African violets are far and away the most popular flowering houseplants in this country, and they could hardly have risen to that lofty spot if they were as delicate as people seem to think. In fact, they're among the easiest of all flowering houseplants, and one of the few that stay in flower all year long. Their botanical name is *Saintpaulia*, in honor of their discoverer, Baron Walter von Saint Paul, who came upon them in 1893 in a warm shady spot in what was then called German East Africa. True to these origins, they want warm temperatures — nights in the high 60s and days 75 degrees or better — and bright indirect light. I usually give my plants either a north- or east-facing window, where the light is bright but not sunny. If you have no choice but to put them in a sunny window, shade them with a gauzy curtain. If you have the opposite problem, and have no place for them but a spot so dark that the normally horizontal foliage begins to reach upward, you will still have a fine collection if you supplement your dim light with artificial. In fact, many ribbon-winning African violets are grown entirely un-

An African violet plant enjoying a flush of bloom

African Violet *(Saintpaulia)*

9

der artificial light. (For more about how to do this, see the February feature.)

African violets are a trifle touchy about their watering routine. They have delicate fibrous roots that are easily damaged if they're allowed to dry out, so keep the soil barely moist all the time. I usually water my plants every day or so and unless I'm fertilizing, I bottom-water, leaving them in a saucer of water for about half a day. The leaves will develop permanent ugly white splotches if cold water hits them, so always use tepid water. Don't let this scare you away from giving the plants regular baths, though. Their foliage will stay bright and clean if they're washed with the kitchen spray — just make sure the water is room temperature or warmer. They appreciate the humidity provided by a humidifying tray, but don't mist the foliage with an atomizer; fuzzy-leaved plants should never be misted.

Most gardeners make the mistake of overfeeding their African violets, which destroys the plants' delicate roots. I find that they're sufficiently nourished if they have monthly feedings of any houseplant fertilizer, diluted to half strength and applied directly to the surface of the soil. If you fertilize by bottom-watering, a white stain is apt to form on the surface of the soil as the fertilizer collects and crystalizes. This problem can sometimes be solved by top-watering carefully for a few days to flush the soil clean, but you're usually better off repotting the plant in fresh soil.

If they're happy, modern African violet varieties are never without flowers; they have flushes of growth, when they're dense with blossoms, and then slack periods when they bear only a few. If your plant isn't blossoming at all, something is wrong, and my guess would be that the culprit is either darkness or chill. It won't flower if it's given too little light. The clue here is that the foliage aims upward, rather than lies flat as it should. African violets won't flower if the night temperatures drop below the mid-60s either; in fact, if the thermometer drops below 55 degrees, they die. Overcrowding might be the villain, too. If you see new crowns of foliage developing, which is a normal occurrence, separate them; just use a sharp knife, and make sure that each rosette of foliage has a few roots to call its own. Finally, a nonblossoming plant may be infested with cyclamen mites; the leaves will be contorted and curled, and look very hairy in the center of the crown. If that's your problem, throw the plant away — it's not worth saving, and it certainly isn't worth infesting your other plants. (You can apply this information to buying a new plant, too. Select one with a single crown of healthy, horizontal leaves, and a good supply of young buds.)

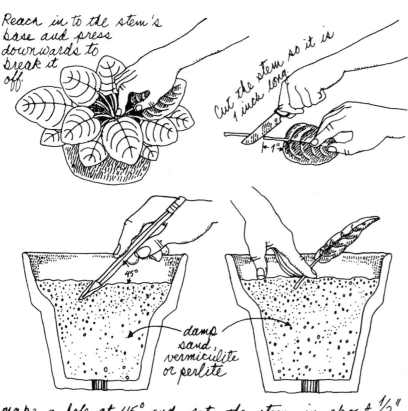

Reach in to the stem's base and press downwards to break it off.

Cut the stem so it is 1 inch long.

←1"→

45°

damp sand, vermiculite or perlite

make a hole at 45° and set the stem in about ½"

African violets are easily multiplied by leaf cuttings — technically called leaf petiole cuttings because they include an entire leaf and part of its stem, or petiole. Start with a leaf that is healthy and of medium growth, neither the plant's youngest nor oldest leaf. Reach in to the stem's base and press it downward. Usually the leaf snaps off cleanly; if a bit of the stem is left behind, cut it off, or it will rot. Then cut the leaf's stem so it's no more than 1 inch long, not including the length of the leaf, and insert it about ½ inch deep in damp sand, vermiculite, perlite, or a mixture of these three. Don't set the leaf stem in straight up; use a pencil to make a hole at an angle of about 45 degrees, and then set the cutting in. In about 3 months, one or more tiny plants will have developed at the soil line. When the leaves of these new plants are ¼ to ½ inch long, dig them up and wash off the roots. If you've gotten more than one little plant for your efforts, carefully separate the crowns into single divisions and plant them in individual pots in African violet soil. These new plants will begin to flower when they're about 5 months old, and they'll continue to blossom month after month until they reach stalky old age, which for African violets is about four years.

11

The second stalk of this amaryllis was in bloom by the time the first flowers faded

 **Amaryllis** *(Hippeastrum)* The botanical name for this plant, *Hippeastrum* (hip-e-*ast*-rum), means horse star, a justifiable reference to the massive size of this starry six-pointed bloom, some 8 to 10 inches across; the plants produce 3 or 4 flowers at a time atop each thick 1- or 2-foot stem. Usually, just as the first flowers fade, the bulb sends up a second gigantic flower stalk. (We once had a plant in the Victory Garden greenhouse that produced two stems, each with 8 flowers, twice the usual number. It was a plant we had carried over from a previous season.)

Amaryllises grow from enormous bulbs — nearly as big as a grapefruit and weighing a couple of pounds. The larger the bulbs, the more expensive they are, and the larger the flowers they produce. Sometimes you'll see bulbs identified only by color — either white, pink, orange, red, or striped. These are seed-started bulbs, and they are not the best choice. The superior varieties are propagated vegetatively, to guarantee identical plants, and are sold by name. Some of the best of these are Appleblossom, a pale pink; Beautiful Lady, salmon orange; Fire Dance, a well-named bright red; Scarlet Admiral, dark red; and White Giant, which is white. So whether you're buying bulbs to pot up yourself, or potted plants just about to bloom, pick large,

12

choose a pot that will leave about 1" around the bulb.

when potted, the bulb should be about halfway out of the soil.

½" Coarse gravel

named amaryllises. You'll pay a bit more for them, but the bulbs last forever, produce more and bigger flowers year after year, and propagate themselves by sending out basal offsets. Think of them as a long-term investment.

Amaryllis plants appreciate tight quarters. If the pot's too large, the leaves develop at the expense of the flowers. I use a standard pot that's about 2 inches larger in diameter than the bulb, which allows a narrow 1-inch margin all around the bulb. When I pot an amaryllis I first put ½ inch of coarse gravel or pebbles at the bottom of the container. When potted, an amaryllis bulb should be about halfway out of the soil. The roots grow from the base of the bulb, so hold the bulb suspended over the pot with the roots hanging down, and then fill in the pot with a well-drained commercial potting soil, firming the soil against the roots. Sometimes, after being stored, the roots are brittle and easily snapped off, so firm the soil carefully. Then water the soil thoroughly and set the pot aside to drain. Too much water in the first days is apt to rot the roots, so don't water it again until the bulb shows signs of growth. There's no way to predict how long the plants will take to produce that first growth; they seem to have minds of their own. Some send up flower stalks right away, others continue to rest for a few months, but eventually all mature bulbs send up blossoms. I usually start in October, and pot up a few bulbs every couple of weeks until December; as a rule I have plants in bloom from late November through March.

The first sign of growth is usually the flower bud itself; the foliage often doesn't develop until the flowers are opening. Once this bud is visible, I put the plant on its normal routine: constantly moist soil, food once a month, at least half a day of sunshine, and mild temperatures, with nights in the 60s and day readings in the 70s. When the blossoms open — the plants bloom for about a month — I shade them a bit from the full glare of the sun, and keep them a little cooler; this keeps the flowers fresher longer.

Hybrid Amaryllis *(Hippeastrum)*

Many gardeners eventually have the same hard-luck story with asparagus ferns. They buy a beauty of a plant — rich, soft, deep green. Within a year they have a sparse, spindly, yellowing plant with dry, brittle stems. The reason for this is simple. The asparagus fern is an extremely fast grower; in a matter of months its roots fill the pot, leaving the soil exhausted and unable to hold water or nutrients enough to keep the plant going. So it becomes spindly, yellow, and brittle. When you find yourself having to submerge your plant in a bucket of water to get enough moisture into it, it's time to divide. If you don't act at this point, the thick succulent roots of the plant — the swollen sections of these roots look like giant white beetles — will continue to seek food and moisture, and they will appear at the surface of the soil. Then it is *certainly* time to divide. I've had plants with such strong, thirsty roots that they've actually burst the pot open.

The division itself is uncomplicated. Just knock the plant out of the pot — watch out for the sharp, thorny foliage — and cut all the stems down to the soil level. (I know some gardeners grow so attached to their plants that they try to divide them without cutting the foliage back, but this produces a lopsided plant.) Then use a sharp butcher knife and slice down from the surface of the soil to the base. Each division should be 3 or 4 inches across. Reset the individual sections in separate 6-inch pots, in a commercial potting soil, and stand back, for the plants will grow quickly. You'll have several handsome plants — rich, soft, and deeply colored — in 2 or 3 months.

Cut all the stems down to soil level, then cut down from the surface to the base with a sharp knife, making each section three or four inches across. Replant the sections in commercial potting soil, each in its own six-inch pot.

Asparagus plants can be started from seed, too. You can either buy the seeds from a seed house (see this month's feature), or you can harvest them from your own plants, provided that you have both a male and a female of the same species. If the tiny pinkish-white flowers are pollinated when they open, which is usually in the spring, the female plants produce ¼-inch berries that turn from white to green to red to black. When they're black, pinch them off and plant them in a moist medium. Most of them will germinate.

⌂ **Calendula** *(Calendula)* This native Mediterranean annual is an extremely versatile plant. Sometimes called pot-marigold, it's a familiar and popular herb that's been used for generations both in herbal medicines and in cooking. And it's beautiful, too. In a cool greenhouse it can be brought into bloom any time of the year, depending on when the seed is planted (its name comes from the Latin *calendae*, meaning "throughout the months"). Each individual flower lasts for weeks, whether left on the plant or cut and arranged in a vase. Calendulas are available in either single or double flowers, and in every shade of yellow and orange imaginable. Standard calendulas grow to be about 20 inches tall, and are

This semi-double calendula, some 3 inches across, will make a fine cut flower

Dwarf Calendula *(Calendula)*

the best choice if you're after cut flowers. The dwarf plants are nicer if you're interested in a pot plant; they grow to be about 8 inches tall, with flowers some 3 or 4 inches across, about the same sized bloom as the standards. The standards grow so tall that their weak stems will be crooked unless they're given three tiers of string-and-wire supports. The dwarf plants don't need any support.

Calendulas need sun all day and cool temperatures — never higher than 50 degrees at night and 65 during the day. That all but limits them to the greenhouse owner. If you don't have a greenhouse, buy a plant ready to bloom and give it the sunniest spot in the house — by which I mean sun virtually all day long. Or you might try starting them off outdoors in August, bringing them in before the first frost and setting them on your sunniest windowsill. Keep them moist, cool, and sunny, and I believe they'll bloom for you.

We have a large greenhouse in the Victory Garden and can keep one corner cool enough for plants like these, so I can usually sow calendula seeds in that cool spot in August or September and I have flowers from November through May. If your greenhouse is still too warm in late summer, start the plants off outside, and then bring them into the greenhouse before the frost. For the dwarf plants I use commercial potting soil and 2½- or 3-inch flowerpots or peat pots, and set 2 seeds in each pot. When the seedlings are about 1 inch tall, I cut off the weaker one. Calendula seedlings grow at quite a pace, so I keep an eye on them, and when the roots fill the small pots I transplant them into 6- to 8-inch pots. They branch naturally so they don't need to be pinched.

The standard-sized plants need different attention. Start them off in pots, but transplant them into greenhouse benches with 8 to 12 inches between them in all directions. When they're about 4 inches tall, pinch out the tips of the main stems to encourage the plants to send out side branches, which means more flowers. Don't forget the string-and-wire supports.

Be careful not to overfeed calendulas, as this encourages succulent, weak stems with few flowers. For signs of hunger, watch the leaf color closely: as long as it's dark green, don't feed; when it begins to show a paler tone, feed with any houseplant fertilizer.

Calendulas develop thick, fuzzy foliage that, during the winter, should be kept as dry as possible to prevent botrytis leaf fungus. A preventive spray of benomyl will keep the leaves free of this unwanted visitor, but I prefer to space my plants so they will have good air circulation and when I water, I'm careful to wet the soil, not the foliage.

18

Camellia *(Camellia)* I have a friend, now in her late eighties, who has a spectacular camellia collection. She lives in a great old New England house, and keeps her camellias in a front hall that's barely heated, where they bear hundreds of flowers every fall and winter. If you have a cool, bright room for them and are willing to attend to their needs, you'll probably have the same good luck, and keep your plants like old friends year after year after year. I've had a number of camellias myself for twenty-six years, and they still blossom profusely every winter. If you can't keep them cool enough, though, they'll only be disappointing.

The best camellias for growing indoors are selections of the common camellia (*C. japonica*), the netvein camellia (*C. reticulata*), and camellia hybrids. Each named variety blooms for about 6 weeks, but by choosing early, midseason, and late varieties, it's possible to have plants in flower from mid-October to mid-April. The blossoms of the common camellia look like roses or peonies and run from 2 to 5 inches across, amid shiny leaves. It comes in both single- and double-flowering forms, and there are hundreds of each available

This lovely camellia blossom was borne on a plant only 8 inches tall

19

Common Camellia *(Camellia)*

from garden centers or through the mail. (The common camellia is an outdoor plant in the South and along the West Coast; sometimes it's known simply as a japonica.) The flowers of the netvein camellia are similar in beauty to the common camellia, but a little larger; the foliage is dull and leathery.

Camellias have evergreen foliage and flowers in white, red, and pink, sometimes aiming toward magenta. As a rule they are not fragrant, but there are a few delightful exceptions: my favorite is a huge pink camellia called Scentsation. All camellias make wonderful cut flowers, and they'll live for a whole beautiful week floated in a shallow bowl of water. Take care when you're working with the blossoms — they'll turn brown if crushed and fall off if they're handled roughly. The safest way to hold them is from underneath the flower.

Camellias do their best in bright indirect light or curtain-filtered sunlight. Their temperature needs vary according to their stage of growth: when they're in flower they need night temperatures in the low 50s and days no higher than 68 degrees; during the late summer, when the buds are forming, they do best with night temperatures in the low 60s and days as cool as possible. I usually set my plants outside in a shady spot during the summer months, and when I bring them inside in the fall the ends of the stems are clustered with fat flower buds. Sometimes I let all these buds flower and other times I disbud the plants — picking off all but one bud from each cluster — which produces enormous flowers but far fewer of them.

Camellias can be started from seed, but I don't recommend it unless you have patience: they won't flower for at least four years — I have waited as long as seven years — and they're likely to revert to the wild species, which is nowhere near as nice as the modern selections. The better and easier approach is to propagate from stem cuttings of firm current season's growth taken in late summer or fall; several mail-order companies sell rooted camellia cuttings and/or young plants. The cuttings grow slowly, too, but they can start flowering when no more than 6 to 10 inches tall. Use a mixture of equal parts moist peat moss and sand, or a commercial potting soil recommended for African violets. The important thing is that the soil should be acid, with a pH of 4.5 or 5.0: if the soil is too alkaline, the foliage turns yellow with dark green veins. If you find yourself with this problem, water the plants with a solution of 1 ounce of iron sulfate, available from a druggist, to 2 gallons of water, or use iron chelate, available at any garden center. The frequency of application depends on the pH of your local water supply; in alkaline areas monthly applications may be required. I keep the soil constantly moist, and I feed them three times a year — in early spring, late spring, and midsummer. An acid fertilizer recommended for camellias, azaleas, and rhododendrons is fine. So is cottonseed meal, a good slow-acting, nonburning organic fertilizer; use about 2 tablespoons to a 10-inch pot at each application.

There is absolutely no reason for camellias to die of old age, provided they're happy. They'll live practically forever, and given a chance they'll grow into small trees. But I think they're nicer kept pruned to 3 feet tall or so; that's the height I keep my plants, by root- and top-pruning, and they're dense with blossoms every year. Cramped quarters help control their growth, too; so I only repot my camellias when they're completely pot-bound, usually every three to four years. The time to repot camellias is immediately after they have finished flowering in the late winter or early spring, just as new vegetative growth begins.

Cape Cowslip (*Lachenalia*) Gardeners in the Southwest are sometimes able to grow these natives of the Cape of Good Hope outdoors, but for most of the country they are strictly indoor bulb plants, and lovely, delicate ones at that. The ribbonlike leaves hug the soil and are sometimes splattered with purple — a trait responsible for one of the plant's common names, leopard lily. Above the foliage each bulb sends up one or two 6- to 8-inch spikes heavy with as many as two dozen tubular flowers in yellow, orange, or red.

Cape cowslips are easily available but for the most part unknown. I think gardeners take a look at the unfamiliar name and decide to stick with the old standbys — daffodils and tulips. It's too bad this happens because Cape cowslips are much easier to grow. The bulbs, each less than 1 inch in diameter, are available in August and September for immediate potting up. I usually put six bulbs together in a 5-inch pan (placed individually, the plants would look insignificant), setting them 1 to 2 inches apart in a soil mix composed of equal parts potting soil, peat moss, and either sharp sand or perlite; I add ¾ tablespoon of ground limestone per quart of this mix. No drainage material is needed for such small bulbs in such a small pot. The potted bulbs should sit about ½ inch below the surface of the soil. Once they're planted, I water them well once and set them on the coolest, brightest windowsill in the house. The night temperatures shouldn't run higher than 50 degrees.

When the foliage appears the plant is ready for its normal culture. It needs at least 4 hours of direct sunlight every day, even when it's in bloom. It wants moist soil, night

The buds at the tip of these Cape cowslips will open as fully as the flowers lower on the stem.

21

Cape Cowslip *(Lachenalia)*

temperatures in the 40s or 50s and days no warmer than 68 degrees. Many bulbs need to recuperate from forcing by spending a few seasons out in the garden, but Cape cowslips can be forced year after year, so I give them a drink of fertilizer every month to help them keep up their strength. The flowers will last up to two months — the cooler they're kept, the longer they'll last — but by this time of the year their flowering season will be drawing to a close. When the flowers begin to fade, gradually withhold the amount of water until the leaves die back. Then let them dry out entirely and set the plant in a sunny hot spot for the summer. When September comes, repot the bulbs in fresh soil and start the process again.

The best way to increase Cape cowslips is by separating the new bulbs that develop next to the old ones. Segregate the bulbs by size. Pot the little ones, too, to give them a chance to grow to flowering size. Cape cowslips can also be grown from seeds sown in the fall; seed-started plants will flower in about three years.

A hybrid cattleya orchid

Cattleya Orchid *(Cattleya)* This is the most familiar of all orchids; it's the one most often used in corsages, the orchid that *looks* like most persons' concept of an orchid. And if you've never grown an orchid before, this is an excellent one to start with. Most of the cattleya (*katt*-lee-a, after William Cattley) orchids available today are hybrids: they're the easiest to grow, produce the handsomest colors, and can blossom as often as three times a year. The hybrids are sometimes labeled as Cattleya alliance. (If you'd like to give the wild species a try, these make good choices: *C. labiata; C. trianae*, known as the Christmas orchid; *C. mossiae*, known as the Easter orchid; and *C. gaskelliana.* The wild species usually bloom only once a year.)

To understand the culture of cattleya orchids, it's helpful to know their habit of growth, which is so different from that of most ordinary plants. As epiphytes or air plants in the jungles of Central and South America, they cling to tree branches, sending along the surface of the branch a zigzag stem called a rhizome. The roots protrude from the lower side of the rhizome, either clinging to the bark or hanging in the air. From the top of the rhizome grow the stems that bear the leaves and flowers. The stems are unique in that the lower part of each is swollen to serve as a moisture reservoir when rainfall is scanty; technically this part of the stem is called a pseudobulb, meaning false bulb. Above the pseudobulb appears one or two long, succulent, straplike leaves that cling to the pseudobulb for a number of years. The flowers are produced at the juncture of the pseudobulb and leaf, appearing first as a flattened sheath of tender tissue; eventually the flower buds push their way through the sheath and open into some of the most beautiful flowers in the world. After flowering, the plants enter a rest period to build up strength for the next season of blooms.

Don't be scared away from orchids on the grounds of expense. There was a time when they were costly indeed, but a new propagation technique — called meristemming — so cuts down on the production time of young plants that it's possible to buy flowering-sized cattleya orchids for as little as $5.00 (or as much as $1,000.00 or more). The very expensive ones are either rare types or especially exquisite new hybrids. If you're a beginner at growing orchids I'd suggest that you indulge in some instant gratification by buying mature plants "in sheath," meaning that the flower buds are nearly ready to open. If you're more experienced and feeling patient, young seedlings are less expensive and more interesting, though they may be several years away from their first bloom. If you do start with seedlings it will be your privilege to be the first to see their blossoms, each of which is somewhat different from all others, even if their seeds come from the same pod. (As babies, they require diligent attention to prevent drying out and need to be shifted to ever-larger pots as they increase in size.)

All year long, whether in active growth or resting, cattleya orchids need at least 4 hours of muted sunshine every day; the full sun is too much for them, so a gauzy shield is in order. They need night temperatures in the mid-50- to mid-60-degree range and 68 degrees or higher during daytime. They also crave high humidity; I place mine on a humidifying tray and let the planting medium become moderately dry between thorough waterings. The frequency of watering depends on the dryness of the atmosphere, the temperature, and whether the plant is in a growing or resting period. During their after-flowering rest period, they should not be fed, nor should they be overwatered. The length of the rest period varies, but its end is signaled by the appearance, just beneath the last pseudobulb, of a fat pointed bud. This means that the growing period has begun, and watering should be stepped up and continued until the next blossoms have opened and faded, signifying the end of a growth cycle. This is the only period — from the first sign of new growth through the appearance of flowers — that I feed cattleya orchids. I do so monthly with a special orchid fertilizer, such as 30-10-10, 18-18-18, or 10-30-20.

Orchids are divided into two categories according to the direction of their growth, and the two types are potted up differently. Monopodial orchids grow vertically, producing foliage along upright stems. Sympodial orchids grow horizon-

Species Cattleya Orchid
(*Cattleya trianae*)

23

galvanized wire extending about 12 inches above the rim to support the foliage.

a layer or two of clay shards on the bottom.

Plant the rhizome at the side of the pot with the newest end pointing toward the center

The rhizome should rest on the surface when finished.

Loosely tie the foliage to the wire support.

tally, sending up from the rhizome a series of pseudobulbs, each topped by one or more leaves, producing a trail of pseudobulbs and foliage across the surface of the growing medium; each pseudobulb and leaf or leaves produces a flower or flowers at the juncture of the pseudobulb and leaf as it matures. The cattleya orchid is sympodial, so I'll provide the directions for repotting this type of orchid here; directions for handling a monopodial orchid are given in the April chapter under moth orchid.

Eventually, as the seasons pass, the rhizomes of sympodial orchids creep clear across the width of the flowerpot. When they start over the edge it's time to divide the plant into pieces of rhizome containing four or more pseudobulbs and plant each division individually. As weak-stemmed plants that grow sideways, sympodial orchids need to be provided with room enough to grow — I use a pot that will accommodate two or three years of growth to delay the next repotting — and a support system for the weak foliage. I use an upright wire stake of aluminum or galvanized wire whose lower end is bent so that it rests snugly on the bottom of the pot and extends some 12 inches above the rim. As the foliage develops I tie it loosely to the stake.

24

Once the stake is in place in the pot, I add a layer or two of pieces of broken clay flowerpots, called shards, to provide the best possible drainage and air circulation for these air-hungry plants and then fill the pot halfway with planting medium. Some growers use shredded tree fern fiber or osmunda fiber as a planting medium; I usually make up my own mix of 2 parts fir bark and 1 part coarse sphagnum moss. Whichever medium is used, it should be thoroughly moistened before being used.

When the pot is half full of firmed planting medium I hold the rhizome over the pot and position it so the oldest end is near the rim of the pot and the newest end is aimed toward the center, leaving the roots hanging down into the pot. Holding the rhizome in place with one hand I fill in around the roots with moistened planting medium, firming the medium as I go along. When I have finished the potting operation, the rhizome should rest just on the surface of the medium, and the roots should be covered. Once the plant is potted, I water it well once, then rather sparingly for the next 2 or 3 weeks until new roots begin to form, at which point the plant is ready for normal culture.

January is often the month of the year when orchid societies across the country hold their annual shows. These exhibits are the perfect introduction to orchids humble and splendid, and are almost bound to send the newly initiated out on a search for these beauties. If you find yourself among this group, don't bother looking in garden centers, as they rarely carry orchids. Instead, visit an orchid grower, or look for firms that sell orchids by mail. Plant magazines usually carry advertisements of these companies. The most complete source of information is the monthly *American Orchid Society Bulletin*, published by the Botanical Museum of Harvard University, Cambridge, Massachusetts 02138.

Chinese Evergreen *(Aglaonema)* If you're looking for a plant for a dark corner of the house, consider a Chinese evergreen. There's a good deal of choice, in terms of the size and coloration of the plants. Here's a sampling. *Aglaonema* (pronounced ag-lay-o-*nee*-ma) *modestum* is the old-timer: it was the first Chinese evergreen to be sold by florists. It grows slowly, rarely becoming taller than 24 to 30 inches, and bears dense foliage of heart-shaped dark green leaves about 3 inches across and 6 inches long. Other good ones are White Rajah, with green-and-white foliage, Pewter, with mottled cream and silvery green leaves, and the popular hybrid called Fransher, whose rich green leaves appear to have been lightly brushed with silver. All of these varieties of *A. commutatum* grow up to 3 feet tall with foot-long leaves.

Chinese Evergreen *(Aglaonema)*

A mature Chinese evergreen, a good plant for dark places or bright

Chinese evergreens do best in bright shadowless light — a north window is ideal. Night temperatures should be in the mid-to-high 60s and days between 75 and 85 degrees. Keep the soil barely moist all the time, and feed every 4 months. (They also grow very well in plain water, especially if a bit of charcoal is added; a drop of fertilizer once a month will help things along, too.) Whenever they become overcrowded repot them in ordinary potting soil. When you want more plants, propagate them either from stem cuttings, from sections of the main stems, or by air-layering. (For more about these methods, see the April feature.)

Miniature Rose *(Rosa)* Hundreds of thousands of gardeners in this country grow rosebushes in their yards, but as far as I can tell only a few have brought their affection for these plants indoors when the chill winds blow. The deterring factor is that most people think roses always grow on large bushes, but these special dwarf varieties grow no more than 12 to 15 inches at best, and some are no more than a third that size. The flowers are about the size of a nickel or a quarter, fragrant and available in every possible

26

rose color: pure white, salmon, pink, yellow, orange, red, and combinations of these colors. As a bonus, miniature roses growing indoors bloom all year long. But they don't bloom *heavily* all year. Every 3 months or so they send up a flush of flowers, then only a few until the next spurt; I usually cut my plants back to 3 or 4 inches from the soil line after a flush of bloom, and then let them bloom fully again.

Miniature Rose (*Rosa*)

Miniature roses are evergreens descended from a rose native to southern China; they are accustomed to warm temperatures, so they do very well indoors. They don't need intense heat, though: nights from 50 degrees to 65 degrees and days 65 degrees or higher will suit them fine. Like all roses, the indoor type is a sun worshipper. It needs at least 4 hours of direct sun every day; the more sun, the more flowers. I keep the soil barely moist and once every other week I add some half-strength houseplant fertilizer to the water. Outdoor roses are prone to every bug and disease going, but indoors these rarely present problems. As a precaution, wash the plants every week — in the morning — with tepid water. Don't invite trouble by leaving the foliage wet overnight.

Miniature rosebushes are available from garden centers and through the mail. If they are sold unpotted, as is sometimes the case, they should be potted up immediately in

The tiny, fully open blossom of this miniature rose is as fragrant as a full-sized outdoor tea rose

27

any commercial potting soil and set aside out of the direct sun for 3 or 4 days until they get their bearings. I usually prune back all the branches slightly after I pot them up, to give them an easier job adjusting to their new surroundings. This is an especially good idea if the plants arrive through the mail damaged; the broken stems or roots should be pruned off before potting.

The best way to propagate miniature roses is by stem cuttings, which can be taken any time of the year from the tips of firm, mature stems.

Ponytail Plant *(Beaucarnea)* *Beaucarnea recurvata* is popularly known both as a ponytail plant and an elephant foot tree, which is not to say that it looks like an elephant with a ponytail. The two names are descriptive of the

A ponytail plant with its maturing bulbous root

28

plant at different ages. When the plant is young the bulbous root protrudes above the soil line, sporting a fountain of grassy leaves tightly clenched at the base: hence, ponytail. As the plant matures the ponytail foliage arches over the rim of the pot, ending with gentle waves at the tips of the leaves, and the basal bulb grows and takes on the color, appearance, and texture of an elephant's foot, which accounts for the second nickname. In their Mexican homeland, ponytail plants grow to be some 30 feet tall, and each grassy leaf 6 feet long, but the tallest houseplant version I've ever seen was only a shade over 5 feet, and it had been growing for years in all-but-perfect surroundings. Most indoor plants are less than 2 feet tall.

This is a very easy-to-grow houseplant, provided it's given enough sunshine. If it gets less than half days of sun, the leaves will be pale, weak, and floppy, and eventually the plant will die. If you notice these problems starting, and suddenly move the plant into brighter sun, though, it may actually suffer sunburn; so move it gradually, over a period of several weeks, to a brighter location. Given the right amount of sunshine, ponytail plants can survive inattention. They withstand night temperatures between 40 and 55 degrees and days as high as 90 degrees or more without suffering at all. They're succulents, and in their native location in the deserts of Mexico, their basal bulb serves as a water-holding reservoir, so give them a chance to dry out a bit between deep waterings. They make a single flush of growth in the spring, and then consolidate that growth during the rest of the year, so I only feed them once, in the early spring, with any houseplant fertilizer. They grow quickly if they're repotted into larger containers every spring, and they slow down if they're left in the same pot. They live practically forever.

As for troubles, they don't have many. I've never seen an infested or sick ponytail plant. Sometimes the tips of the leaves yellow a bit, but I just cut off the dry part of the leaf, and prune the remaining green part to a new slender tip.

Ponytail Plant *(Beaucarnea)*

⊟ **Sweet Olive** *(Osmanthus)* I can't say enough nice things about sweet olives. The only problem is that they're in short supply. At first glance you'd be apt to miss the fact that the sweet olive is a flowering shrub, its white blossoms are so tiny. But on first whiff, you'd know this was no ordinary foliage plant. It's sweetly fragrant all year long — it smells a little like orange blossoms — thanks to those modest flowers. A native of southern China and southern Japan, it will grow 3 to 5 feet tall in mild climates outdoors, but it

Sweet Olive *(Osmanthus)*

does very well pruned to a modest height indoors, even if it's kept very small. I've seen little plants no more than 4 inches tall already bearing flowers.

Because they're native to relatively warm climates, they're well suited to indoor growing. Nights in the 50s and days in the high 60s or low 70s suit them perfectly. They do well in sun or very light shade. I usually let sweet olive plants become fairly large by growing them in tubs; when summer comes I move the tubs outdoors to a spot where the plants are protected from the midday sun. The soil should be barely moist all the time, and the plants need a monthly feeding with any houseplant fertilizer.

Sweet olives can't be started from seed but they're easily propagated from stem cuttings taken any time of the year. Commercial soil is fine for them, but the plants need good drainage so I usually use a lumpy mixture of 1 part

30

commercial potting soil and 1 part rather coarse compost or peat moss.

⊟ **Urn Plant** *(Aechmea)* The urn plant (*A. fasciata*) belongs among the council of houseplant elders: it was discovered in the rain forests of Brazil over 150 years ago. It's a bromeliad, and it has the unorthodox qualities that distinguish bromeliads from other plants. Most of them are epiphytes, or air plants. They cling to the branches of trees and take their nutrients directly from the air. (They aren't parasites, though; they don't ask for life from the trees, merely support.) Most bromeliads, including the urn plant, have stiffly arching leaves that form, at the base of the plant, a tightly compact cup that collects water and holds it in reserve until the plant needs it.

Urn Plant *(Aechmea)*

The leaves of the urn plant are spiny-edged and as much as 2 feet long; they're basically a rich green, but they're strikingly marked with silvery stripes that dominate the plant's appearance. It's the combination of the silvery color of the foliage and the water cup that has earned the plant one of its common nicknames, the silver vase plant. From the center of the plant, growing from the vase or cup, rises a spike of bright pink and purple flowers. This spike can live for as long as 6 months on the plant, but once it starts to fade, it should be cut off at the base, leaving the foliage to continue growing. This is the plant's period of regeneration, when new rosettes of foliage appear alongside the original. Then, to the shock of the unsuspecting gardener, the original part of the plant dies, leaving its offspring behind. When the new rosettes are about 8 to 10 inches tall they should be cut from the plant and potted individually to flower themselves when they're about 18 inches tall.

It's one of the oddities of the urn plant that, although it grows naturally clinging to the limbs of tall tropical trees, it can also grow in the terrestrial setting of a flowerpot. It doesn't need soil, of course, but it does need support, and the support needs to be light enough for the air to circulate easily through it. Some growers use a combination of equal parts sphagnum peat moss and coarse sand. Others use osmunda fiber, the tough, wiry roots of the osmunda fern; this is often used as a planting medium for epiphytic orchids.

Whatever planting medium is used, it's critical that it stay neither wet nor dry, but just barely damp. When it comes to watering, the gardener has to imitate nature. In the wild, the cup or vase acts as a reservoir, trapping rainwater that the plant uses slowly, as it needs it. When the urn plant is grown indoors, that cup must be kept full of water, preferably rainwater, all the time.

31

The long-lived flower head of an urn plant known as Foster's Favorite

Bird's-eye view of an urn plant's central cup

Feeding has to accommodate the plant's natural habits, too. In the wild that vase of water collects stray insects. As the insects die and decay they release the small amount of nourishment the plants need. It isn't necessary for the home gardener to keep a ready supply of dead flies on hand, but it is important to provide the same service in another way. What I do is to put 2 or 3 drops of liquid fertilizer into the reservoir once a month or so. The plants also take up nourishment from their roots, so it's a good idea to apply a houseplant fertilizer, diluted to half strength, to the planting medium once a month.

Urn plants need bright indirect light; they can't take the full sun. They can't take too much shade, either; it makes the leaves grow too long and lose their silvery streaks. The night temperatures should be in the low 60s and the days in the 70s.

It is possible to grow urn plants from seeds, but you'll wait three years, sometimes longer, before the plants begin to flower. It's easier and faster to cut off and pot separately the shoots that appear at the base of the plant after flowering. This can be done at any time of the year.

Q&A

Q: I've successfully pollinated my amaryllis and now have three huge pods that have opened, revealing hundreds of seeds. What do I do now to get more bulbs?

A: Plant the seeds ¼ to ½ inch deep, keep them moist, and nearly every one will sprout. The hitch is you may wait five or six years for the first flower, and you'll be shifting them to ever-larger pots in the duration. Which is why I advise to buy flowering-sized bulbs. They're expensive, but worth it.

Q: A friend has given me a plant labeled Yesterday, Today, and Tomorrow. What have I got here?

A: You have a *Brunfelsia,* a beauty of a houseplant that, under good conditions, is nearly everblooming. The common name is in reference to the fact that the new flowers turn from purple to lavender to white over a 3-day span. During the winter months, give it as much sunlight as possible; for the rest of the year give it filtered light. Keep the soil barely moist and feed your plants with half-strength fertilizer every other week.

Q: I love bird's-nest ferns. Are they impossible houseplants?

A: They're not easy because they need so much humidity, but they'll do quite well with partial shade, a humidifying tray, and regular misting. The botanical name is *Asplenium nidus.*

Q: I bought a terrific-looking calathea to dress up the house for Christmas, and now it's in obvious distress. Any suggestions?

A: Calatheas demand indirect light, moisture, and warmth. Keep your plant in a spot where the night temperatures fall no lower than the high 60s, and set it on a humidifying tray. Once you've had the plant for 3 months, begin feeding it every 2 weeks with a half-strength fertilizer.

Q: Is it possible to grow pansies indoors?

A: Only if you have a greenhouse. They need cool temperatures and full sun. Try winter-flowering and climbing pansies in your greenhouse, rather than the typical garden varieties. Seed catalogues list them, and they blossom very profusely.

SOWING AND GROWING FROM SEED

A few of the essentials needed for sowing seeds indoors

Starting Houseplants from Seeds Most gardeners, I know, don't bother starting houseplants from seeds. They buy full-grown plants from a garden center, or they start new plants from cuttings. When only one plant is needed, or when a full-grown plant is needed to dress up a corner before the weekend guests arrive, these are the best, and sometimes only, choices. But if you're interested in saving money, or in having a collection of the same plant, sowing your own seeds is by far the cheapest route, and surely the most interesting. Some houseplants are all but impossible to start from seed, but many others are just child's play. Some of the best choices are coleus, begonia, Arabian violet, gloxinia, impatiens, primrose, nasturtium, and silk-oak, as well as cacti and other succulents.

Although it's possible, in some instances, to collect seeds from your houseplants, most of them do not set seeds indoors.

You'll have a far better turnout for your efforts if you buy seeds from a reputable seed house. Fern spores are sometimes sold through these houses too; they can also be harvested from certain types of homegrown ferns. (See below.) Here are some seed houses that I've been doing business with for some time, and that have my confidence.

Buell's Greenhouses
P.O. Box 218
Eastford, Connecticut 06242

Burnett Brothers
92 Chambers Street
New York, New York 10007

W. Atlee Burpee Co.
(in three regional offices)
Warminster, Pennsylvania 18794

Clinton, Iowa 52732

Riverside, California 92509

DeGiorgi Company, Inc.
Council Bluffs, Iowa 51501

Park Seed Company
Greenwood, South Carolina 29647

Stokes Seeds
(in two regional offices)
P.O. Box 548
737 Main Street
Buffalo, New York 14240

P.O. Box 10
37 James Street
St. Catharines, Ontario 6R6 Canada

Thompson and Morgan
P.O. Box 100
Farmingdale, New Jersey 07727

The necessary equipment for sowing seeds is neither complicated nor expensive; it consists simply of pots, soil, and seeds. Any ordinary flowerpot will do, but a pot known as a pan is better; it's twice as wide as it is deep, and this added roominess works to the little seedlings' advantage. If the pot's been used before, it should be cleaned by soaking in a solution of 1 part laundry bleach to 9 parts water for 10 minutes, then rinsed. In general, clay pots do not make as good containers for starting seeds as do plastic pots because they are so porous that they draw moisture from the soil, and therefore from the seeds. If seeds dry out, even once, they do not germinate. If you're devoted to clay pots, though, soaking them for several hours in a bucket of water will wet the clay thoroughly, reducing this problem but not eliminating it.

I usually make up my own soil mix for sowing seeds, using equal parts sifted leaf mold or peat moss, pasteurized garden soil, and coarse sand. It's a particularly good medium because it provides nutrients to the seedlings and holds water well without becoming soggy. If you use soil from your garden as one of the ingredients in your soil mixture, be sure to pasteurize it first to kill insects, bacteria, and weed seeds. Pasteurizing soil is not quite the production that it may seem: it amounts to putting the soil in a covered baking dish in the oven. Stick a meat thermometer in the soil: when it has registered 180°F. for 30 minutes it's "done." And warn the family, because there will be an "earthy" fragrance

during the operation! If all this seems like too much bother, use any sterile packaged potting soil or soilless mix; the only disadvantage of commercial mixes is their cost.

There is nothing difficult about seed sowing. I begin by filling a pot with soil, and firming it down with the bottom of a clean flowerpot until the soil level is about ½ inch below the rim of the pot. Then I sprinkle the seeds sparsely over the soil surface and cover them lightly — to a depth about twice the seed's diameter — with a fine grade of vermiculite or finely ground milled sphagnum moss. To assure an even coverage of the seeds, I sift the vermiculite or moss through a ⅛-inch screen. (If the seeds are tiny, the size of a grain of sand or smaller, I put the moss or vermiculite over the soil and then sprinkle the seeds on top.)

A handy little homemade screening tray

Plastic bags keep moisture circulating while the seeds sprout

Milled sphagnum moss resists cold water, so before using it I sprinkle it with hot tap water, which it takes up eagerly.

Once the seeds are sown I set the pot into a bowl of warm water, and leave it there until the moisture has worked all the way to the surface. (This takes about 20 minutes and has the advantage over top-watering of not disturbing the newly planted seeds.) Then I remove it and let it drain for an hour or so. Moisture and humidity are so important to germinating seeds that I slip each pot at this point into a plastic bag, which I seal shut. If the pot is set into an area where the temperatures are in the 70s, the seeds usually germinate without any additional water. (If you use this plastic bag arrangement, set it in bright light but don't put it where the direct rays of the sun will hit it. Otherwise the bag will function like a solar heating unit, the sun raising the temperature inside the bag so high that the seeds will die.)

Pots of seedlings growing in the Victory Garden greenhouse

even with the addition of bottom heat, to see the seedlings through to germination without additional watering. Should the soil surface begin to dry out at any time, mist it lightly with warm water.

When the seeds sprout, the plastic bags or coverings should be removed, and the seedlings set into the recommended light and temperature for the species. While the seedlings are young the soil should be moist but not wet; I always water in the morning so that the surface of the soil is dry before nightfall, which helps prevent damping-off disease.

A plant's first growth is known as its seed leaves; they are, literally, the leaves that emerge from within the seed. All the later leaves that the plant produces are known as true leaves. When the seedlings begin to produce their true leaves I prick them out of their bottom-heated container, holding them gently by one of their leaves, not their stem, and relocate them in individual pots and the recommended potting soil for their species.

All seeds germinate best — and cuttings root best — if they are planted in warmed soil. There are two devices sold by garden centers and hardware stores that can be used to provide bottom heat. Both have plugs that fit into regular electrical outlets and thermostats to turn the heat on and off to keep the soil temperature constant at around 70 degrees. If the seeds are planted in individual pots, rather than flats, the best choice is a heated pad made of black insulated rubber. A pad is tidy and easy to use: just lay it on a table and set the pots of seeds on it. Don't try to substitute regular heating pads — the type used to relieve backaches — for these specialized pads. They're not insulated, making them electrical hazards whenever the seeds are watered.

Soil-heating cables are more efficient than heated pads because they are placed in the soil just beneath the seeds. They're available in several lengths; from 36 inches to several feet; and can be used either in garden flats or on greenhouse benches. The cable has to be laid out in a uniform pattern with no overlap, and then secured. I usually use wooden flats so I can tack the cable into place with insulated staples; if you're using plastic flats, vinyl tape is the best material to hold the cable in place as it can stand up to moisture without losing its grip. Once the cable is in place, I lay over it a sheet of heavy-gauge galvanized screening called hardware cloth, cut to fit loosely in the bottom of the flat; usually sold in ¼-inch to ½-inch mesh sizes, this screening will protect the cable from an inadvertent jab with a trowel. Then I add the soil or soilless mix and sow the seeds. Heated soil dries out much more quickly than unheated soil, so I check the flat daily to make sure the soil is moist enough. If the seeds dry out, they won't sprout. Cover the flat with a piece of clear plastic or glass, the equivalent of the plastic bags used with individual pots; this will usually retain enough moisture in the system,

36

Starting New Ferns from Spores Because ferns do not flower, they don't bear what are rightly called seeds; instead, they develop spores that serve the same function and are treated nearly the same. Ferns produce spores during the warm months of the year, from late spring through early fall, in a tidy arrangement along the undersides of the fronds. The spore cases often look like dots marching in formation; if they were not so neatly arranged, they would look very much like tiny insects.

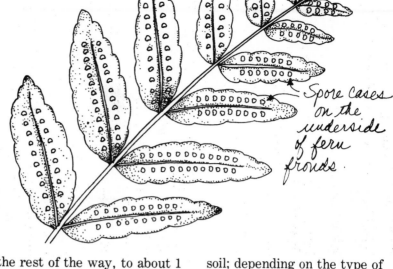

Spore cases on the underside of fern fronds.

Some seed houses sell spores, but they're easy to collect from certain ferns, such as maidenhair and table ferns. (Some ferns, such as the Boston fern, do not produce viable spores; this particular species reproduces by sending out runners similar to those put out by most kinds of strawberry plants.) When the spore cases ripen and turn dark, take a frond off the plant and put it into a paper bag for a week or so, during which time the spore cases will dry and the spores will fall out. Then empty the bag onto a piece of white paper, pick out the dry pieces of the frond, and you'll be left with hundreds of tiny, dusty dots — the spores.

Fern spores like their own special soil mix, designed to keep them happily moistened. My basic recipe is just equal parts of pasteurized garden soil (or potting soil) and either peat moss or leaf mold. Drainage is as important as water retention — the soil should be moist, not drenched — so I fill a plastic pot about ⅓ full of this mix. Then I sift more of the soil mix through a fine mesh screen or kitchen strainer and fill the pot

the rest of the way, to about 1 inch below the rim. With the coarser material on the bottom and the finer soil on top, the water balance in the soil should be just about right. It's important to firm the soil mix and leave the surface as level as you possibly can; a surface that might look only gently lumpy to you would seem like the Himalayas to the tiny spores.

Now it's time to scatter the spores as lightly and evenly as you can over the surface of the soil. Work carefully and close to the pot so the spores don't blow away. (You might want to prepare the pot before you empty the bag of dry spores on to the white paper, in order to give them less opportunity to be carried off by an errant breeze.) Then set the pot into a dish of water (if you water from the top, you'll flood the spores), and when the surface of the soil is moist, set it into a saucer of water and seal the whole affair in a plastic bag; put it out of the sun in a spot where the temperature is a constant 65 or 70 degrees. And wait.

The first sign of action will be a seaweedy green slime developing on the surface of the

soil; depending on the type of fern, it will take anywhere from a few days to several months for this to appear. This slime is the environment in which the males and females mate and produce a new fern. This mating takes place very enthusiastically, and the green slime will soon be dense with tiny but identifiable new ferns. When the fronds of the new plants are about 1 inch tall, remove the plastic bag. The young ferns will be too closely packed to leave them growing together, and too delicate to separate entirely, so transfer ¼-inch-square patches of young ferns to a flat or another pot, giving each patch a margin of 1 or 2 inches all around. (Some of the slime will still be visible at this point, but it will be gone soon.)

You can either leave the ferns together and let them develop into a large specimen, or you can divide them and pot them individually when they're about 2 inches tall.

FEB

Calceolaria
Cape Primrose
Geranium
Marigold
Petunia
Pineapple
Prayer Plant
Primrose
Purple Passion Vine
Silk-Oak
Striped Inch Plant

Feature: Gardening Under Lights

Polyanthus primroses

FEB

February is a busy and satisfying month for the indoor gardener. After their short winter in the cold frame or bulb trench, the first of the potted spring bulbs come into bloom this month, promising to the winter-weary that spring will come after all. Beyond the windows, winter's hold is breaking: the days are lengthening, and the sun is a little warmer, a little brighter. All plants respond to this encouragement, and grow more quickly than they have through the dull days of winter. This is the best time to prune, repot, and propagate most plants, so they can take full advantage of the long months of spring and summer to grow and establish their roots. Umbrella plants, for instance, should be repotted now if they're overcrowded; these are bog plants that need constantly wet soil, so be especially attentive to them now that the warmer, brighter spring weather dries the soil more quickly. This is the best time of the year to propagate a Boston fern by pinning a runner to moist soil; if you haven't done so in the past year, by all means divide your Boston fern this month. Maidenhair ferns can simply be repotted now, or you can cut all their fronds down to soil level, divide the roots, and plant the divisions separately. If you have a camellia that is completely pot-bound, February is the time to repot it, assuming that the blossom period is over. And plants that make yearly flushes of growth, such as boxwood, euonymus, and gold-dust plants, should be pruned every year at this time to make way for the new stems and leaves and to control the shape of the plants.

If you were given an azalea for the holidays, it's probably nearing the end of its blossoming season now. When the flowers fade, trim the plant back, repot it, and give it a light feeding with azalea fertilizer. Don't forget to treat the plant every 3 or 4 months with iron sulfate or iron chelate to prevent the pale-foliage condition known as chlorosis.

Remember that some plants can take the full force of the winter sun but need to be protected from the spring and summer sun. This includes most foliage plants and ferns, and some flowering plants like browallias and fuchsias.

Calceolaria *(Calceolaria)* Knowledgeable gardeners look forward to February and March, because this is the normal indoor flowering season for calceolarias. Individual plants bloom for about 4 weeks, producing, above the foliage, a solid mass of pouch-shaped flowers, each about 2 inches across. Because of the shape of the blossoms, they're often called pocketbook flowers. In color they range from red, pink, and maroon to bronze and yellow, and look as though they had been sprinkled with cinnamon. Most of the calceolarias offered by florists are annuals that mature at 6 to 12 inches.

Calceolarias (kal-see-o-*lair*-ia) are native to the cool mountains of western South America, and they continue to crave those crisp temperatures even when they're potted and grown indoors. The cooler they are, the more numerous the flowers and the longer they last. They should never be subjected to temperatures above 60 degrees and they do best with night temperatures some 15 to 20 degrees cooler. Obviously they're too demanding for most home gardeners to grow from seeds, so I suggest that you buy a plant with buds, enjoy the month-long blooming period, and then throw the plant away. While they're in bloom they need little more

A calceolaria, its blossoms so dense they all but obscure the foliage

41

Calceolaria *(Calceolaria)*

than bright light and a cool spot; too much moisture may encourage rotting of the leaves, so I keep the soil barely moist and water from the bottom.

If you're lucky enough to have a cool greenhouse where the day temperatures seldom rise above 60 degrees and the nights are between 45 and 50 degrees, you can start calceolarias from seeds without any difficulty. I usually do this in August or September so the plants are in flower in the early spring. I start out with a shallow flowerpot filled with potting soil covered with a ⅛-inch layer of damp milled sphagnum peat moss or vermiculite. Then I sprinkle the dustlike seeds sparingly so they'll nestle down within the moss. Calceolarias are very susceptible to damping-off if the growing medium is too wet, so I make sure the moss is kept only barely moist. The seeds germinate in about 2 weeks when kept at 70 degrees. When the seedlings develop their first true leaves, I move them to individual 2½-inch pots, and give them night temperatures of 50 to 60 degrees. As the plants grow I repot them into successively bigger pots until the mature plants are in individual 6-inch pots. Let me caution you again that calceolarias are fussy about excess moisture, so I only water them lightly, and always early in the day so the soil dries out by evening. And I never let the leaves become wet, as it can cause a serious case of crown rot. Air circulation around the plants helps them release moisture, so don't cluster the plants too closely together. Once a month the plants get a feeding of liquid fertilizer diluted to quarter strength, except when the plants are in flower, when they get no food at all. Aphids, by the way, would trudge across town for a bite of calceolaria. And being so prone to rot, the weekly bath and shower aren't advisable. Instead, spray your plants weekly with a combination of pyrethrum and rotenone; these naturally derived insecticides are both safe and effective.

If you have a greenhouse you may want to grow a perrenial shrubby calceolaria, *C. integrifolia*, that was very popular three decades ago. It grows 18 to 24 inches tall and has masses of small yellow, pink, or red-brown flowers. It's a colorful plant for use in the summer in garden beds, window boxes, and hanging baskets. It also makes a lovely pot plant for the winter months. Named varieties are propagated from cuttings taken during early summer. There are also some fine seed grown strains.

Cape Primrose *(Streptocarpus)* The Cape of Good Hope section of South Africa is home to many handsome ornamental plants, none more beautiful than the Cape primrose. But it's not very well known and as a result it's hard to find. I think the botanical name sounds too much like a sore throat, and the common name isn't intriguing enough to draw people's attention.

There are three types of Cape primrose, all very different, and all worth growing. One is *S. saxorum:* it has much smaller leaves than the other two; they're about 1 inch long, a fuzzy gray green, and roughly oval in shape. The leaves overlap to form a low-growing mat; it bears trumpet-shaped lavender flowers, and is sometimes called the Dauphin violet. It isn't a violet, of course, but then again it isn't a primrose either, being, instead, a gesneriad related to the African violet and gloxinia. It blooms for months, primarily through the summer and fall.

Another group is the Wiesmoor hybrids. Their 1½- to 2-inch flowers come in white, pink, red, purple, and shades

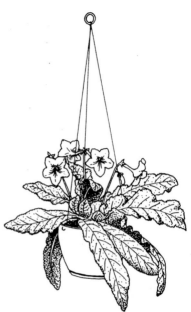

Nymph Hybrid Cape Primrose
(Streptocarpus)

A Wiesmoor hybrid Cape primrose

in between, frequently with markings of contrasting colors. Plants grow 6 to 8 inches tall; their leaves are tongue-shaped, as much as 10 inches long, and the wiry flower spikes rise above the foliage. They stay in bloom for at least 2 months, and they can be made to bloom any time of the year, coming into flower 6 months after the seeds are sown. Commercial growers generally sow seeds in early spring to have flowering plants for sale in late summer and fall.

Members of the third group, called the Nymph hybrids, probably will give you the most satisfaction because the plants bloom over the longest period. They're larger than the Wiesmoor hybrids: they become 10 to 12 inches tall, with individual flowers 1 to 2 inches across, again on slender stems that rise above tongue-shaped foliage. The first of this type on the market was a deep sky-blue flowered plant called Constant Nymph, which blooms without stopping from April through September. As is so often the case with plants that have a heterogeneous background, Constant Nymph has mutated enthusiastically, and there are now Nymphs available in a variety of blue-to-purple shades, as well as white.

All Cape primroses need essentially the same care. They want bright, indirect light — a north-facing window is perfect. If they don't get enough light their leaves are excessively floppy and the flowers droop into the foliage. These are tropical plants, so the night temperatures should be in the high 60s and the days 10 degrees or so warmer. Use a potting medium with good drainage; I generally combine 2 parts peat moss, 1 part potting soil, and 1 part sharp sand or perlite. They're slow growers, so they don't need repotting too often, but when they do, the job can be done at any time of the year. All Cape primroses need to be kept constantly moist and fed monthly through their growing season. For the *saxorum* group, which has no rest period, continue this routine all year long. But both the Wiesmoor and the Nymph hybrids go through a semi-rest period after they flower, and they need less water and no food during that time. Cape primroses can take quite a bit of punishment. They can wilt right down to the soil line, which would kill many plants, and completely revive a few hours after a good drink. That's not a license to abuse them, just a testimony to their toughness.

The *saxorum* plants are best started by stem cuttings, but they can be propagated by seed. The best way to multiply a collection of Wiesmoor hybrids is by dividing the crowns, but if you want to start new plants, you can do so from seed. They're usually sold in packages of mixed colors. Keep in mind that the seeds are as fine as dust, and can be easily blown away or drowned. Sow them either in a mason

44

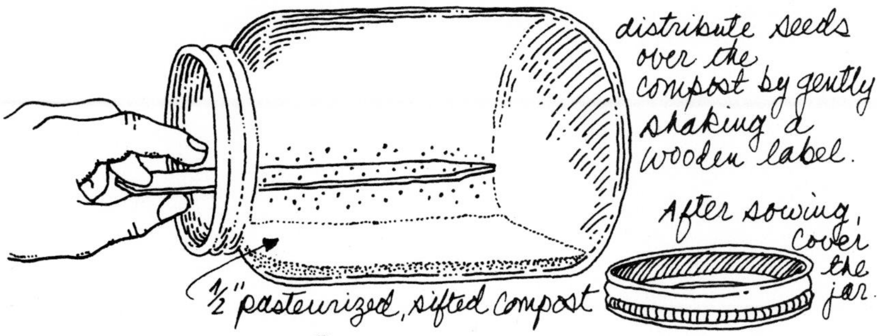

distribute seeds over the compost by gently shaking a wooden label.

After sowing, cover the jar.

½" pasteurized, sifted compost

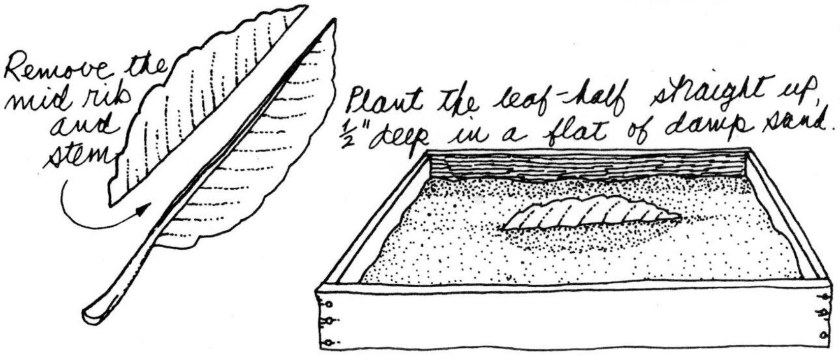

Remove the mid rib and stem

Plant the leaf-half straight up, ½" deep in a flat of damp sand.

jar laid on its side in a bed of sand, or in a flowerpot. The crucial thing is to keep the container sealed, either with the top of the jar or with a plastic bag over the pot; in that way the tiny seeds don't have to be watered while they are germinating. Keep them in a warm, bright, sunless spot.

The Nymph hybrids can't be started from seed, but they can be divided; the best time to do this is in the early spring, before the new growth starts. New plants can also be started by leaf cuttings. Just take a mature leaf from the plant and remove the midrib and the stem. Prepare a flat of damp sand and set each leaf-half in edgewise with the midrib edge about ½ inch deep in the sand. You may have up to a hundred tiny plants growing along the lower edge of the leaf, well nourished by the parent. So well nourished, in fact, that after this generation of plants is potted up separately, the same leaf-half can be used again to propagate a second generation. If you want only a few plants, take a section of a leaf-half 2 or 3 inches long, and set it into a flowerpot filled with moist sand.

■ **Geranium** *(Pelargonium)* If there's one secret to growing good-looking geraniums, it's sunshine. Those that aren't in the sun at least half the day lose their flowers and become leggy; after a while, they're just stalky creatures with a few pathetic leaves clustered at the tips of the branches. The more sun they get, the more flowers they produce. In a greenhouse, where they're in the sun constantly, they bloom all year long, but in the best of conditions in-

45

doors — a south-facing window, that is — they only bloom part of each year, beginning in February when the days are noticeably longer and continuing until early November when days become short and cloudy. Geraniums also need cool temperatures, in the 50s at night with days around 70. Let the soil become moderately dry between good, thorough waterings. Feed them twice a month from February through October, and once a month through the winter.

Despite their popularity, geraniums can't be called easy-to-grow houseplants. Stress causes their foliage to become yellow and dry, and eventually to fall off. Geranium stress is usually caused by shade, but if your plants are getting enough sun, make sure that the soil and the air around the plants are moist enough, and that the foliage is clean.

I know that many gardeners run out when the first frost threatens and dig up their outdoor geraniums, hoping to pot them up and save them to grow indoors. This just never works to my satisfaction: the plants survive, but so many of their roots get left behind in the garden that they end up as windowsill invalids. The best idea for the home gardener is to buy fresh young plants, or to grow new plants yourself. Any of the varieties of *Pelargonium hortorum,* sometimes known as the zonal geranium, make good choices: they bloom from late winter through the following fall indoors, producing red, white, pink, or lavender flowers. (This is the same kind that's usually grown outdoors.) Geraniums usually dominate the market in May, when gardeners are shopping for plants for summer window boxes, but they can be bought any time of the year.

For years, hobby and commercial growers alike have started their geraniums from cuttings. And this has contributed to one of the problems that nags this plant. Virus diseases linger in the cells of certain plants, and are passed on from generation to generation by way of the cuttings, reducing flower production by as much as 75 percent. That's quite a loss. Commercial growers work around this problem by a process known as culturing, which produces plants labeled as indexed plants. The cuttings are put into growth chambers, where intense heat and light force them to shoot upwards. They wouldn't live long under this kind of stress, but they don't need to. When they have grown about 1 inch, the growers take off a tiny slice at the tip, and because the virus can't keep up with the accelerated growth, this tip is disease-free, and can be used to produce disease-free plants. Commercial growers have to repeat this process every year in order to sell healthy plants.

Obviously, though, this isn't a job for the indoor gardener, who simply wants to take cuttings and have some

Geranium *(Pelargonium)*

Opposite: A double-flowered geranium grown from a cutting

47

new plants. Now there's an alternative — starting geraniums from seed. Actually there have been geranium seeds on the market for some time, but they germinated erratically. Now it's possible to produce reliable, disease-free, free-blooming plants from seed; each year plant breeders introduce ever-better varieties. If the seeds are started in January, the plants will blossom in June. Commercial growers have begun to sell seedlings, too, along with cutting-grown plants. Small seed-started plants are sometimes known as "green geraniums" because they're too young to show any color when they're sold, from 3 to 6 inches tall, in May. The seed-grown plants will still be dense with blossoms in the fall, when a diseased plant will have petered out. They also have the advantage of having been bred with natural basal branching, so they produce many branches and many flowers without pinching.

Eventually I think seed-grown plants will dominate the market, but there are still a few snags. The flowers, though plentiful, are mostly singles, and not as showy as the usual double-flowered blooms on plants started from cuttings. The flowers are also very fragile, and shatter if touched. So cutting-grown plants are still the standbys. Cuttings form roots in about 1 month, and begin to blossom about 2 months after they're potted up in any commercial potting soil. Cuttings need to be pinched back in order to encourage branching; each pinch delays flowering for at least 1 month, but the plants are bushier, with more branches and therefore more flowers. Rooted geranium cuttings can be bought through the mail from several sources.

■ **Marigold** *(Tagetes)* Most people, even those with armloads of marigolds in their summer gardens outdoors, never consider growing these plants inside. But they're wonderful houseplants, and trouble-free as long as they are given a spot that's airy and sunny for most of the day. They have to be started from seed, but there's nothing at all to that effort; practically all the seeds germinate, and they do so quickly. Do take caution in selecting the seeds. Make sure to buy dwarf strains such as so-called French marigolds or French-African hybrids rather than African marigolds, or you'll have tall, gawky plants that are slow to come into blossom. The Nugget series is my own favorite: their 2-inch yellow, orange, or red-orange colors are cheery and the plants blossom continuously. They are sterile hybrids and do not produce seeds.

Marigolds can be brought into flower at any time of the year, but I usually sow my first seeds in August to have plants in full swing after frost has wiped them out of my out-

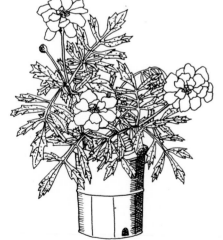

Marigold *(Tagetes)*

A Nugget hybrid marigold, double-flowered as is the whole Nugget series

door garden. Since I usually want only a few plants, I just drop about a dozen seeds into a 4-inch pot filled with commercial soil, cover them ¼ inch deep, give them a drink of water, and keep them warm while they germinate.

Marigolds tolerate a wide range of temperatures: when it's cool, they simply grow more slowly. They take well to normal house temperatures when they're grown indoors. The soil should be allowed to dry moderately between thorough waterings, and I usually boost their growth with a monthly feeding of any houseplant fertilizer at half strength. Most of the fragrance of marigolds, by the way, is released only when the foliage is touched. I'm fond of the scent of marigolds, but if you don't like their smell, don't bruise their leaves. There are some marigolds bred to have no scent, but they're tall-growing types that don't work out nicely indoors.

One final note: red spider mites are even fonder of marigolds than I am. They line up on the undersides of the leaves, spinning webs and sucking the plant's juices. So be especially diligent to give your marigolds a weekly shower of cool water. I use the spray at the kitchen sink to wash the mites away.

Petunia *(Petunia)* This is another plant like the marigold — a mainstay of the outdoor garden, but seldom seen indoors. Evidently they're so common that they're overlooked. But as a matter of fact, petunias are in some ways better off inside than out. For one thing, they're not rained on, so they don't fall victim to flower and leaf blight, the scourge of outdoor plants. Gardeners in areas where the winters are severe are accustomed to considering petunias as

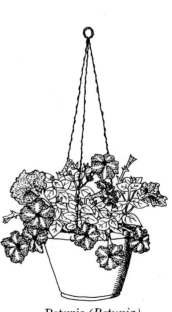

Petunia *(Petunia)*

49

A hanging pot of petunias reigning over the Victory Garden greenhouse

annuals, but they're not; they're nonhardy perennials, and indoors they'll go on and on and on. There are no insects in the house to pollinate them, so they don't set seed. As a result, the individual flowers don't have to be picked off to keep the plant alive, as they do outdoors. They're also easy to grow and inexpensive. What's more, they're available in a staggering variety of colors and shapes.

A new collection is best started by seed; if they're sown in midsummer the young plants will be in flower by fall. If you have a plant in your garden that you're particularly fond of, you can dig it up before frost, slip it into a 6-inch pot, cut the stems back to about 4 inches from the soil line, and you'll have flowers again in about 2 months. (I can remember the time when all double-flowered petunias had to be started from cuttings; they still can be, but there are now seed-grown varieties available, too.)

Petunias need at least a half day of sunlight, day temperatures near 70 and nights no cooler than 50 degrees; the buds don't form if the night temperatures are any cooler. Feed them every 2 weeks with any houseplant fertilizer, and let the soil become slightly dry between thorough waterings.

50

Pineapple *(Ananus)* As long as you've got a spot that's sunny half the day, you can grow a pineapple in your house. You can buy a dwarf variety — more and more florists and garden centers are stocking them — or you can buy a pineapple at the grocery store and start a plant of your own. If you decide on the latter, buy a fruit that's been freshly picked, and is still green. If the fruit has been picked too long, it's not apt to have viable growing tissue to propagate a new plant. If the leaves pull easily from the fruit, it's too ripe.

A miniature pineapple bearing its small edible fruit

To start a new plant, slice off the top ½ inch of pineapple, with the foliage attached. Clean all the fruit out of the tip so only the outer skin is left. Then leave it on a sunny windowsill for 2 weeks; it'll look terrible but if it's not given a chance to dry out, the tip will rot in the soil. When it's thoroughly dry, set the tip about 2 inches deep in potting soil and put it in a sunny spot. That's all there is to it.

The plants need nights no cooler than 60 degrees and days 70 or higher. As bromeliads, they like water applied directly to their foliage, which I do with a fine spray of warm water every day or two. But unlike many bromeliads, pineapple plants aren't air plants. They need to be grown in a good soil; I use 2 parts peat moss, 1 part potting soil, and 1 part sharp sand or perlite. Keep the soil just barely moist and feed them every month. They're practically indestructible, but they can do you some damage if you're not careful; they have brutal spines along their leaves. This is more of a problem when the plants are large because there's almost no safe way to move them.

Ordinarily, a pineapple plant has to be 3 or 4 feet across before it's large enough to blossom and set fruit. But

Variegated Pineapple *(Ananus)*

51

you can trick a young plant into premature blossoming. Wait until it's about 18 inches tall, then slip it, pot and all, into a large clear plastic bag along with two ripe apples. After 2 or 3 weeks, the ethylene gas given off by the apples will have persuaded the pineapple plant to begin to form a flower stalk instead of more leaves. Several months later its fruiting period will begin when a slender spike bearing a cluster of red buds appears in the center of the long arching leaves; the buds open into purple flowers, followed by a fragrant edible pineapple.

Prayer Plant *(Maranta)* By day the foliage of prayer plants extends straight out from the stems, but with the approach of dusk they raise their leaves skyward, and it's this reverent habit that has earned them the name prayer plants. Even under the gentle light of a table lamp they will lift and lower their foliage in response to the amount of light they receive.

There are two popular varieties of prayer plants, sometimes dubbed with names nearly as colorful as the plants themselves; neither grows taller than about 12 inches,

A prayer plant, its leaves extended in the bright light

so they're good plants for low splashes of rich color. The red-spotted prayer plant, also known as rabbit tracks (*M. leuconeura kerchoveana*), has gray-green oval leaves about 6 inches long; when the leaves are young, two rows of reddish-brown spots appear parallel to the central ribs, as if a rabbit had scampered across them. As the leaves age the tracks turn dark green. The beige or Massange's prayer plant (*M. leuconeura massangeana*) has a fishbone webbing of veins in the leaves, which are purple on the undersides. In the comfort of a greenhouse, and occasionally in the home, both of these plants sometimes send out slender spikes of tiny lavender flowers.

Prayer Plant *(Maranta)*

Prayer plants do best if they're divided and repotted in fresh soil every year in the early spring. Ordinary potting soil will do for repotting, but I like to add a bit of homemade compost, about one third by volume; it seems to bring an added luster to their leaves. Most plants are vulnerable to overwatering after repotting and until new roots begin to grow, and this is particularly true of prayer plants; so until new growth starts I keep the soil only lightly watered.

Prayer plants need a warm spot (nights between 65 and 70 degrees and days in the 75- to 85-degree range) but they need only indirect light, or 400 foot-candles of artificial light 14 to 16 hours daily. During the summer half of the year, from the spring through the fall, I keep the soil moist all the time and feed the plants every 2 months with any houseplant fertilizer. Their winter diet is more restrained: I don't give them any food at all, and I water them only when the soil has had a chance to dry out a bit.

■ **Primrose** *(Primula)* February is the primroses' proudest moment, the month when many of them are in beautiful blossom. There are three kinds of primrose that do very well by the home gardener. The fairy primrose (*P. malacoides*) is the most popular. The flowers — white, pink, or red — sit in tiers over the foliage. If they're kept cool enough, fairy primroses are able to bloom for 3 or 4 months, sending up a few stems at a time.

The obconica primrose (*P. obconica*) looks nothing like the fairy primrose. The flowers are larger, and are borne in clusters over hairy leaves. (I've never seen a case of this myself, but some people who are sensitive to plants have been known to develop skin rashes from the obconica primrose.) This plant stays in blossom for as long as 6 months and has clusters of 1½-inch pink, red, white, or lavendar flowers.

The polyanthus primrose (*P. polyanthus*) is usually thought of as an outdoor perennial; it's a hardy plant that

The buds in the center of these fairy primrose clusters will develop into the next tier of flowers

53

blossoms in the spring. It has the largest flowers of the three types, mostly in shades of yellow, but including pink, red, lavender, purple, and creamy white. If outdoor plants are potted up in the fall and brought inside, they'll bloom for about a month indoors.

All primroses like permanent spring: cool temperatures, moist soil, and bright light. They like their nights in the 40s or 50s and the days below 70. Keep the soil slightly moist and feed them every other week with half-strength fertilizer. (Don't bother feeding the polyanthus primrose when it's growing indoors.)

All primroses can be started from seeds, but if you can't manage the cool temperatures, you're better off buying a florist-grown plant and replacing it after the bloom period. The fairy primrose is an annual and dies after flowering, so it must be grown from seeds; the obconica and polyanthus primroses can also be propagated by division of the crowns.

Purple Passion Vine *(Gynura)* Purple passion vines literally shine. Their leaves are covered with velvety purple hairs that glisten in the sun. The foliage is wine-red

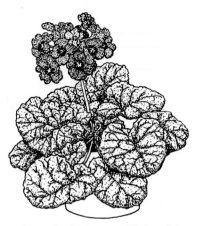

Obconica Primrose *(Primula)*

A richly colored, well-grown purple passion vine

on the undersides, and the stems are red too. Their botanical name is *G. sarmentosa;* they're related to Java velvet plants (*G. aurantiaca*) and require the same care. Both species send out tiny orange daisylike flowers and are native to Indonesia.

Purple passion vines are extremely popular and very easy to grow, but they become weedy and generally sorry-looking if they're not kept pinched back regularly. The foliage is intensely purple when it's young, but as it ages it tends more toward green, so if you're growing it for the purple color, you'll have more of it if you keep the plant pinched so most of the growth is young. This also helps the shape of the plant, making it more bushy than gangly. These plants thrive in a warm, sunny spot where they have at least 4 hours of sunlight every day; if they are grown without enough sun, the leaves will be greenish rather than purple, and the sun-hungry stems especially gawky. The night temperatures should be in the high 60s and the days between 75 and 85. Keep the soil barely moist all the time and feed them once a month with half-strength fertilizer. When the plants become overcrowded you can repot them in ordinary commercial potting soil. The young plants are better-looking than barbered old ones, though, so you might be better off rooting cuttings from the stem tips and starting new plants.

Purple Passion Vine *(Gynura)*

Silk-Oak *(Grevillea)* In their native Australia, silk-oaks are towering forest trees, 150 feet tall. In some warm parts of this country, notably California, they're grown as shade trees for streets and sidewalks. As houseplants they last for years because they can be pruned to fit the space they occupy, making small trees with 6- to 18-inch lacy fern-like leaves. (They don't look anything like oak trees.)

Silk-oaks do fairly well in bright indirect light (or 300 foot-candles of artificial light 14 to 16 hours daily), but they prefer 4 or more hours of direct sunlight every day. They're comfortable with night temperatures in the mid-to-high 50s and days around 70 degrees; they don't like to be cold. I let the soil dry out somewhat between thorough waterings, and feed the plants every 2 or 3 months, giving newly bought or repotted plants a 3- or 4-month waiting period before feeding.

Silk-oaks are eager growers; their botanical name is *G. robusta,* and with good reason — they often increase in height by a foot or more a year if given rich soil. In fact, they're a little too eager, so I usually prune back half the length of their branches in February, and then let the new growth appear. They can be repotted at any time that there is no new light-colored growth showing. Any commercial

Silk-Oak *(Grevillea)*

The fernlike foliage of a silk-oak plant

Striped Inch Plant *(Callisia)*

potting soil is suitable. If your silk-oak gets out of hand and shapeless simply buy a new plant as a replacement or grow some from seeds at any time of the year. Seedlings grow very quickly.

Striped Inch Plant *(Callisia)* The striped inch plant (*C. elegans*) is relatively new to the indoor gardening world, but it's already a favorite because it does so well in today's cool houses. It's at its best when the night temperatures are between 50 and 55 and the days in the 68- to 72-degree range. It prefers bright indirect or filtered light to the full rays of the sun. (If the plant must rely entirely on

56

The striped inch plant's crisply marked leaves

artificial light, it needs only 400 foot-candles to grow contentedly.) The plants do demand a constant supply of water; so I keep the soil barely moist at all times. I also feed established plants every 3 or 4 months, waiting about 6 months before feeding a newly bought or potted plant.

Callisias (pronounced kal-*iss*-ia) bear a close family resemblance to their relatives, wandering Jews, but their coloration is darker and more varied. Their deep green-and-white striped leaves, about 1 inch long, are purple on the undersides. I usually pot striped inch plants in hanging containers so all these colors can be seen at once. They have a tendency to become woody and unattractive as they age, so it's a good idea to cut them back close to the soil line whenever they become straggly and either repot them into larger containers or divide them into smaller plants.

Q: It may be my imagination, but it seems to me that my variegated plants are much harder to keep healthy than their one-color counterparts. Am I right?

A: You are. Variegated plants simply don't have as much chlorophyll in their leaves as all-green plants, and it's chlorophyll and light that build a plant's strength.

Q: My geraniums have many leaves but no flowers. And the leaves don't have the dark green rings I see on other plants. What am I doing wrong?

A: Some geranium varieties don't have ringed leaves at all, but your problem sounds like one of too little sunshine. Geranium plants need sunlight to form flowers and to develop the rings in the leaves. You might be keeping the soil too wet, too.

Q: I've just visited the South for the first time, and I still can't get over the sight of oleander bushes nearly 20 feet tall. I fell in love with them, but I live in the north and can't grow them outside. How do they do as houseplants?

A: I remember my first glimpse of an oleander, too; it was on my grandmother's sunporch where the daytime sun was all but constant and the nights cool. They bloomed through the spring and summer and rested through the winter. (In a greenhouse, where the night temperatures can be kept above 60 degrees all year long, and where there is full sun, they bloom intermittently all winter, too.) So, if you've got the sun, they'll do very well indoors. They'll start to blossom when they're no more than 18 inches tall, and you can keep them pruned to whatever size you want. Their botanical name is *Nerium oleander*. They have been grown as ornamental plants for thousands of years, but I should caution you that all parts of the plants are poisonous to eat.

Q: I have a forsythia plant in my yard. How do I force it to bloom indoors?

A: The forsythia is perhaps the easiest of all flowering shrubs to force indoors, with the possible exception of pussywillow and flowering quince. Branches from these shrubs can be cut as early as 2 to 2½ months before their normal outdoor flowering season. Choose a day when the temperature is above freezing, wrap the boughs in damp newspaper, and plunge the ends of the stems in deep water in a cool room. Leave them there for about 2 weeks. By that time the buds will have begun to swell, and you can arrange the branches in a vase and enjoy the lovely flowers indoors. Remember, though, that in cold areas forsythia flower buds are sometimes winterkilled. You'll never know for sure until they begin to swell.

Opposite: Tending to the greenery while the snow mounts outside

GARDENING UNDER LIGHTS

The artificial light arrangement in the Victory Garden office

Every week gardeners tune in to watch *Crockett's Victory Garden,* and they see me working outdoors, my hands in the warm soil, or inside the bright and sunny greenhouse surrounded by life and color. How lucky this guy is, they think, and they're right, I am. But I haven't hardened to the grim and often dim realities of growing plants in less-than-perfect circumstances. Upstairs in the WGBH studios there's a small windowless room that functions as the Victory Garden office. There's no natural light there at all, but the staff and I spend most of our time in that room, and we won't be without plants. So we've rigged up an inexpensive fluorescent light over one of the desks, and it's given us thriving African violets, gloxinias, wax begonias, and several small foliage plants as well. We're the envy of all our neighbors.

It's a very simple arrangement. We bought a standard hanging fluorescent fixture, 4 feet long and shaded by a metal canopy. We've mounted it so that we can raise and lower the light according to the needs of the plants. Our fixture holds two 40-watt lamps: we use one cool white and one warm white, a combination that is both inexpensive and ef-fective in producing healthy plant growth. There are much more elaborate fixtures available, including some that are actually pieces of furniture with lights hidden away in the structure of the piece itself. Many of these are spacious and handsome, but they're also expensive, and some have a serious drawback: the distance between the shelves and the lights is fixed, which means there's no way to vary the amount of light the plants receive without raising individual plants on supports so they can be closer to the light. If you know exactly what plants you want to grow, if you don't intend to change the plants, and if you can find a setup that provides the right distance between the plants and the lights, one of these more elaborate structures is probably worth the money. Otherwise I think you're better off putting together your own system. In either case, and regardless of the type of bulb, the lights should be on 14 to 16 hours a day. Make sure you have a timer to switch the lights on and off. Plants need darkness in order to rest, and with a timer they'll have it whether you remember to tend them or not.

The essential element of an artificial lighting system is the bulb itself. Fluorescent bulbs are best for several reasons. They provide light without much heat, so plants can be put close enough to light to benefit from its full intensity without burning. Fluorescents are more expensive than incandescent bulbs, but they use less electricity and last 12 to 15 times longer, so they're a better buy in the long run. You should have good luck if you combine a cool white 40-watt fluorescent with a warm white 40-watt fluorescent. You might also try one of the lamps or tubes sold specifically as "grow lights," though these will be more expensive.

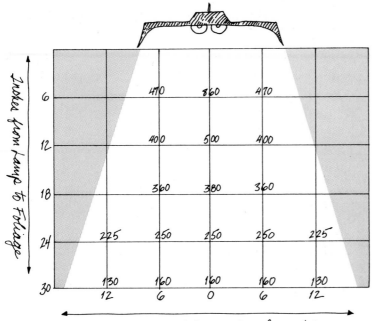

Inches from Lamp to Foliage (vertical axis)

6	470	860	470	
12	400	500	400	
18	360	380	360	
24	225	250	250	250	225
30	130	160	160	160	130
	12	6	0	6	12

Inches of Plant from Center Line

When it comes to setting up the lamp, the crucial factor is the distance between the lamp and the plants. This is because the intensity of light varies dramatically, even within a small area, and this difference in intensity is the difference between life and death for plants. The chart above shows how light intensity varies as the distance from the light source increases. The light source in this case consists of two 40-watt fluorescent bulbs, mounted within a reflector canopy.

Light intensity is measured in foot-candles, so using this chart, and the foot-candle information given in the alphabetical entries, it's easy to determine how far a plant should be from the source of light. A prayer plant, for example, needs 400 foot-candles of artificial light, so it should be 12 inches below the light source, and 6 inches to either side of center. Shade-loving flowering plants, like African violets and gloxinias, can be grown under artificial light, too. Set the plants no more than 8 inches from the light source for 14 to 16 hours a day. (Sun-loving plants such as cacti cannot be grown easily under artificial lights.)

Sometimes of course plants receive some, but not enough, natural daylight, and all the gardener need do is add enough artificial light to meet the plant's needs. In order to know how much to add, you have to know how much you have to begin with. There are foot-candle meters available for about $25.00, but if you have a camera with a light meter, it will do the job. The procedure sounds fearfully complicated, but it isn't really. First of all, set the film speed dial to ASA 25, and the shutter speed to 1/60. Then put a sheet of white opaque paper in front of the plant, and aim the camera at the paper, making sure that the camera is no further from the paper than the paper's narrowest dimension. (In other words, if you are using a piece of paper that is 15 by 20 inches, the camera should be no further from the paper than 15 inches.) Then adjust the f-stop until the meter indicates the correct exposure. If the f-stop is f/2, the illumination is about 100 foot-candles; f/2.8 is about 200 foot-candles; f/4 about 370; f/5.6 about 750; and f/8 about 1,500.

Fluorescent lights are useful up to a distance of about 3 feet; beyond that the light is too weak to do much good. Adding more fluorescent bulbs will help, but it can become an awkward solution. There is an answer, though, for that dark forlorn spot where no fluorescent bulbs would work: a 150-watt incandescent spotlight, which casts a shaft of light bright enough to maintain foliage plants that don't need much light. (Flowering plants are out of the question with only spotlights.) If some natural light reaches a plant and all that is needed is a supplement, an incandescent floodlight, which gives a wider, more diffuse, light helps, but it is too weak to maintain any but the most shade-tolerant of foliage plants. Whether you're buying a spotlight or a floodlight, make sure you buy bulbs labeled as plant lights. Ordinary bulbs won't give off the bluish light that plants need.

After all is said and done, sunlight is still the best light for plants, even for shade-loving plants that need those strong rays softened somewhat. But when it's impossible to give plants the natural light they need, artificial lights can save the day.

MAR

Parlor palm

MAR

With the arrival of March, the indoor gardener begins the busiest time of the year. Many plants should be put onto their growing-season diet of increased water and fertilizer. This includes, among others, burro's tails, string-of-beads, cast-iron plants, zebra plants, orchid cactuses, and bougainvilleas. I usually find that the sizable job of pruning, repotting, and propagating plants, begun in February, continues through this month. (I give my newly transplanted and propagated plants a 2-week rest before I set them on their growing season diet; they need a chance to adjust to their new surroundings, as we all do.) There are several popular houseplants that can tolerate only rare feedings, for instance, ponytail and monstera plants, fatsias, and fatshederas. If these plants are fertilized now, they will be able to put the nutrients to work through the warmer, brighter weather in the months ahead.

Of course the indoor gardener continues to plan for upcoming seasons. If you want your gold-dust plants to bear their bright red berries in the fall, pollinate the flowers this month by lightly touching the center of each bloom with a camel's hair brush. (Remember that you must have both male and female plants.) Flamingo flowers and bird-of-paradise plants can be started from seed in March, if you're patient enough to wait the three or more years they will need to reach flowering size. By contrast, oxalis bulbs planted this month will be in flower by April; make sure you provide these light-sensitive plants with plenty of sunlight, or they won't open their flowers. If you have favorite plants of the Nymph hybrid Cape primroses, propagate them by root division this month, or increase your collection dramatically with new plants started from a leaf cutting.

For those of you with a greenhouse, March is the month to start tuberous-rooted begonias back into growth. If you don't have your own tubers in storage, you'll find them in abundance in garden centers now. This is the best time of the year to start cuttings of chrysanthemums and princess flowers. Carnation cuttings should also be rooted early in the month, then set into the open garden in April and moved into the greenhouse in early summer so that they will begin to blossom in October.

⬟ **Anemone** *(Anemone)* Many biblical scholars are now convinced that the "lilies of the field" were not lilies as we know them today, but poppy-flowered anemones. Today's cultivated varieties would prove an even greater embarrassment to Solomon: they are available in pink and violet in addition to the red, blue-purple, and white of biblical times; they bear larger flowers with more petals than their ancestors; and they're available in single, double, and semidouble flowering forms. Of the many species that exist, only *Anemone coronaria*, the poppy-flowered anemone, is grown as a florist crop: Creagh Castle, de Caen, and St. Brigid are the most popular varieties within this species. Other anemones are mostly treated as garden flowers or as wild flowers.

Each flower of a cultivated anemone is about 3 inches across, atop stems 12 to 18 inches tall. They're long-lasting flowers, whether they're left on the plant or cut and used in a bouquet. Unfortunately they require the combination of full sun and cool temperatures that makes them impractical for most indoor gardeners. They need carefully controlled greenhouse conditions in order to thrive.

Poppy-flowered anemones of the St. Brigid strain

65

Poppy-flowered Anemone
(Anemone)

Anemones are tuberous-rooted plants that can be grown either from the roots, called tubers, or from seeds, the tubers being the speediest route to flowering plants. (Plantsmen usually ship the roots in September or October for immediate planting.) The tubers should be planted with their claw-ends down, about 2 inches deep in a soil that is 3 parts rich sandy loam, 1 part peat moss or compost, and 1 part coarse sand; the soil pH should be 6.0.

Anemones are very vulnerable to crown rot, a problem caused by excess moisture, so ½ inch of plain coarse sand sprinkled over the soil after planting is a wise move, as it will dry out quickly after each watering and help the plants stave off this curse. As an extra measure against crown rot, many commercial growers start their tubers in 4-inch clay pots. When the plants have begun to make strong root growth these growers take a hammer and break away the bottoms of the pots. Then they transfer the plants, bottomless pots and all, into the bench, spacing them about 4 inches apart in rows 10 inches apart. Drainage is crucial, so the broken pots are set only halfway into the soil. (Excess moisture is even more of a problem in the winter, when there is less sun and heat to keep the plants dry.) The care's a little fussy, but if they're pampered, tuber-grown anemones will begin to blossom in January and continue until late in the spring.

But there's a problem in starting with tubers. The material shipped through the mail is often infected with disease, and sometimes the plants either die or grow poorly. My preference is to start the plants from seeds, which is safer, if slower. Sow the seeds in pots in April or May in the soil mixture mentioned above, and then prick them out and transplant them directly into flats or greenhouse benches when the seedlings are about ½ inch tall. The plants demand good drainage, so when I use this technique I usually make sure the plants are growing in a good 4-inch bed of soil. Seed-grown anemones begin to produce a few flowers in October, with ever-increasing numbers as the season advances, and the most abundant flower production in March and April.

Anemones need full sunshine and cool temperatures — in the 40s at night and in the high 50s during the day. As I've said, moisture can be a threat, so when I water them — the soil should always be barely damp — I try to water the lower root system, and not, if I can help it, the crown or the foliage. When the flowers have faded I let up on the watering until the plants wither. Seed-grown anemones will have developed disease-free tubers by the end of their first growing season, so when the leaves turn yellow and fade I dig the tubers out and store them in a cool, dark place until the following fall, when I begin the routine all over again.

■ **Azalea** *(Azalea)* If I had to write a one-sentence summary of azalea care, it would be this: keep them cool, keep them moist, and keep them after they flower. An English gardening magazine once published a photograph of a 150-year-old azalea that had been growing in the same pot, regularly fed and trimmed, of course, for 50 years. In Japan, where most evergreen azaleas are native, gardeners regard an azalea of that age as a mere stripling!

The kinds of so-called florists' azaleas grown as houseplants are flowering shrubs with small evergreen leaves; their flowers, single or double, are usually white or a shade of pink or red. Yellow and orange azaleas are for the most part deciduous and are generally grown in outdoor gardens. Normally florists' azaleas bloom in the spring but plant specialists, by altering temperatures, are able to bring them into flower at any time of the year. Because of the great demand for flowering plants during the fall, winter, and early

Open flowers and buds of a florists' azalea

67

Florists' Azalea *(Azalea)*

spring, the bulk of azaleas are brought into bloom and sold in flower shops between November and May. Given the right care through their rest period, they then resume their normal spring-blossoming schedule. It's the after-blooming care that I like to emphasize because it's entirely possible for the home gardener to keep azaleas growing for many years with an ever-increasing abundance of flowers.

Most people buy azaleas as bud- and blossom-laden plants just as they are about to flower. While they're in bloom, and in their vegetative period as well, they need a cool, brightly lit spot; an east-facing window with night temperatures about 50 degrees is ideal. The cooler they can be kept the healthier they will be and the longer their flowers will last. (If they're kept in too warm a spot, their growth becomes etiolated, meaning that the leaves are widely spaced along tall slender stems.) It is vital that the planting medium be kept constantly moist all year.

The critical time in an azalea's life is after the flowers fade. Too many gardeners seem to think that the plants are worthless at this point, and put them out with the Thursday trash. But as I've said, if they're properly attended they'll last for years, and improve with age. The first step in good after-flowering care is housekeeping. I go over an entire plant and snip off the dead blossoms and the seed pods. Then I trim back any branches that stray beyond the plant's natural shape, making my cuts down inside the foliage so they don't show. Then I repot the plant into a 1-inch-larger pot, using a medium of sphagnum peat moss or a mix of half peat moss and half coarse builder's sand; the peat moss provides the plant with the acidity it craves, and it serves to hold moisture as well. When it's repotted I water it, adding a little azalea fertilizer, available at most florists and garden centers. This is one of only three yearly feedings: the second follows the first by about 2 months, and the third and final feeding is in midsummer, when the flower buds have formed.

Once an azalea's flowers fade, the plant begins a handsome new stage of vegetative growth, and it's then that the foliage takes its turn at showing off. (Unlike many flowering plants, the azalea is a beautiful foliage plant during the months when it's not in flower.) When this new growth reaches maturity, but before it gets hard and woody, new plants can be easily started from 2- to 3-inch cuttings taken from the tips of the stems.

When summer approaches and the danger of frost is past, I move my azaleas, pots and all, outside to a shady spot, where I plunge them into a bed of damp sand or peat moss. This procedure serves two functions: it keeps the soil cool and helps to conserve moisture; and it prevents the plants from being toppled by high winds. I always try to locate them near a water source to reduce the effort involved in keeping them constantly moist during the blistering days of summer. In the fall when a frost threatens I bring them in and set them in a cool bright windowsill. They're at their best when the nights are in the 40- to 55-degree range and the days no warmer than 68.

Azaleas are subject to a few problems, all either curable or preventable. If the water they receive is too alkaline, the leaves develop chlorosis and their color pales to a light green as the veins darken. This can be solved by watering them with a solution of 1 ounce of iron sulfate crystals — available from a druggist — dissolved in 2 gallons of water. It's probably a good idea to give the plants this treatment every three or four months whether they have chlorosis or not, just as a preventive measure. Or use iron chelate, another excellent material to keep foliage dark green and healthy; it's available from garden centers, and because it's a powder it can just be sprinkled on the surface of the soil to work down in as you water the plant. Iron chelate is sometimes sold as sequestered iron.

Invasions of red spider mites are sometimes a problem. The answer to this one is good hygiene. Whether the plants are indoors or out, they should be washed weekly, aiming a good strong spray all around the foliage, especially on the undersides of the leaves. When my plants are indoors for the winter I fill a sink halfway with warm sudsy water and swish the foliage around in it. Then I rinse them with clear warm water. This not only keeps the mites at bay, it keeps the foliage clean and shiny, too. (If the red spiders are given the opportunity, they'll suck the life out of the plant, so if the infestation is out of hand, use a miticide such as Kelthane or Dimite, following label directions carefully. I like to spray my plants outdoors where there is good air circulation.)

Finally, it's normal for all plants to drop their old leaves, but when they drop the new ones too, it means trouble. Usually the problem is too little moisture, but too little light will have the same effect. Keep the soil beneath the plants moist at all times, and if this doesn't seem to help, move them to a brighter spot.

The perfect stage at which to buy an azalea plant, just as the buds are about to open

◆ **Carnation** *(Dianthus)* My father liked all kinds of flowers, but carnations were his all-time favorite. I don't know whether it was the spicy fragrance that appealed to him, or the clear, bright colors, but at any rate, because he loved them, I love them too. And I'm not alone. Next to roses, carnations are the most popular year-round flower in

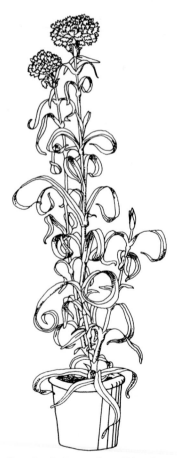

Standard Carnation *(Dianthus)*

America. That's partly thanks to Anna Jarvis, a Philadelphian who was responsible for naming and popularizing Mother's Day; she loved carnations, and she considered them the perfect gift for that day.

Carnations are grown only as cut flowers rather than as pot plants, and professional florists grow them in huge cool greenhouses. They usually grow the standard-sized carnations, but miniature carnations are becoming more popular each year. Both grow about 3 feet tall, necessitating a support system of strings and wires to keep the stems straight. Standard carnations naturally produce 3 or 4 flower buds atop each stem: the professionals remove all but one, which

70

then grows to be a very large flower, often 3 inches or more in diameter. It's always a surprise to a first-time greenhouse visitor that there are so few flowers showing at one time.

I think the best way for the hobby greenhouse grower to get pleasure from carnations is by growing the miniature varieties. They're no shorter than their standard-sized relatives, but they have a quite different growth habit. They form a multitude of stems, all of which bear many clusters of flowers, so they don't need to be repeatedly pinched back to increase production. Commercial growers don't disbud the miniature plants, and hobby greenhouse growers shouldn't either. The flowers are about 1½ inches across, roughly half the size of the standard-sized flowers. The main thing in favor of the miniatures is that they bear so many flowers, far more than the standards. Both types need full sun and a cool greenhouse.

Modern carnation varieties are the result of years of breeding and careful selection, and they have to be reproduced by cuttings. There are companies that serve the hobby greenhouse trade, and many of them offer cuttings that are already rooted, ready to pot into soil for growing on. But if you buy some cut flowers, you can remove any of the side shoots and root them without any trouble. The shoots snap away easily and root well in either sand or perlite. Commercial growers put their carnations in benches, but I think you'll have better luck just growing a single plant in an 8- or 10-inch pot. Let the soil become moderately dry between thorough drenchings and feed them every other week with a commercial houseplant fertilizer. Provide each plant with 4 bamboo stakes and the support of some green twine to help them keep their heads up.

Carnation cuttings are best started early in March. Set them into the garden in April and leave them until July, keeping the tips pinched the entire time so the young plants don't send up flowers. Then dig them up and bring them into the greenhouse. They'll come into blossom the following October and continue to flower continuously thereafter, but you'll find that when summer comes, and the nights are warm, the blossoms will be noticeably poorer. That's why you're better off starting new plants every year and enjoying the blossoms through the cool months.

■ **Cineraria** (*Senecio*) I've never outgrown the boyish wonder I felt when I first met a cineraria. I thought I'd found a velvet daisy. These plants are sold in flower shops from late fall until late spring. They're annuals, so after they blossom, they set seeds and die and the plants have to be thrown away at that point. They're not a frivolous invest-

Cineraria *(Senecio)*

71

The numerous velvety blossoms of a cineraria

ment, though. The colors are intense, in purple, red, pink, and white, and there are so many flowers that they all but hide the foliage. Think of them as a long-lasting bouquet. Keep the soil constantly moist, and put the plant on as cool a sunny windowsill as you can find — 45 or 50 degrees is ideal. Without sun the foliage will quickly turn yellow. Because the canopy of foliage and flowers is so dense, water the plants from below to avoid crown and leaf rot.

If you have a cool or intermediate greenhouse, you can grow cinerarias quite easily from seeds. The seeds have to be sown between August and October, when most amateur gardeners' attention is on the vegetables and flowers growing outdoors, but this sowing will produce plants in flower from midwinter to spring. There are standard-sized plants that grow to be some 2 feet tall, and just as wide, but they're not the best choice for the grower with a cramped greenhouse. The dwarf strains, which peak at about 10 inches, are a far better idea; they're smaller, and more flowery-looking than the standard-sized plants. Keep your eye out for aphids; they love nothing better than cinerarias for dinner.

72

Hydrangea *(Hydrangea)* Hydrangeas originated in Japan and China but for a number of years most of their cultivated forms were developed in France. This is partly why the plants are often referred to as French hydrangeas; the other reason, in my opinion, is that the word French lends the plants, and, of course, their owners, a touch of class.

Late March to mid-May is the hydrangeas' season of glory, when they produce their enormous blooms, the size of

A richly colored hydrangea plant

your hand or larger. They're usually sold when they're about 18 to 24 inches tall and just coming into flower. They'll retain those commanding blooms for 6 weeks or more if they're given the right conditions: bright indirect light, and constant attention to moisture. The leaves of hydrangeas are so large and thin that they lose moisture very quickly. It's not uncommon to have to water them more than once a day, but setting the pot into a humidifying tray helps the gardener stay ahead of things. If they do begin to dry out, and the foliage wilts, plunge them, pot and all, into a pail of water for a few minutes and then set them in a cool shady spot; they usually revive in an hour or so. They do well in average household temperatures, with the nights in the high 50s and the days around 70 degrees. They shouldn't be fed while they're in blossom. Bright sun will bleach the flowers, so keep the plants in a lightly shaded spot when they're in bloom.

Hydrangea plants can be kept over for years if you have an intermediate or cool greenhouse, and they will increase in the number of stems and flowers. As soon as the weather is mild enough, set the plants outside in a sunny spot for the summer, and feed them every other week. Then bring them in when frost threatens. In the fall, while the fat terminal buds are forming, keep them at no more than 65 degrees for about 6 weeks, until the buds have formed. At this point the plants become dormant; for the next 6 weeks they should be kept just above freezing (certainly no warmer than 45 degrees) and in darkness to force them to lose their leaves. Then cajole them back into action by setting them in a spot where the night temperatures are about 60 and fertilizing them every 2 weeks. They should bloom in about 3 months. (If you'd rather they bloomed in late spring, keep them just above freezing until late winter.)

If you don't have a greenhouse, and live in an area where the winter temperatures usually stay above zero degrees, you can set your plants into your flower garden. Their fat terminal buds, the ones that produce flowers, are sensitive to cold weather, and if these buds are damaged only the foliage buds will survive and the plants will not blossom.

If you don't have a greenhouse, if you live where the winters are fierce, and if you have the patience of Job, try this technique to see if you can bring your plant into flower a second time. After it has finished flowering, cut the plant back to two nodes from the soil level and repot in ordinary potting soil. Set it outside for the summer, keep it moist, and feed it twice a month with any standard houseplant fertilizer. In the fall, while the leaves are still on the plant, give it at least 6 weeks of night temperatures below 65 degrees. Then after the leaves drop, give it another 6 weeks of night temperatures between 35 and 45. Then set the plant into a protected cold frame — one that's been hilled up with soil and leaves and covered with a tarp to prevent repeated freezing and thawing of the plants inside — until January. Bring it inside where the nights are in the low 50s, feed it every other week, and it should blossom in about 2½ months. Good luck.

Hydrangea plants will go on happily for years if they're shifted to ever-larger pots, but they become so large that they take up an inordinate amount of space. So I like to start fresh young plants each year with cuttings taken in the spring from the stems of flowering plants. I usually root them in moist sand, warmed from below with bottom heat to about 70 degrees. In early summer I pinch back the central stem, which encourages branching. I let them grow on, and new buds form at the tips of the branches. Then they need the winter care described above.

During the height of the era of the French hydrangea, naive folks thought that pink hydrangeas were female and blue ones were male. In fact the color of the bloom is determined partly by the amount of available aluminum in

Hydrangea *(Hydrangea)*

the soil. Most soils contain large amounts of aluminum, but if the soils tend toward the alkaline, the aluminum is "tied up" chemically in the soil and plants cannot use it. When the soil is only slightly acid or neutral, with a pH of 6.2 to 7.0, the flowers tend toward pink. Truly acid soil, with a pH of 4.5 to 5.5, produces blue flowers. Soils with an intermediate pH of 5.5 to 6.2 produce mauve-colored blooms. (White-flowered varieties are unaffected by the composition of the soil.)

To make the soil more alkaline to produce pinker flowers, add ground limestone to the potting mixture. If you want to make the soil more acid to get bluer flowers, water the soil with a solution made by dissolving 1 ounce of iron sulfate to 1 gallon of water and apply it six times at 10-day intervals during the forcing period prior to the opening of the blossoms. Plan to enhance the color — not change it — by adjusting the acidity of the soil. If you try to make a blue-flowering plant turn pink, you'll end up with a muddy color. The same is true for the pink plants.

Lipstick Plant (Aeschynanthus) This plant from the Asian tropics is a welcome gift for the indoor gardener plagued by too much shade; it's a gesneriad that wants

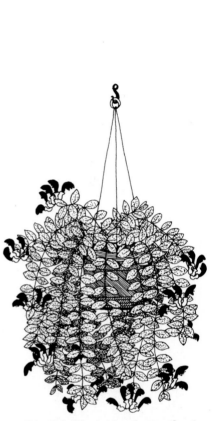

Lipstick Plant *(Aeschynanthus)*

A lipstick plant with its tubular flowers fully open

bright indirect light. It will live happily, and bloom, right along next to wax begonias and African violets on a north windowsill. Lipstick plants bear unusual tubular flowers, mostly at this time of the year (some hybrids, like Black Pagoda, are practically everblooming), from buds that resemble lipsticks, at least to some eyes. Depending on the variety, the flowers may be red, orange, or yellow; there's one that's deep brown. Even when the flowers are gone the plants are still good-looking. Because of the gracefulness of their pendant stems, these plants look their best if they're potted in hanging containers; they're sometimes called basketvines for this reason. They are, by the way, amazingly similar to columneas. Even professionals have a hard time distinguishing between them. You should certainly try to keep track of which plant you buy, but both these gesneriads need the same care.

Lipstick plants appreciate warmth. Ideally, they should have night temperatures in the high 60s and days 75 degrees or higher. The roots need to be surrounded by constant moisture, so I use a highly organic potting mix, either one sold for African violets, or my own recipe of 2 parts peat moss, 1 part packaged potting soil, and 1 part sharp sand or perlite. The planting medium should be moist all the time. Once a month I feed them with any standard houseplant fertilizer. If, when a plant finishes flowering, it is too long and straggly to suit me, I cut it back to about 2 inches from the soil line and repot it in fresh soil. I also root the stem ends, and then pot up 3 cuttings together so they make a bigger plant.

▭   **Palms** Palms are probably more easily and more accurately recognized, even by people who pay no attention to plants, than even the most common of indoor greenery. They're increasingly popular as indoor houseplants, just as they were thirty or forty years ago. The reason, of course, is their distinctive foliage. There are many different kinds of palms, involving many different plant families, but they require the same care, so for the sake of convenience they're grouped according to the shape of the foliage, either fanlike or feathery. The parlor palm (*Chamaedorea elegans*, formerly *Neanthe bella*) is one of the most commonly grown, and also one of the best for dim light. It's a dwarf palm with feathery foliage, and rarely grows taller than 2 feet in the house. The European fan palm (*Chamaerops humilis*) can tolerate cool temperatures particularly well; its leaves are fan-shaped. The miniature date palm (*Phoenix roebeleni*) is one of my favorites: it has feathery leaves so long that they curve back in on themselves.

A group portrait of easy-to-care-for palms

Palms are very easy to take care of, and very tolerant. But they're big feeders and drinkers. Keep the medium constantly moist and during the spring and summer, when they do most of their growing, feed them once a month with a houseplant fertilizer. (No food the rest of the year.) They like bright light, but because they spend their life indoors where light is dim, they can't take the full rays of the sun except during the winter. Palms can grow for years in the same pot; they may look — and be — overcrowded, but they'll survive. The best time to repot them is in the early spring. Use a medium made up of equal parts sharp sand, loam, and peat moss, plus a half part of dried cow manure. During the summer, set them outdoors in a shady, windless spot; spray them with the garden hose now and then to help them collect themselves for the winter indoors.

Parlor Palm (*Chamaedorea*)

■ **Paphiopedilum** (*Paphiopedilum*) There are thousands of orchids in this world, and three in this book. That's not to say that there aren't many more that can be grown successfully, but the three included here are certainly the

The blossom of a hybrid paphiopedilum orchid

Species Paphiopedilum Orchid
(*Paphiopedilum insigne*)

easiest and among the most satisfying. (See the cattleya entry in January and the moth orchid in April.) All three can be grown indoors, even by a beginner.

There was a time when paphiopedilums (paff-ee-o-*ped*-i-lum) were classified as cypripedium orchids, the genus name of similar North American wild flowers. They are often called ladyslipper orchids, from the moccasinlike shape of the blossoms, although this common name is correctly applied only to the *Cypripedium* genus. But the tropical versions of this orchid were different enough to warrant a name all to themselves, and the paphiopedilum was born. To confuse matters further, differences were noted between paphiopedilums native to southeast Asia and those native to South America, so the latter were dubbed phragmipedilums. Most current reference books have caught up with all these changes by now, but older reference materials still list the former names.

There are over fifty species of paphiopedilums, mostly native to Southeast Asia, a hot and humid area of the world. The species do quite well indoors; but in general, the hybrids make better choices. They're usually stronger, with more unusual colors and larger flowers of greater substance and longevity both on the plants and as cut flowers. They also tend to blossom more than once a year, which the species usually do not. The hybrids don't grow much taller than 15 inches.

Paphiopedilums are terrestrial orchids, and they need a highly organic medium in which to grow. I plant them in a mix of 4 parts fine fir bark and 1 part coarse sand. This medium shouldn't be allowed to dry out because these orchids have no water-storage organs, so keep it constantly moist. They need duller light than most orchids, and do best in semi-shade; if the foliage starts to yellow, they're probably getting too much light. They want warm temperatures, in the high 60s at night, and into the 70s during the day. Grown indoors, they need a humidifying tray; humidity can spell the difference between success and failure indoors, so don't overlook this.

Paphiopedilums bloom for a 2- or 3-month period. The hybrids may send up another flower stem right away, or they may wait a few months. The species are done for the year after that blossom period. These orchids can go on for some time in the same pot, but after about three years they need a bigger space. These are sympodial orchids, so see the cattleya entry (in the January chapter) for directions. You can divide them at that time, too, just pulling the roots apart with your fingers, making sure that each division has 3 or 4 leaf clusters of its own.

A well-grown poor man's orchid growing in a hanging pot

🔲 **Poor Man's Orchid** *(Schizanthus)* Fast growing and bright with color, the poor man's orchid, sometimes called the butterfly flower, would seem to have enough going for it to achieve real popularity. But it's burdened with a botanical name that sounds like a disease — one that few people even try to pronounce (sky-*zan*-thus). Yet, it is an outstanding plant and I highly recommend it. An annual native to Chile, it must be grown anew each year from seeds, but it's well worth the small trouble it entails. In the greenhouse poor man's orchids bloom from midwinter through spring, sending up great flower clusters in lush shades of violet, purple, red, salmon, yellow, white, and pink. When grown outdoors as summer annuals, they get strong enough sunshine so that they produce stiff, erect stems, but when they're grown in a winter greenhouse their stems are weak and need support to give straight-stemmed cut flowers. I usually grow mine in hanging pots and let the growth cascade over the edges. Seedsmen offer several strains, some as tall as 3 feet. I prefer the dwarf varieties.

I sow my first seeds in August, then follow up with successive crops every month through January; that gives

Poor Man's Orchid *(Schizanthus)*

79

me blossoms from mid-February through May. Flowering time can be advanced slightly by keeping the plants pot-bound and the soil somewhat dry, but usually the first flowers appear in mid-to-late February regardless. The earlier sowings grow into taller plants, and need 7- or 8-inch pots; the later sowings produce plants that can mature in 5-inch pots. I use commercial potting soil, and plant only a pinch of seeds at each sowing. (Too many plants would overwhelm my small greenhouse.) When the seedlings develop their first true leaves I move them on into individual 3-inch pots, and then into the larger pots. After each 3-inch increment of growth, I pinch out the tips to make the plants branch; the last pinch has to be taken 6 weeks shy of the predicted time of bloom or the flowers will be delayed. Give them excellent air circulation and a little fertilizer once a month. They need full sun and prefer cool temperatures, with nights in the high 40s or low 50s and days no warmer than 60, limiting their growth to a cool greenhouse. Some plants can't adapt to adversity; the poor man's orchid has trouble with prosperity. It's apt to be weak and succulent if it's given too much water and fertilizer during the winter months in the greenhouse.

A close-up of the water-holding central cup of a queen's tears

Queen's Tears *(Billbergia)* Bromeliads, of which queen's tears is an outstanding example, offer some of the easiest-to-grow houseplants you're apt to find. Queen's tears, *B. nutans*, is a little gentler-looking than many of its relatives, having long, slim grasslike foliage and not the stiff, straplike leaves that mark so many bromeliads. The leaves grow in clusters, and each cluster forms a narrow cup in the center; these cups aren't visible unless you look down inside the foliage, but it's important to find them because they have to be kept full of water at all times. In the winter queen's tears produces slender stalks bearing slim, delicate, pendant flowers marked with green, blue, and red — a most unusual color scheme. Because there are several leaf clusters to a plant, there are several flowers at a time.

Queen's Tears *(Billbergia)*

Queen's tears is as durable as it is graceful, and very easy to please. It wants sun for half the day, with some protection against the harshest midday rays in the summer. The night temperatures should be in the low 60s and the days 70 degrees or warmer. It's an air plant, but it also grows well in a pot with a highly organic medium — I use a mixture of equal parts coarse sand and peat moss. In addition to making sure that the cups at the base of the foliage clusters are always full of water, preferably rainwater, keep the soil constantly moist, and feed the plant every couple of weeks with any houseplant fertilizer. Once a month or so, add a drop of liquid fertilizer to the water in the cups. New plants can be propagated from the shoots that appear at the base of the plant after it ends its flower season.

Rat-Tail Statice *(Limonium)* Many gardeners think of statice only as a dried flower or as a fresh cut flower with flat clusters of dry-feeling, usually purple, bracts, but there are many other kinds of statice to enjoy. The rat-tail statice is especially satisfying when grown in an intermediate winter greenhouse. I've grown them for years in the Victory Garden greenhouse and they have brought many compliments. This statice is grown in deep soil benches by commercial growers seeking long stems and large crops, but I've been happier growing mine in pots: they're more compact and I can move them about if necessary.

Rat-tail statice is related to but very different from the annual and perennial statice sold as fresh or dried flowers. The rat-tail statice (*L. suworowii*) takes its name from the slim 18-inch spires of rosy-pink flowers produced one after another during the blossom season. The flowers are delightful — they look a bit like king-sized pipe cleaners — and they make fine cut flowers. After a flower is cut, the remaining stem will often branch and produce more flowers.

Rat-Tail Statice *(Limonium)*

The tall, graceful flower spike of a rat-tail statice

I plant my seeds in October for flowers from midwinter to late in the spring. I find that there's a better show of blossoms if the plants are allowed to flower in 6-inch pots. They need bright sun, night temperatures in the 50s, commercial potting soil kept barely moist, and a monthly feeding. They're annuals, so after their long flower period, discard them to make way for new plants.

⊡ **Rubber Tree** *(Ficus)* The *Ficus* family is huge and varied. It includes not only the rubber tree, but the popular weeping fig trees (see the November chapter), and some plants that are far from houseplant candidates, like the tropical banyan tree with its multiple trunks. In the early years of the nineteenth century the rubber tree was found growing in the remote sections of Assam and Burma. It was harvested for years for its latex-bearing sap, allegedly used mostly for erasers. (This rubber tree is rarely tapped for latex nowadays, having been superseded by a more productive genus from Brazil called *Hevea*.) The original rubber tree (*F. elastica*), with its rather slender 4- to 10-inch leaves, has been overtaken in popularity by a mutation found in Java, the broad-leaved India rubber tree (*F. elastica decora*), whose larger leaves open from a surprising red sheath. Doescher's India rubber tree (*F. elastica doescherii*), is a variegated plant.

One of the reasons that these trees are so popular is that they tolerate either sun or shade — though their water needs have to be carefully watched if they're grown in the sun. The ideal temperatures are in the high 60s at night and the days a little warmer. If they're kept cooler than this, they enter a semi-dormant period, and all but stop growing. A feeding every 6 months is sufficient; they grow too large if they're overfed. The only element they're very fussy about is water. The soil has to be kept barely moist all the time. If they have either too much water or too little their leaves turn yellow and drop. Most gardeners overwater and for this reason the plants are best off in small pots, which won't hold enough water to drown them. Leave repotting until the time when the new leaves seem stunted; the best time of the year is in the early spring. (All of this information also holds true for the fiddle-leaved fig, *F. lyrata*.)

Rubber trees are usually sold when they're from 2 to 4 feet tall. But of course they grow, and eventually they get too big. When this happens, any problem with moisture or light, combined with the plant's natural growth pattern, usually makes for a plant with a bare lower stem, and all the leaves clustered forlornly at the top. When your plant reaches this state, gather up your courage and cut the plant back to 4 or 5 inches from the soil line (the best time is early spring); give it some fresh soil, and put it back in the same pot, or one only slightly larger. You'll see some white sap oozing out from the cut, but don't worry about it. It's possible to kill the remaining roots with too much moisture, so water them very cautiously, and don't feed them at all; without their large leaves, they just can't put very much water or nourishment to use. When the new growth starts from the bare leaf scars below the point of pruning, gradually increase the water supply. By the way, if you can't bear to part with the tree for the months it will take it to rebuild, you might want to air-layer the top of the plant (see the

Rubber Tree *(Ficus)*

A broad-leaved rubber tree that I air-layered in the Victory Garden greenhouse

April feature) before you cut the original back. The rubber tree takes beautifully to this technique, and you'll have several fine plants for very little effort.

Q&A

Q: I'm fascinated by bonsai plants, but a friend tells me I'd have to devote my life to them. Is he right?

A: Just about, I'm afraid. Bonsai is the cultivation of plants, usually hardy trees like spruce, cypress, pear, or quince, in such a way that their size is dwarfed while they continue to look like their full-sized counterparts, weathered and impressive. The dwarfing is achieved by reducing the supply of nutrients, moisture, and soil; in fact, by keeping the plants ever on the borderline of starvation. They have to be tended like infants; this can mean watering the plants several times a day during the summer because they use their small supply of water so quickly. And because they're outdoor plants to begin with, they have to be kept outside; they can be brought in for applause for a day or so now and then, but living as houseplants is impossible. (There's some interest in this country in developing tropical bonsai. They wouldn't live as long as the hardy trees, but they can be kept inside for constant enjoyment.) I stand in admiration of Oriental gardeners who have mastered bonsai care, who have kept these plants thriving for a century or more, passing them on from generation to generation as living heirlooms.

Q: What is it that florists do to make cut flowers last so long?

A: Nothing that you can't do on your own. Before they arrange the flowers, they remove from the stems any leaves that would be below the water line. Then they cut off a bit of the bottom of each stem; this cuts away the slimy bacteria that will attack the cut cell tissues, decaying and plugging them so water can't pass up the stem. They use lukewarm water in the vase, not cold. And they add a cut-flower food, which inhibits the growth of decay bacteria, adjusts the acid-alkaline balance of the water so that it nearly matches that of the soil sap, and provides nutrients that the flowers would have taken up from the roots. These cut-flower foods are sold in garden and flower shops, so you can take all these steps and have long-lasting cut flowers, too. Be sure to add water to the vase each day to replenish that used up by the flowers.

Q: I've always had good luck growing citrus seeds into small trees, but all of a sudden this year I've had an attack of scale that has wiped out all the little lemon trees and is headed straight for the grapefruit. Is all hope lost?

A: Not at all, but the winter cure for this problem is a tedious one: go over every inch of the plants with alcohol and a swab. In the summer, you can take the plants outside and spray them with malathion, but the weather's still too cold in March for this outdoor treatment. (Don't use malathion inside — it's much too potent.) By the way, I suspect that the infestation arrived on a newly purchased plant. From now on, quarantine your new plants for a week or two so you can spot problems before they spread.

PINCHING, PRUNING, AND REPOTTING

Pinch off the tender tips of stems to promote full growth.

Master these three techniques of good plant-keeping and you've gone a long way toward guaranteeing yourself a healthy, shapely collection of houseplants.

Pinching and Pruning

Pinching, or pinching back, is the term applied to the technique by which the tender tips of stems are removed to guide the growth of plants. The only "tool" required is a thumbnail to nip off the succulent new growth. Timely pinching encourages a compact, bushy habit of growth capable of bearing more foliage and flowers than would be borne were a plant allowed to grow in a straggly, though normal, manner. Pinching differs from pruning only in a matter of degree: pruning involves the removal of stems so thick and tough that shears are required. Pinching at the proper time often trains a plant's growth so well that pruning is never required.

Pinching back works because every plant has dormant buds that lie at the point where a leaf joins a stem. If the tip of the stem is removed, one or more latent buds begin to grow, resulting in two or more stems where there was only one. If the tips of these new stems are removed, even more branches develop and the plant becomes compact and bushy rather than tall and straggly. All plants are more attractive when their foliage is dense, but this is particularly true of flowering plants that only produce flowers on the tips of their stems; the more stems there are as a result of judicious pinching, the more flowers the plant will bear.

Pruning is a rather infrequent task when dealing with houseplants or even greenhouse plants. It usually is necessary only when a plant has become so large that the only alternative to pruning it back is to discard it because it has overgrown the space allotted to it. Most woody plants can be pruned severely — nearly down to the soil line — and come right back. Other plants can die if all their leaves are cut off. Check the alphabetical entries for pruning information specific to each plant.

Plants react to pruning in exactly the same manner as they do to pinching. Dormant buds spring into life below each cut, causing the plant to have more branches. As a general rule, the best time of year to prune a plant, especially if drastic pruning is required, is in early spring. March is an ideal month for this job because plants are just entering into a new season of growth. During the months that follow, the new growth will increase in size rapidly. To prevent it from becoming too tall all over again, resort to pinching out the tips of the new stems, forcing them to take on the compact, bushy habit of growth that is so desirable.

Repotting

It's a rule of life that all things grow or die: nothing stands still. So it is with plants that, sooner or later, they need larger pots. The speed with which this happens depends on the kind of plant, its stage of development, and on the particular conditions under which it grows. Some plants need to be repotted every year at a specific time, often in the early spring as they are about to enter a new period of growth. Others can be repotted whenever they appear to be in need. If the foliage seems stunted, if the plant wilts between normal waterings, if the lower leaves turn yellow, or if the roots appear at the soil surface or peek through the drainage holes, it is probably time to move the plant to a larger pot.

The first step in doing this is to knock the plant out of its current pot; it helps to water the soil a few hours before the operation is to begin because the soil ball and roots will release more easily when moist than when dry. With plants in pots 8 inches or less in diameter, this involves no more than holding one hand over the surface of the soil, straddling the stem with the fingers if possible, turning the pot nearly upside down, and knocking the rim of the pot sharply against the edge of a table. Large plants may need more encouragement: wrap the rim of the pot with a cloth pad, lay the plant on its side, and rap against the pad with a wooden or rubber mallet. Then turn the plant a few degrees and rap again. You may have to repeat this a few times, but the plant will eventually slip out of its pot.

Once the plant is free of the pot, take a look at the soil ball. If you can see a clear network of roots around the outer perimeter of the soil, the plant is crowded and needs more room. The general rule is to move the plant into a 1-inch-larger pot, or a 2-inch-larger pot for plants already in pots 10 inches or larger in diameter.

Whenever a plant is repotted, it is essential to reset the old root ball at the same level at which it has been growing. In other words, the stems of the plant should be neither more covered nor more exposed than they were in the old pot. So the first thing to do is to fill in the bottom of the new pot with whatever potting soil is recommended for the plant. (Drainage material, like pebbles or clay shards, is unnecessary unless the plant is being moved into a pot 6 inches or larger in diameter. In that case put in ½ to 1 inch of drainage material and cover it with some of the potting mix.) Firm the potting mix so that it will not settle when the plant is placed on it. Once the bottom is ready, set the plant in to judge

Firm the soil around the roots as you fill the pot

There should be about 1" of new soil around the old root ball

fill to original soil line

whether you need more or less soil to bring the plant to the proper level. Then fill around the root ball with soil, firming with your fingers as you go along. During this operation I tap the pot on the table top several times to help the new soil settle snugly around the old root ball. If there is space between the old soil ball and the side of the pot, use a slender stick to firm the soil you cannot otherwise reach. The importance of firming the soil around the old roots cannot be overemphasized. New soil is always lighter and airier than the soil ball in which the plant has been growing; if this new soil isn't firmed down well, any water added to the plant will wash so quickly through the light new soil that the original soil ball and roots will not be moistened. Make sure that the plant is given a thorough watering after potting is completed, but for the week or two following, be careful not to overwater because it is during this period that new feeder roots and root hairs are forming in the fresh potting soil, a process that requires air as well as water in the soil.

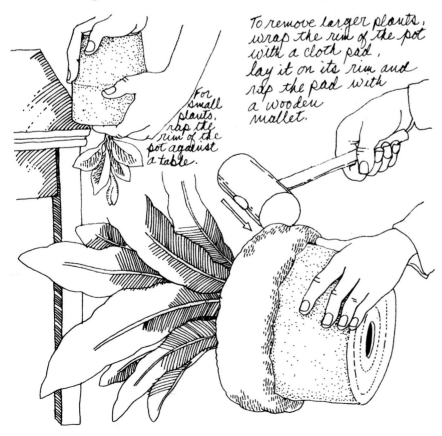

For small plants, rap the rim of the pot against a table.

To remove larger plants, wrap the rim of the pot with a cloth pad, lay it on its rim and rap the pad with a wooden mallet.

APR

Feature: Vegetative Propagation

Impatiens

APR

April is one of the show-off months for indoor flowers. The Nymph hybrid strains of Cape primroses come into blossom in April, and continue to send up their flowers through the summer. Hydrangeas are in bloom this month; make sure if you buy a potted hydrangea that you attend to its watering needs, as the soil moisture will be lost very quickly through the plant's large, thin leaves. An azalea plant that's been kept cool through the winter will come into its natural blossoming period now. Late-season camellias may still be in flower. And the flowering maples cut back in January will begin to blossom this month, too.

Most plants need some attention through the spring, so if you haven't finished the pruning, repotting, and propagating jobs that you lined up for yourself, attend to them as early in the month as you can. April is the midspring month, and some of these jobs are best done a little earlier in the season. Don't put them off, though; there's still a long summer stretching out before the plants, and they will grow luxuriantly in its warmth. Wax plants should be pruned for fuller growth this month, but be sure to leave the leafless stubs of the old flower stems, as these will bear flowers next season too. Palms of all types do most of their growing through the spring and summer, so start feeding them regularly now. Echeverias should be given their single yearly feeding this month, and put on their growing-season watering routine. If you'd like to have some unusual and colorful window box or windowsill plants this summer, start some fancy-leaved caladium tubers into growth early this month; they'll be ready to set out when the warm weather arrives.

Greenhouse gardeners should set the carnation cuttings taken last month into the open garden. Make sure to keep the tips pinched back so these precocious youngsters don't have an opportunity to set flowers and drain their strength. Pinching back will make them husky and many-stemmed. Anemone seeds sown in the greenhouse this month will produce their first flowers in October. And if you're thrifty and sow freesia seeds this month, you'll have corms by fall that can be potted up to produce flowers the following winter.

Bougainvillea (*Bougainvillea*) The first bougainvillea, a species with pale lavender floral bracts, was found growing in Brazil in the 1760s by Philibert Commerson, a ship's naturalist sailing under a French flag; he named it in honor of his captain, the explorer Louis Antoine de Bougainville. Eventually several species were discovered and crossbred to give us dozens of dazzling hybrids. They need at least half a day of sun to thrive indoors: they blossom from March through September, sending out great clusters of red, pink, yellow, copper, or white bracts. Bougainvilleas bloom nearly year-round in a warm greenhouse where conditions are perfect, just as they do in the tropics. I've had two varieties in all but constant bloom for twenty years: Barbara Karst, which bears red flowers, and Texas Dawn, whose flowers are coppery pink.

Bougainvillea (*Bougainvillea*)

Bougainvillea (boo-gen-*vill*-ya), true to their tropical origins, want warm, rather dry, sunny conditions. They can grow to be very large plants, but indoor specimens are best looking if they're kept pruned and pinched to a height of about 2½ feet. Nights should be no cooler than 60 degrees, and the days 70 or higher. In the home, where they'll most likely rest through the winter, feed them every other week

A cluster of bougainvillea flower bracts

91

during their growing season and water them thoroughly every few days, giving the soil a chance to become moderately dry between waterings. When they stop flowering, cut them back, eliminate food from their diet entirely, and give them only enough water to keep the foliage from wilting. Then in the early spring, just as they resume growing, repot them in commercial potting soil, working carefully so you don't disturb the roots, and resume the growing season's watering and feeding routine. If you keep the tips pinched, the plant will be bushier. The cuttings will root easily for a new generation of plants.

Coffee (*Coffea*)

■ **Coffee** (*Coffea*) A healthy coffee plant is a beautiful sight. When the leaves are young, they have a bronzy tinge that deepens to a rich shiny green as the leaves age. The plant can grow 4 feet tall, or more, if left unpruned, and it bears tiny white flowers that give off a heavenly fragrance before they develop into bright red berries. The berries in turn house two beans which, when cured and roasted and ground, are the source of your morning cup of coffee.

Coffee plants are relatively easy to grow indoors, but without the humidity, warmth, and sunshine of a greenhouse, they'll seldom be more than conversation pieces. Their foliage is thin, and the leaves turn brown if they're brushed up against, which is hard to avoid with an indoor plant. They'll keep growing, and they'll survive, though not always handsomely. (They're like avocados in this respect — interesting curiosities, but not especially good houseplants.)

We grew a few coffee plants (*C. arabica*) from seed one year in the Victory Garden greenhouse. They're slow-growing plants, so we didn't expect them to germinate quickly, but there was still no progress at all two months after the seeds were sown. We decided to add some bottom heat, about 80 degrees' worth, and there were sprouts within 3 weeks. (Since then I've learned that in coffee-growing countries where they boast of mountain-grown coffee, the seedlings are started in the hot and sultry lowlands before being moved to higher elevations for fruiting.) Coffee plants continue to need those warm, humid conditions through their life. They want night temperatures no lower than the low 60s and days in the 70s at least. They need gentle, filtered sunlight all day long, and constantly moist soil. From October through March, when their growth is slow, feed them monthly with any houseplant fertilizer; from spring through fall feed them every other week. They're gross feeders and when grown in a greenhouse they need regular repotting to give them adequate room for their dense root system.

92

A sturdy and happily warm coffee plant

Coffee plants can be started from cuttings as well as from seeds. Use only the upright growing tips, as cuttings from the side branches are apt to produce straggly plants.

☕ **Easter Lily** *(Lilium)* Easter lilies, known botanically as *Lilium longiflorum,* are everywhere at this time of the year, sending their message to the world by way of their fragrant, snowy white, trumpet-shaped flowers. If you're given a plant already in bloom, it will stay in blossom for a week or more if it's given bright indirect light, cool nights (in the 40s or 50s) and days no warmer than 68. Keep the soil constantly moist, and spray the tiny buds with tepid water to help them open in the dry indoor air. (Some gardeners remove the orange stamens to prevent staining the white flowers.)

Easter lily bulbs are seldom forced a second time, so don't try to hold them over for another year indoors. You can save them for your outdoor garden, though. First of all, make sure to remove each flower as soon as it fades so the plant has no opportunity to waste its energy setting seeds. If the weather is still cold when the last flowers fade, set the plant on a sunny windowsill until the leaves mature and wither away, keeping the soil moist the entire time. This may take 4 to 6 weeks. If, on the other hand, the outdoor night temperatures are reliably in the 40-degree range when

Easter lilies, with the orange stamens visible in the centers

the last flowers fade, plant the lily in a sunny spot in the garden. It may rest a year and bloom the following summer, or it may send out a few flowers later the same year.

Casual gardeners are usually advised to avoid the demanding job of forcing Easter lily bulbs. But really, the difficulty is related only to the florists' economic need to bring

94

them into bloom right on time for Easter Sunday. If you're willing to let them blossom whenever they please, they're no more difficult, and often easier, than other forced bulb plants. Commercial growers use specially precooled lily bulbs, the refrigeration helping to shorten the forcing time; these cooled bulbs are not easy for the amateur gardener to come by, but the standard lily bulbs are, and they should be bought in the early fall, when they're relatively dormant. The shorter-growing varieties, those that seldom exceed 3 feet at maturity, are the best proportioned for indoor forcing: Nellie White, Croft, and Ace are good choices. (Professionals, by the way, use chemicals to keep lily plants short. This is no process for the home gardener to undertake, so expect your homegrown plants to be taller but far more graceful than those you buy from a florist.)

Standard lily bulbs produce blooms by late March or early April if they're potted up as soon as they're available in the fall. I use one 6-inch standard pot for each bulb, and begin by placing a 1-inch layer of gravel in the bottom of the pot. Lily bulbs are particularly vulnerable to rotting, and excellent drainage is a must, so I set the bulb in directly on the layer of gravel. Then I fill in around the bulb with a mix of equal parts potting soil and compost boosted with about 1 teaspoon of slow-release fertilizer, which provides all the nutrition the bulb needs. I fill the pot to within about ½ inch of the rim, firming the soil mix against the bulb with my fingers as I go along, and making sure the bulb is covered by at least 2 inches of soil. Then I water the bulbs thoroughly and from this point on keep the soil constantly barely moist, but never soggy. Full sun and night temperatures of 50 to 60 degrees will bring the plants along slowly, but with sturdy growth that will produce long-lasting flowers.

Easter lilies are the most popular of the lilies forced for indoors, but they're not the only ones that can be treated this way. In fact, lovely as the Easter lilies are, there are others that I actually prefer because they bring such vivid colors indoors through the winter. Among those that have outward-facing flowers, like Easter lilies, are Corsage (pink), Paprika (deep red), and Prosperity (lemon yellow). Lilies with flowers that face upward include Cinnabar (deep crimson), Enchantment (orange-red), Joan Evans (yellow), Pepper (deep red), Rainbow hybrids (several colors), and Tobasco (dark maroon-red). All of these lilies grow to be about 2 feet tall.

There is a second group of lilies that can be forced indoors. These are taller, at 4 to 6 feet, and are called Oriental lilies. Some of them are hybrids, and all of them bear outward-facing flowers. They include Auratum or Gold Band lil-

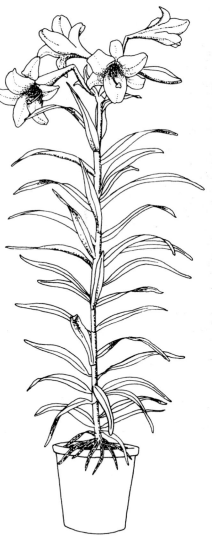

Easter Lily (*Lilium*)

95

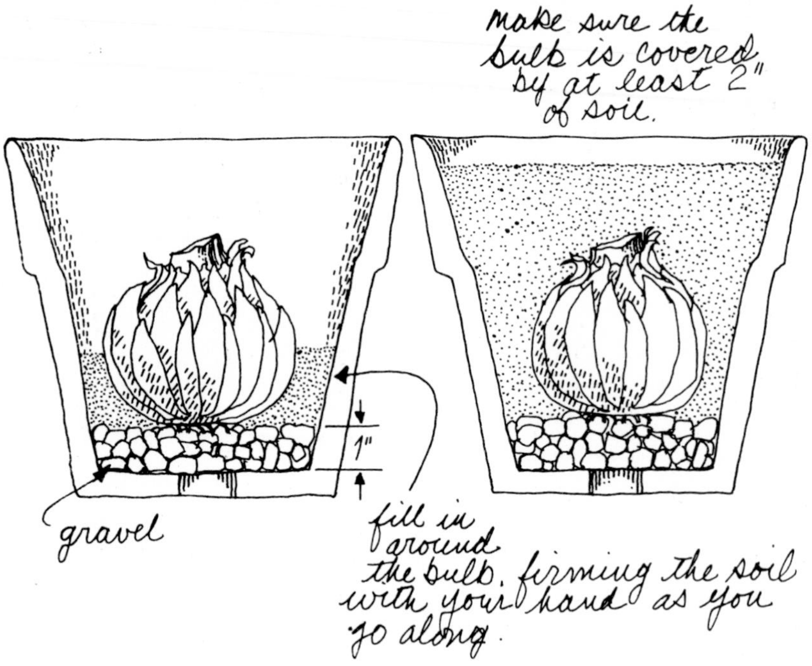

make sure the bulb is covered by at least 2" of soil.

gravel

1"

fill in around the bulb. firming the soil with your hand as you go along.

ies (crimson, golden yellow, silvery white, and pink), Imperials (white), Allegra (crimson), and Jamboree (bright red). Because of their height they are more commonly grown in home greenhouses than on windowsills.

English Ivy *(Hedera)* Ivies have been around as cultivated plants for centuries and grow wild in Europe, North Africa, and Asia. Bacchus, the ancients' god of wine, was fond of wandering the mountains and forests with nymphs while wearing a crown of ivy and laurel. Ivy isn't seen much on headgear these days but it is a staple in even the most modest of houseplant collections. The reason is that ivy plants are a snap to care for and there are dozens of types from which to choose, offering different shapes, coloration, leaf size, and spacing on the stem. The Canary Island or Algerian ivy, *H. canariensis*, has three-lobed leaves about 2 inches across; in my opinion the best of this species is *H. canariensis variegata*, sometimes known as the Gloire de Marengo, which has softly mottled green-and-white foliage.

The English ivies, *H. helix*, are a numerous lot. The original species isn't my favorite, as the leaves are 2 to 4 inches across and widely spaced along the stems, giving the plant a thin and hungry look. But many of the offspring of *H. helix* are dense, vigorous-looking plants: Hahn's Self-branching belongs in this group, as do Maple Queen, Lady

Kay, and Needlepoint. These varieties all have dark green foliage, but there are others whose leaves are variously marked with yellow, white, and even pink.

If they had their way, ivies would spend all their days in the English countryside, where the sun is gentle, the days cool, and the air moist. But barring such bliss, they tolerate an impressive range of less-than-perfect conditions. They're at their best in bright indirect light, or 800 foot-candles of artificial, but they'll grow in full sun or fairly heavy shade. They're happiest when night temperatures fall in the upper 50s and days about ten degrees warmer, but they'll survive readings below freezing. Heat, on the other hand, does pose a problem. For one thing it tends to dry out the atmosphere, setting up a miniclimate favorable to red spider mites. To keep these pests at bay, wash the foliage in warm sudsy water once a week, rinsing with a cold shower from the kitchen spray. This serves the triple purpose of leaving the foliage bright and shiny, adding moisture, and flushing

Canary Island Ivy *(Hedera)*

97

away any possible advance guard of spider mites before they have the time to lead in the troops. Keep the soil barely moist and mist the foliage religiously. Resist the temptation to overfeed them; they'll do fine with a light feeding of any houseplant fertilizer every 3 or 4 months.

All ivies have roots along the length of the stem that can cling to any notches or bumps on a vertical surface. As a result they can be grown as a tree with a stake or trained as a sort of indoor topiary around wire frames filled with sphagnum moss. My own preference is to leave them alone and let them trail over the rim of a hanging pot, pinching them back regularly to keep them bushy. The pinched stems root easily and the plants can be repotted at your convenience at any season, using a standard commercial potting soil.

False Aralia *(Dizygotheca)*

False Aralia *(Dizygotheca)* A healthy false aralia is an airy, willowy plant with foliage that is distinctive not only for its shape but for its color. Indoor plants eventually stand from 3 to 5 feet tall, bearing leaves that look like hands with slender jagged fingers. The leaves are coppery-colored when they first unfold, turning to a rich leathery dark green when they're fully open. It's one of the few foliage plants that will grow well in full sun, and it will do well in bright indirect light, too. Its correct botanical name is *D. elegantissima* but it's sometimes labeled *Aralia elegantissima.*

These plants are native to New Caledonia and other South Pacific islands, so they want warmth and humidity when they're grown indoors. The night temperatures should be in the upper 60s and the days well into the 70s. Keep the soil constantly moist and the air humid. Feed them with half-strength fertilizer every other week from spring through fall when they're doing the bulk of their growing; don't feed them at all for the rest of the year. False aralias can be propagated from stem cuttings taken in the spring or summer. When plants outgrow their quarters, repot them in standard potting soil.

One problem with these plants is that they have a tendency to drop their lower leaves if they don't have enough humidity and warmth. These are two difficult elements for the indoor gardener to control. They're upright-growing plants that don't tend to branch; so when the lower leaves are gone, not much can be done about it. Additionally, they're susceptible both to red spider mites and to scale, and the scale is particularly insidious because the plant's mottled stems provide a camouflage for them, and by the time they're noticed they often have a good head start. Nevertheless, an observant gardener, wary of these pests

and willing to cope with them, will find a false aralia a handsome and extremely satisfying foliage plant.

A close-up of the fingery foliage of the false aralia

Impatiens *(Impatiens)* Impatiens have been grown as houseplants for years and years, since long before there were florists serving home gardeners. My grandmother grew them, and when people came to visit, she'd send them home with a cutting. Her friends did the same for her, so many people had several impatiens plants each. These little flowering plants were much loved and appreciated because they blossom constantly, but they weren't as good-looking as today's plants. They were long-jointed, with the leaves sparsely spaced along leggy stems. The flowers were mostly a washed-out pink. Modern varieties, by contrast, are short-jointed and dense. They're also self-branching, which produces more stems, and more flowers at the tips of the stems. What's even more exciting, they're available in pink, red, orange, purple, gold, white, or multicolors. They have a pendulous habit of growth, so they're usually potted in hanging containers. (A few years ago several new species of impatiens were found in New Guinea. These plants have been in-

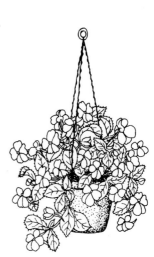

Impatiens *(Impatiens)*

99

terbred to produce plants known as New Guinea hybrids. They're attractive, but I still prefer the more common types. The flowers of the New Guinea hybrids are the same shape, and larger, but there are considerably fewer of them. To offset this, however, their large leaves are commonly marked with attractive cream-colored areas.)

Impatiens have simple needs. They flower best in bright, indirect light. The night temperatures should be in the low 60s and the days in the 70s. Keep the soil constantly moist and feed them every 2 weeks all year long. Gardeners in most of the country have to treat outdoor impatiens as annuals because they're not hardy enough to survive the harsh winters. In fact, impatiens are perennials native to Central America, and indoors they'll stay in constant bloom throughout the year.

The uncommon flowers of a common impatiens

When impatiens seed pods ripen, they explode and fling their seeds out to drop into soil and germinate; it's this trait that's responsible for the plant's botanical name, as well as one of its common names, Busy Lizzie. (It's also known as Patient Lucy, a contradiction I can't explain.) But as eager

100

as the seeds are to escape, they're very slow to germinate, and this is not the easiest way to increase your collection. Impatiens do grow very well and very quickly from cuttings, though, and you can manage your entire indoor and outdoor impatiens collection by taking cuttings when old plants become straggly. To build up a collection, I suggest that you sow impatiens seeds indoors in midwinter; use the plants outdoors as bedding plants or in window boxes, then take cuttings of the best of them before frost in the fall and grow these plants indoors through the winter. In the early spring, take cuttings of your indoor plants so you will have plenty of young plants to set out when the weather permits. As long as you have enough colors to keep you happy, you'll never need to buy another impatiens plant.

Monstera *(Monstera)* Botanically, this plant is known as *Monstera deliciosa*, a reference to its enormous leaves, and to the delectable pineapple-banana-flavored fruit that monstera plants bear in the wild. This is a vining plant native to the jungles of Central America, but unlike many other vining plants, which are potted in hanging containers to allow the foliage to tumble over the rim, these large plants are usually grown in an ordinary pot and provided a slab of wood upon which to climb. Roots develop aerially along the stem; when they're long enough they either cling to the bark or reach down into the soil. Some gardeners find them unattractive and cut them off, but I prefer to stick their ends into the soil as an extra source of nourishment for the plant. At maturity the leathery 8- to 10-inch leaves are deeply notched and perforated, the trait responsible for one of the plant's common names, Swiss cheese plant. Young monstera plants are sometimes mistaken for philodendrons, and sold as *Philodendron pertusum*, or as the cut-leaf or split-leaf philodendron, because when the leaves are young they are a simple oval shape similar to philodendron foliage. Monstera plants are usually known in the tropics as ceriman, a name applied to both the plant and its fruit.

Their preference is for bright indirect light, or at least 400 foot-candles of artificial light. If they have insufficient light, the growth becomes weak and the leaves are spaced far apart. They like their temperatures on the cozy side, in the high 60s at night and between 75 and 85 degrees during the day. They'll live at readings below 60 but they won't make much progress. Keep the soil barely moist all the time and give them a feeding of any houseplant fertilizer twice a year, once early in the spring and again in midsummer. They can be repotted any time of the year, using commercial potting soil.

Monstera *(Monstera)*

Monstera plants are naturally vining; they'll grow up and up and up, and even if they're pinched regularly, they rarely form side branches. They hold on to their bottom leaves for years, but eventually they do lose them. As a result it's not uncommon to find a plant that's been part of the family for longer than anyone can remember, having grown too tall and lost its lower foliage. There's no way to restore this plant to good looks because it simply won't put out new growth on its denuded stems. However, you can propagate it by leaf-bud cuttings and improve upon it enormously. Just cut the stem into sections, making sure each section has one leaf to it; such a stem section may also have an aerial root as a bonus. Put three or four of these sections into a pot with commercial potting soil. There's no need to root them first; the new plant will grow from the junction of the leaf and stem. By setting a few cuttings in together, the resulting plant will have a bushy look that no single plant could ever manage. (If you'd prefer one large plant, air-layer the top of your overgrown specimen, and then cut the plant back severely after you remove the air-layer. The original stem will send up new growth just below the point of pruning. See this month's feature for more about these methods of vegetative propagation.)

Moth Orchid (*Phalaenopsis*) What a beautiful flower this is, so uncluttered, so graceful and simple that it makes many other flowers seem gaudy by comparison. Its blooms are borne, dozens at a time, in long clusters on 2- to 4-foot stems. For foliage it bears only a few flat leathery basal leaves. The white moth orchids are the best known — they've been a staple in bridal bouquets for years — but there are delicate yellow, pink, and pink-striped varieties, too, as well as white ones with bright red lips.

The hybrids make the best choices because, when they're happy, they stay in almost constant bloom. I'd suggest that you buy a plant "in spike," meaning that it has formed buds that will open in a few weeks. If you can, order one that will come already potted up; if you can't, pot it up when it comes. A 6-inch pot is the right size for most plants in spike.

Throughout its life (and it will never die of old age), give your moth orchid the warm shade of its native locale in the tropics of Southeast Asia. The night temperatures shouldn't fall below 65 degrees, with the days into the 70s. During the summer, give it fairly dim light; it can take brighter light the rest of the year, but never sun, which is apt to burn the foliage. It needs excellent air circulation, but don't set it in a drafty spot, or one subject to sudden

Opposite: Monstera plant trained to a bark-covered slab

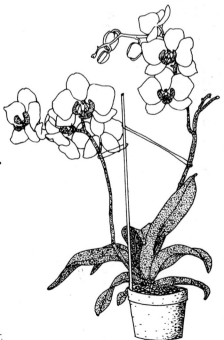

Moth Orchid (*Phalaenopsis*)

103

changes in temperature. The moth orchid doesn't have a pseudobulb, but it does have a water-holding spongy outer layer over its roots, and this covering helps to tide the plant over from one watering to the next. Be careful not to over-water it. Just keep the medium barely moist all the time and set the plant on a humidifying tray. You'll notice that as the plant grows, the bottom leaves will eventually turn yellow; they won't pull off easily, so cut them neatly from the plant.

As it grows, the moth orchid will develop aerial roots. When there are so many of these roots creeping over the edge of the pot that it's apparent the plant is getting pot-bound, it's time to move it to larger quarters. This will be necessary at least every other year, and the best time is in the spring. Moth orchids are monopodial, meaning that their growth is vertical; this is in contrast with cattleya orchids, and many others, which are sympodial and grow from rhizomes that creep along the surface of the soil. Sympodial orchids need a special location in the new pot when they're repotted (see the cattleya entry in the January chapter), but monopodial orchids can simply be set in the center of the pot. I use a planting medium composed of 2 parts fir bark and 1 part coarse peat moss, with a very small amount of slow-release fertilizer added to the medium.

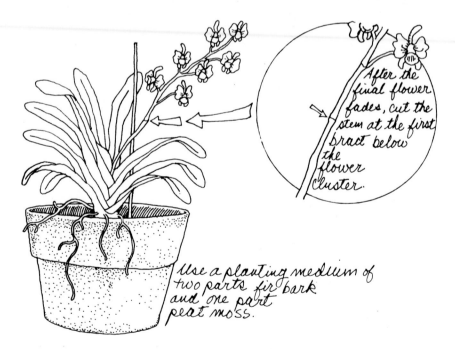

After the final flower fades, cut the stem at the first bract below the flower cluster.

Use a planting medium of two parts fir bark and one part peat moss.

The first bud to open will be the one closest to the base of the stem; each bud will open in succession out toward the tip of the stem. The time will come when there are so many buds and flowers that you will need to provide a stake to help the stem stay gracefully arched. When the final

flower on the stem fades, cut off the end of the stem at the first tiny leaflike bract below the flower cluster. You'll get another stem and flower cluster, or maybe two, from that original stem.

There is more information about orchids in general in the cattleya entry in the January chapter.

The tip of the moth orchid flower stem, its last flowers open

🏠 **Painted Tongue** *(Salpiglossis)* Rarely does a flower as lovely as a *Salpiglossis* suffer under the burden of two such awkward-sounding names. But I urge you not to let this put you off! To my mind, this is one of the most beautiful and graceful of flowers, whether grown in a winter greenhouse or a summer garden. It's related to the petunia and has blossoms of a similar shape, but there the resemblance ceases. Each salpiglossis flower, no matter what its color — pure yellow, pansy purple, creamy white, pale or deep blue — is cunningly marked with a fascinating network of golden veins. The plants themselves grow 18 to 30 inches tall and make superb cut flowers. Like their petunia cousins from Argentina, their stems are sticky, but it's a small price to pay for such delightful flowers.

Painted Tongue *(Salpiglossis)*

The velvety flowers of a painted tongue

Painted tongues (*S. sinuata*) are annuals, and have to be started anew from seeds every year. They need 5 or more months to reach flowering size, depending on when the seeds are sown. If the seeds are planted in September and the plants are kept in a greenhouse at 50- to 55-degree nights, they will blossom in March, April, and May. (You can bring the September sowing into bloom in midwinter by giving them an extra 5 or 6 hours of artificial light in the late fall, until the buds form.) Plants sown in January in the greenhouse blossom in June.

I'm partial to the September sowing because the blossoms open before the outdoor garden is colorful. I start the seeds in a cold frame, and then transplant them into commercial potting soil in 3-inch pots, and finally into 6-inch pots, feeding them monthly with any houseplant fertilizer. I move them into the greenhouse before the freezing weather arrives, and I keep the soil barely moist all the time. Until the buds appear I keep pinching off the leading stems to encourage bushiness. As they need it, I provide a support system for their relatively long stems.

Podocarpus *(Podocarpus)* Gardeners in the South and West think of the podocarpus as a dual-purpose plant. It's a handsome evergreen for the garden, where it is sometimes called "southern yew," and it is a fine, versatile, durable houseplant as well. In fact, it's hard to find a single negative thing to say about it. It tolerates a wide range of light conditions, from full sunshine through bright indirect light (its preference) to deep shadows; the darker the spot it grows in, the deeper green is the foliage and the slower-growing the plant. Its new foliage is always a paler green than the old, and the combination of colors is very striking. The podocarpus is a semitropical tree from Japan and thrives as well in cool spots as in warm ones; it can stand night temperatures as low as 40 degrees and days as high as 85. Ordinary potting soil is perfectly suitable; keep it constantly barely moist, and feed the plants twice a year, once in the early spring and again at the beginning of the summer, with any mild houseplant fertilizer.

A close-up of the evergreen foliage of a podocarpus

When podocarpuses grow wild in the native habitat they're often used as forest trees because they reach maturity quickly with a minimum of branches. When they're grown indoors, though, they move very slowly and can be pinched back and made to branch repeatedly into dense, bushy plants. This requires both time and effort on the part of the commercial greenhouse staff; as a result, large well-grown plants are often expensive. (Small plants, which do very well in a terrarium, are sold very reasonably.) Sometimes, in an effort to cut down on cost and still produce a good-sized plant, growers overfeed podocarpuses. The excess

Podocarpus *(Podocarpus)*

107

Column Stock *(Matthiola)*

Double-flowered, column-type stock

nitrogen does indeed produce large plants fairly quickly, but not strong ones; often they're too weak to support their own weight without a stake. My advice is to stay clear of these and buy a smaller, well-grown plant. Help it keep its shape by pinching back the tips (the cuttings will root easily in the fall), and pruning it in the spring before the new growth starts. The primary variety for indoor culture, *P. macrophyllus maki*, grows so leisurely that it can be left in the same pot for years.

■ **Stock** *(Matthiola)* Happily, there are several kinds of plants for the gardener who wants both fragrance and flowers in the winter greenhouse, but there aren't many that are easier to grow than stocks or, to my thinking, more rewarding. Wild stocks, native to southern Europe and northern Africa, are biennials or perennials, but the cultivated forms are treated as annuals that can be brought into flower in a cool greenhouse any time from January to early June depending on when the seeds are sown.

Two types of stock are particularly contented in the greenhouse. The first is the column-type stock, a single-stemmed plant that shoots up great 1- to 3-foot spikes of mostly double flowers; Column and Trysomic Giant Imperial are both fine varieties. The second type is the branching-type stock, which bears double flowers on numerous stems that range in height from 12 to 30 inches, depending on whether the variety is a dwarf or a standard; this type is available either as 7- or 10-week stock, referring to the time needed between seed-sowing and flowering. Both types bear dense flower spikes in white, pink, rose, buff, or lavender.

Stocks do not like heat. It encourages disease, like mildew, and it discourages the setting of buds. In fact, the buds won't set if the temperatures are above 65 degrees for more than 6 hours a day. Stocks do, I grant you, grow faster in warmer temperatures, but not as well. They're at their best in night temperatures around 50 and days below 65.

Stocks do not appreciate dampness, either. They're susceptible to diseases that lurk in moisture, and much of their culture is directed toward keeping them dry. If only a few plants are wanted, grow them in individual pots; I usually want a good hearty crop, so I put them into a deep bed — about 6 inches — of commercial potting soil. Column-type stocks are more tall than wide, so I sow 2 to 3 seeds in groups 6 inches apart; the branching type are bushier, so I allow them a spacing of 8 inches.

I keep my eyes on all stock when they emerge from the soil, and make sure to thin out any that are noticeably darker-leaved than the rest. The dark seedlings usually produce single-flowered plants, while the pale ones make double flowers that are more colorful, longer-lasting, and just as fragrant as the singles, if not more so. When they're thinned to their final spacing, column-type seedlings should be about 6 inches apart, and the branching type about 8 inches apart. Here is a timetable for Column stock: a late July sowing will produce flowers in January; an October planting blossoms in April; and an early February sowing means flowers in June.

As I've said, dampness invites problems. The most serious is stem rot, which shows up as a dark-colored rot down at the base of the stem. Don't worry about this problem if your temperatures are cool enough and your watering routine fastidious. I usually water my plants on the morning of a sunny day, making absolutely certain that no water splashes up on the foliage. When the soil is moderately dry, I water again. I rarely see a sign of stem rot, but if I spot what I think may be a problem starting, I pull out the infected seedling and destroy it. Every couple of weeks I give the plants a feeding with any half-strength houseplant fertilizer. It's wise to provide stocks with stakes or wire-and-string supports to assure straight stems.

⬭ **Sword Plant** (*Vriesia*) *Vriesias* are among the best of the bromeliads, and the sword plant (*V. splendens*) is surely one of the best of the *Vriesias*. A native of British Guiana, its long, thin leaves are a handsome bluish-green, marked with broad, dark stripes. The true flowers are insignificant, but they're housed in a spectacular, reddish-orange spike, shaped like a sword, that rises above the foliage and holds its color for months. It's an excellent houseplant because the foliage is good looking, even without blossoms. In fact it's worth growing for the foliage alone.

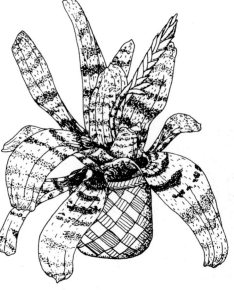

Sword Plant *(Vriesia)*

It also has tolerance in its favor. It's at its best in a warm, bright spot, where the night temperatures are above 60. It should be potted in a combination of equal parts sphagnum peat moss and coarse sand. Keep this medium just barely moist all the time, and make sure there is always water in the cup formed at the base of the plant, where the leaves enter the soil. Use rainwater if you can. And once a month add a drop or two of liquid fertilizer to the water in the cup. (Sword plants are terrestrial — they grow naturally in soil — while most other bromeliads are epiphytic, and normally grow in the crotches of trees. When they're potted up indoors, though, both types are treated the same.)

Sword plants can be propagated from seed, but the quicker route to full-sized plants is to start them vegetatively from suckers. The suckers develop very close to the base of the plant, often actually within the foliage rosette of

109

Sword plants in flower

the old plant, and have to be removed carefully once they've reached a height of about 4 inches. Try first to persuade the sucker to leave the parent by bending it back to an angle of about 45 degrees; then twist it gently side to side. Don't force it. If it doesn't come off with this motion, slice the sucker free with a sharp knife and give it a pot of its own.

Try to remove a sucker from the Sword Plant by bending it back to a 45° angle and gently twisting it from side to side.

Q&A

Q: My friends and I like to give each other cuttings of our plants. What's the best way to package them so they don't suffer in transit?

A: You're gardeners after my own heart — I do the same with my friends. Just moisten a facial tissue and wrap it around the base of the stem. Then wrap aluminum foil around the tissue so there's no leak. In cold weather, wrap the cutting in two or three layers of newspaper for insulation. Many plants, and their cuttings, die instantly in the cold, so don't overlook the newspaper.

Q: I've never been clear on what hybrids are or why they seem to behave differently from older versions of the same plant. Can you explain?

A: Hybrids are the result of mating two related species of a genus; by mating, especially among orchids, two genera; or by mating true-breeding strains of any kind of plant, such as petunia. Some hybrids are far more attractive than their parents and often display greater strength, hence the term "hybrid vigor." The first generation seedlings of hybridization are called F_1 hybrids and are often uniform in outward appearance. Their offspring, called F_2 hybrids, often revert to less attractive plants.

Q: I have an avocado plant that refuses to branch. I keep pinching it back, but it keeps growing up and up and up. Obviously, I'm fighting a losing battle.

A: Yes, you are. Avocados don't have much tendency to break, that is, to form branches. It's interesting to watch the plants grow from the pit, but they aren't very satisfactory as houseplants.

VEGE-TATIVE PROPA-GATION

Plants have a whole battery of reproductive techniques that operate as defenses against the extinction of their species. When gardeners reproduce plants, they are usually only making it possible for the plant to act according to its nature.

Most plants can reproduce sexually, meaning that male and female parts of the blossoms unite to form seeds by way of the transfer of pollen to ovaries. Indeed, most plants have blossoms that are simultaneously both male and female, but on some plants, such as holly and aucuba, the male and female flowers are produced on separate plants. When the seeds germinate they display traits from both parents in a unique genetic combination that marks each plant as an individual. As a result there is no predicting, except in the case of F_1 hybrids, exactly what seed-grown plants will look like.

So if you have a favored plant, and want to reproduce an exact replica, you have to take advantage of the plant's ability to reproduce asexually, without the aid of a partner, just by contributing a part of itself — a leaf, a stem, a piece of root. The resulting plant isn't really an offspring of the older plant, merely a younger identical extension of it. This procedure is known as vegetative propagation. It's familiar to most gardeners, by process if not by name, and with good reason: it's the quickest way to produce full-sized plants and, especially since the introduction of rooting hormones in recent years, all but foolproof. There are several types of vegetative propagation, described below.

Division This is the simplest of the techniques of vegetative propagation. Called either root or crown division, it involves nothing more than dividing a plant into two or more smaller plants, and potting each division separately. It can be used with any plant that sends up more than one stem through the surface of the soil, like Swedish ivies and Boston ferns. Division is best done when the plants are just beginning to produce new growth,

normally in the early spring. Flowering plants should be divided when they're dormant; if they don't have a dormant period, try to divide them when they're showing no flowers, or only a few.

The procedure is a breeze. If you're dividing a plant like an asparagus fern or a Boston fern, cut all the foliage right down to the soil level before you do anything else. This probably sounds dreadful, especially if you've grown particularly fond of the greenery, but if you don't cut it back each division will have lopsided foliage, all hanging over one side of the pot. If you're dividing a multicrowned plant like an old African violet, whose leaves are roughly horizontal and relatively permanent, leave the foliage as is.

Then knock the plant out of the pot and shake or wash off as much soil as possible so you can see the roots. There's no hard-and-fast rule about how large a division should be, but I usually find that I divide plants into 2 or 3 sections. The important thing is to make sure

Dividing a Boston fern grown too large for its quarters

that each division has its share of the plant's roots. Often you will find that the centers of old plants are dead or weak: unless I'm in desperate need of all the new plants I can get, I usually cut out and discard the inner core of old growth.

Some plants can be easily pulled apart by hand; others are more resistant, and call for a clean slice with a sharp knife. The roots start drying out as soon as they're exposed, so after the divisions are made repot each new section in the recommended potting medium. As a rule, each division should be set into a pot about 2 inches greater in diameter than the root ball, to allow for new growth; the exceptions are very fast-growing plants, such as asparagus or Boston ferns, that do better in pots that are 3 to 4 inches broader than the division. Make sure the repotted division sits at the same level at which it grew in the larger pot and that you firm the new soil well around the roots. Water the new plants immediately and put them in a bright spot out of direct sunlight, then water them only sparingly until the new foliage is firm and healthy. At that point return the plant to the conditions recommended for the species.

Stolons and Suckers or Offsets Some plants reproduce themselves by sending up complete new young plants either as suckers at the base of the old plant or as new plants that appear at the end of long trailing stems known as stolons or runners — the spider plant is probably the most familiar example. (By the way, about the only significant difference between stolons and runners is that stolons grow underground and runners above.) When this

Pin the plant at the end of the stolon to the soil in a small pot. When its roots are strong enough to hold it in place, cut the stolon.

type of plant grows in the wild the new little plants nestle down on the surface of the earth, and the runner or stolon, acting as an umbilical cord, nourishes the offspring until its roots take hold and it can live on its own. In the home, the little plant will root if you set a pot of soil next to the parent and, when the stolon is long enough, pin the young plant lightly to the soil with a hairpin or paperclip. Keep the young plant watered; when it looks healthy and is firmly held in place by its own new roots, cut the runner or stolon off and discard it.

Other plants, like many of the bromeliads, send out new plants right from their own bases, huddling close by the larger parent. Sever the young plant from the older one — cut as close to the parent as possible without damaging it — and

plant it in the recommended potting soil for its species; then give it the recommended conditions and it will develop into a handsome plant on its own. Don't separate the offset until it has a small root system of its own.

Cut the young plant from the old one as close as possible without damaging the parent.

Air-Layering This is a slow but exotic and easy technique for reproducing plants such as rubber trees, dracaenas, and dieffenbachias. It's often used with plants that have grown too tall, with all their leaves congregated ungracefully at the top of the stem. It's a peculiar-sounding procedure, but it works because it takes advantage of the plant's circulatory system: a small cut is taken in the stem that acts as a dam to the plant's circulating nutrients. When the nutrients bottleneck in sufficient quantity, they induce the plant to send out roots at the cut; then the stem is cut below those new roots and a short but full-foliaged new plant is born.

The first step in an air-layer is to identify a portion of a plant that will make a handsome short specimen, and make an upward cut about one-third of the way through the stem, at the spot where you want the roots to be. Then slip a toothpick or matchstick sideways into the cut to prop it open a bit and dust the newly cut surfaces with rooting powder. The roots need to emerge into a moist medium, so the next step is to take a fist-sized wad of moistened long-fibered sphagnum moss and tie it around the plant's stem, covering the cut. Then tie a sheet of clear plastic around the moss to hold the moisture in, and let the plant go to work. Continue to care for the plant, giving it the recommended amount of water, light, food, and heat. After a few months, when you can see roots coursing through the moss, take the plastic wrapping off, cut off the stem just below the new roots, and pot the new plant, root-filled moss and all, into the recommended potting soil in a pot sized to fit the new plant.

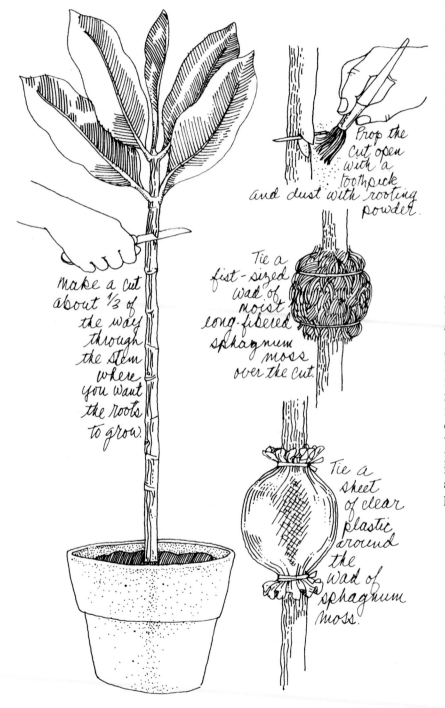

Make a cut about ⅓ of the way through the stem where you want the roots to grow.

Prop the cut open with a toothpick and dust with rooting powder.

Tie a fist-sized wad of moist long-fibered sphagnum moss over the cut.

Tie a sheet of clear plastic around the wad of sphagnum moss.

Taking geranium cuttings in the greenhouse

Cuttings If you're a beginning gardener, you have probably just breathed a sigh of relief: at last a technique you've heard of, and maybe tried. Cuttings are the most common type of vegetative propagation, involving nothing more than snipping off part of a living plant and allowing it to root and develop on its own. Not all cutting techniques can be used with every plant, but there are few plants that can't be reproduced by at least one of them.

The particular techniques vary, but some things are constant with cuttings. Plastic pots are preferable to clay because they hold moisture more efficiently. The rooting medium should be one that holds a good deal of water but is coarse enough to allow air to circulate freely: I think perlite produces the best results, but sharp sand, peat moss, sphagnum moss moistened with warm water, vermiculite, or equal combinations of any of these two, can also be used. It's best not to use the same rooting material more than once, to avoid spreading disease.

Stem cuttings: These are usually called slips, and they're the most common type of cuttings: they work well with any plant that has firm semimature stems, not too tender and succulent. As a rule the best stem cuttings are 3 to 6 inches long; the important thing is that they have at least 2 nodes (places where leaves are attached), but no more than 6. The cuttings should come from the mature tips of the current year's growth — not old woody stems — and should be taken when the plants are in active growth, usually in the spring or summer. (If you're taking a stem cutting of a flowering plant, snip off any flowers or buds; the plant should not expend energy for flowers at this point, but for root production.)

The cutting should have some leaves, but too many will overtax it, so I usually remove all but about 3 or 4 of the top leaves, or even 2 if they're large. It's especially important to remove any leaves that would be below the surface of

1. Use a pencil to make a hole in the rooting medium in a plastic pot.

2. Moisten the end of the stem, dip it in rooting powder and set it in the hole — firm the medium around it.

3. Mist the foliage lightly and cover the pot with a clear plastic bag, keeping the plastic off the foliage with sticks or labels.

the rooting medium, as they would only rot. Some cuttings root eagerly; others stubbornly resist, and need to be treated with a rooting hormone. Although some cuttings root in plain water, the roots that develop are called "water roots" and are fine if the new plant is to be grown hydroponically. If, however, the plant is to be grown in soil, a moistened coarse earth-based rooting medium is preferable. Perlite is often my first choice, but vermiculite, as well as other materials, are also used. An old standby, and very satisfactory for most plants, is plain coarse sand, sold either as sharp sand or as builder's sand by garden centers and masonry suppliers. Don't use beach sand; it's too fine and too salty.

Here's the procedure: Fill a plastic pot moistened with rooting medium, and use a pencil or a label to make a hole in

the medium for the stem. Moisten the bottom of the stem, dip it in rooting powder, set it into the hole, and firm the medium around it so it's well supported. If you want to start several cuttings at once, space them so they don't touch. When the cuttings are in place, mist the foliage lightly, and seal the whole thing, pot and all, in a plastic bag; don't let the plastic rest on the foliage. Sticks or labels, taller than the cutting, can be used to hold the plastic out of the way. For the period while the cutting is taking root, the pot should be in a bright spot where the temperatures are at least 60 degrees — 75 or 80 is better. Bottom heat will get it moving along quickly.

Don't put the pot in direct sunlight, however, as the plastic bag will act as a solar heating unit, and the temperatures inside will rise so high that the cutting will cook. The cutting should be removed from the plastic bag and transplanted to the proper growing medium and light and temperature conditions when the roots are about 1 inch long. Some cuttings form their roots in less than a week, and others take a few months. You'll know the cutting has sent out roots when the plant develops new top growth, but it's important to make sure that the roots don't get too long before the new plant is transplanted. Roots much longer than 1 inch in length are very apt to be broken during the transplanting operation. The most foolproof check is to take the cutting out of the rooting medium and look at it. If the roots aren't long enough, return the cutting to the medium, water it lightly, and give it some more time.

Cane cuttings: Some plants, such as dumbcane and dracaena, can be propagated by a variation on stem cuttings called cane cuttings. A 6- or 8-inch section of the stem or cane is laid flat on a bed of moist sand, so that it's partly covered. If the sand is kept moist, new plants will grow along the stem. If these plants are cut from the stem when they're about 2 inches tall and set into rooting medium, they will form roots and become husky, well-shaped young plants.

Leaf cuttings: Some plants, such as African violets, gloxinias, and Cape primroses, produce each leaf at the end of a long stalk called a petiole; these plants are usually propa-

gated by leaf cuttings, known technically as leaf petiole cuttings. The best candidate is the mature leaf, neither the youngest nor the oldest on a plant. If the plant has long-stemmed leaves, like an African violet for instance, cut the stem so it's only 1 or 2 inches long, not including the length of the leaf. Then use a pencil to make an angled hole in the moistened rooting medium, insert 1 inch of the stem, and firm the medium around the base of the stem. The angle helps prevent the emerging plants from being shaded by the larger leaf.

Plants whose leaves have very short stems, or none at all, can be inserted directly into the medium. Once the cutting's in place, slip the pot into a plastic bag, set it in a bright spot out of the sun, and wait until new leaves form around the original cutting and grow

to about a third the older leaf's size. This is the time to repot the new plant; sometimes you'll find that you have more than one little plant growing — each individual rosette of foliage is a separate plant — in which case you should gently pull or cut them apart at the roots and pot each individually.

Leaf bud cuttings: Leaf bud cuttings consist of the leaf, the leaf petiole or stem, and a section of the plant stem. A new plant grows from the latent bud where the petiole and stem join. This cutting is treated like a stem cutting, but it usually takes longer for a leaf bud cutting to develop roots.

One final note: If you're rooting plants at home, it's best to put the cuttings into individual flowerpots, or set a few together in a flat. But if you have a greenhouse, you may want to devote a section of a bench to rooting cuttings. If you do, make sure you put in a dividing wall to isolate the rooting medium from the soil in the rest of the bench. Provide some sort of shade so the cuttings don't sit in the full intensity of the sun and enclose the cutting bed area with clear plastic to help maintain high humidity. Commercial growers call such a structure a "propagating case" and their term for the high humidity is a "close atmosphere." The most important thing is to be fastidious with the rooting medium. Either change it regularly or soak the soil with a fungicide between each batch of cuttings.

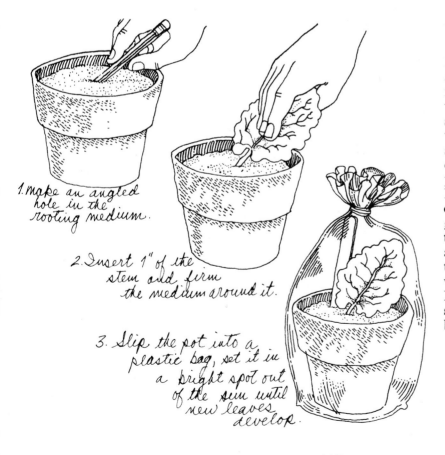

1. make an angled hole in the rooting medium.

2. Insert 1" of the stem and firm the medium around it.

3. Slip the pot into a plastic bag, set it in a bright spot out of the sun until new leaves develop.

MAY

Feature: Water and Food

Fancy-leaved caladiums

MAY

May is an unpredictable month throughout much of the country. It can be cool and rainy and springlike, or warm and dry and summery. If the weather tends toward the warm side, remember that plants will dry out more quickly. Keep an eye especially on the plants that will suffer most if their soil dries out, such as calla lilies, umbrella plants, hydrangeas, fuchsias, and ferns.

Though they're available at any time of the year, geraniums generally dominate the market in May, candidates for outdoor gardens and window boxes. You'll see calamondin oranges in flower this month, too; if you set these plants outside through the summer, they'll be pollinated by the insects, but if you keep them indoors, you'll have to pollinate them by hand with a camel's hair brush if you want them to bear their tart, edible fruit.

Next winter's crop of Arabian violets should be started from seed now. And if you have a greenhouse, this is the month to dig up the anemone tubers, after the leaves have faded. Store them in a cool, dark place through the summer. Greenhouse gardeners also enjoy the last of their calendulas this month, the result of seeds sown the previous August or September; the hot summer months bring these cool-loving plants to an abrupt end.

As soon as the outside weather warms up enough, most houseplants should be set outside for the summer. I make a point to prepare the spot in May so I'm ready to put the plants out as soon as the nights are predictably warmer than 55 degrees. I pick a partly shady spot that's protected from the wind and near enough to my water source that the frequent midsummer waterings will be easily handled. I find that houseplants are more apt to stay cool and moist and healthy if they're plunged into the ground, so I dig a trench for them — 6 to 8 inches deep and large enough to accommodate all my plants without crowding. I give them some drainage by setting in a 3- or 4-inch layer of gravel, and then fill the rest of the trench with peat moss, which will hold moisture around the pots. This is the ideal health spa for summering houseplants, a place where they can recover from the poor growing conditions of a winter indoors.

Aluminum Plant *(Pilea)* If there is one secret to handsome houseplant collections, beyond healthy plants, that is, it's combining a variety of shapes, sizes, textures, and colors. The aluminum plant (*P. cadieri*) and its relatives are helpful on several of these scores. The aluminum plant is small, scarcely ever more than 12 to 15 inches tall, and its fascinatingly quilted leaves have upper surfaces that appear to have been lightly brushed with bright aluminum paint. Aluminum plants are rapid growers and soon become gawky and lose many of their lower leaves. Don't try to save old plants like these: simply take cuttings from the tips of the stems and grow a crop of new husky plants.

Aluminum Plant *(Pilea)*

Other kinds of *Pileas* have dramatically different foliage: the one called Pan-American friendship plant or panamiga (*P. involucrata*) grows 6 to 8 inches tall and has copper-colored leaves. The silver panamiga (*P. pubescens*) becomes as much as 10 inches tall and, as its botanical name implies, its silvery leaves are fuzzy. The Silver Tree panamiga, an 8- to 12-inch hybrid, has leaves whose bronze upper surfaces have a broad silvery stripe, while the undersides are covered with reddish hairs.

All the members of the *Pilea* family are native to tropical areas, and they need similar conditions when they're grown indoors. They want a bright spot out of the sun, or 400 or more foot-candles of artificial light. The night temperatures should be in the high 60s, and the days in the 70s or warmer. The soil should be barely moist all the time. (The small stature of some species and their need for humidity make them fine terrarium plants.) Because of their size, mature plants are usually grown in 3- or 5-inch pots; they grow

An aluminum plant, kept carefully pinched and shaped

121

Burro's Tail *(Sedum)*

The fat, succulent leaves of the burro's tail

in ordinary potting soil but they're better off in a mix of equal parts potting soil and either peat moss or leaf mold. Feed them every other month with half-strength fertilizer. All *Pilea* species root easily from cuttings.

Burro's Tail *(Sedum)* The burro's tail (*S. morganianum*) is a trailing plant that bears fat, blue-green 1-inch leaves crowded along the foot-long stems. Of all the plants included in this book, the burro's tail is probably the easiest to care for, which makes it an excellent gift for people who appreciate greenery but don't have the thumb to match.

Many sedums are familiar hardy garden plants that can be left out year after year, even in areas where winters are severe. But the burro's tail is a native of Mexico, and it's not hardy. It is a rugged houseplant, though. Shy of a freeze, it will stand extreme temperatures, from as low as the 40s to as high as 100. It will grow in bright light or in sunlight. It does most of its growing from spring through fall, so during these months let the soil become moderately dry between thorough waterings; the rest of the year, give the plant only enough water to keep the leaves from shriveling. The leaves are succulent and can retain water for weeks, so don't make the mistake of overwatering. Feed it

three times a year, once in very early spring, once in late spring, and once in late summer.

Burro's tails don't need repotting frequently, and because the leaves are easily dislodged, it's better to water and feed an old plant more often, rather than repotting it. If moving it to a larger pot is necessary, make a mix of equal parts potting soil and sharp sand, and add 1 tablespoon of ground limestone and 1 tablespoon of bone meal for each gallon of this mix.

This plant is one of the easiest of all plants to propagate. Just remove a few leaves and barely insert the basal ends — the end where the leaf attaches to the stem — into damp sand. They'll root in a matter of days. They're very slow growing plants and it would take some time for a single plant to grow to a good size. I suggest, for a speedier effect, that you plant 3 or 4 rooted leaf cuttings together in a hanging container.

■ **Caladium** (*Caladium*) The fancy-leaved caladium is a big splashy plant that outcolors many a flowering plant. One relatively demure caladium (kal-*ay*-dium) bears creamy green leaves with dark green veins and borders, but the more familiar fancy-leaved varieties look as if they've been specially packaged for Christmas. Each leaf — shaped like a rounded arrowhead — is splattered with red, pink, silver, green, and white; the pattern of color varies from plant to plant, and even from leaf to leaf on the same plant. The caladium (*C. hortulanum*) is actually a flowering plant, but the flowers, which look like weak, translucent calla lilies, are hidden beneath the foliage and aren't particularly good-looking. At 15 inches tall, the plants are short for their foot-long leaves, giving them a dense, full, bushy look all their own.

Modern caladium varieties are the descendants of two species native to the jungles of Colombia, and today's plants carry within their genetic memory their jungle-climate life cycle: they rest completely for part of each year, withering away to their thick roots. Wild plants are triggered into growth again with the arrival of rainy weather. Today's varieties are still part-time foliage plants, needing a 4- or 5-month rest every year, but the timing of that dormancy is related to when the plants are started into growth, not to the seasons of the year. So you can have mature plants all year long by starting new ones every 5 or 6 months. They take about 3 months to reach full size, so those started in the spring are at their best in midsummer, then fade in the fall.

Caladiums are easy houseplants once they're about 6 inches tall, but in the beginning they need attention. Just as

Fancy-leaved Caladium
(*Caladium*)

Fancy-leaved caladium at a brightly lit window

Coleus *(Coleus)*

Opposite: A flat of several types of coleus seedlings

it is in the jungle, water is the key to initiating a new period of growth. To start the rhizomes into growth, prepare a bed of equal parts peat moss and damp sand or vermiculite and plant them about 1 inch deep. Bottom heat of 75 degrees is very helpful in getting the tubers started into growth. Maintain the bottom heat until the growth is about 4 inches tall. At that time, pot them up in their permanent soil mix, again 1 inch or so deep, in a 6-inch pot. I usually mix my own soil using 2 parts loam, 2 parts peat moss, 1 part well-rotted or dried cow manure, and 1 part sharp sand. If you prefer, use equal parts of potting soil and either peat moss or leaf mold. African violet soil is fine, too. Even though they're moisture responsive, they're a bit sensitive in their youth, so for the first few days after potting them up, water them sparingly to give them a chance to adjust.

While they're growing, caladiums need night temperatures in the high 50s and days hovering around 80, constantly moist soil, and fertilizer every other week. They're at their best in bright indirect light, or 400 or more foot-candles of artificial light; a north or east window is ideal. They can take full sun if they're introduced to it gradually, but if not the leaves are apt to burn. They can't take dim light at all; it makes the stems long and weak. They do beautifully outdoors for the summer; in fact, one of the best-looking shady window boxes I've ever seen was plush with them.

About 7 or 8 months after they're started into growth, the foliage will begin to wither. Don't fight their urge to rest by aggressive watering or feeding. Instead, gradually withhold water until the foliage dies completely. Then knock the plants out of their pots, shake the soil off the roots, cut off any withered stems and foliage, and dust the rhizomes with a fungicide/insecticide. Bury them in dry peat moss, vermiculite, or perlite at 55 to 60 degrees for 4 or 5 months, then start them into growth again. If you want more plants, divide the roots before you repot them, making sure each section of the tuber has at least one "eye."

Coleus *(Coleus)* For generations, there were two types of coleus available: the common coleus, and a trailing type known as the Rehnelt coleus. Now there are many more types, with more leaf colors, more shapes, and more leaf configurations. Most of them have stems weak enough so that they can be grown in a hanging container, and in my opinion that's the best way to display their colorful foliage.

Coleuses are tropical plants native to Java. They're one of the nicest plants for shady spots outdoors, or for brightly lit areas in the house. They'll tolerate sunlight, but I think their color is better in bright sunless light. The soil

should always be barely moist; they're apt to dry out rather quickly if they're grown in the sun. They're extremely sensitive to cold, and want nights in the high 60s or more and days around 80 to do their best. They're also very sensitive to fertilizers, and if they're overfed the roots will burn; a half-strength feeding with any houseplant fertilizer every 3 months will meet their needs. They'll be fuller if you keep the stem tips pinched back. Coleuses occasionally bear long spikes of pale blue flowers. I like them, so I leave them on the plant, but if you don't, just pinch them out.

Coleuses grow very quickly, and can become pot-bound in 3 or 4 months. You can repot them into packaged potting soil, but eventually you'll have a huge woody plant on your hands. There's no reliable way to rejuvenate a plant once it gets in this shape; if you cut it back, the new growth is apt to come in sparse and weak. It's a much better idea to take cuttings from the tips and throw the old plant away. The cuttings will root very quickly.

You can also start coleuses from seed. The seeds are tiny, so I sow them directly onto sifted milled sphagnum moss over a layer of potting soil. Then I bottom-water them with warm water (the moss won't absorb cold water easily, and the seeds won't appreciate the chill either). I set the pot into a plastic bag so I don't have to water them again before they sprout. If you're going to sow seeds, it's important to know that all coleus seedlings emerge from the soil a muddy green color. They don't take on their mature color until they're about 2 inches tall, so wait until they're that size before discarding any plants to avoid unwittingly sacrificing your best seedlings. In general, the slower-growing seedlings develop into the most colorful plants.

By the way, keep your eye open for mealybugs; they love coleuses. I eliminate them with a cotton swab dipped in alcohol.

■ **Gardenia** *(Gardenia)* I was once visiting a friend who asked me to take a look at her gardenia, which was giving her some trouble. I expected to see a sickly specimen with yellow foliage that hadn't blossomed for years. What I found was a beauty of a plant, 3 feet across and dense with blossoms. Her problem, as she called it, was trying to keep the plant in bounds. Now gardenias aren't plants for the casual gardener, in fact they're quite a challenge, but as my friend's success indicates, they can live and bloom repeatedly indoors if they're given the right care.

Gardenias are flowering shrubs from Japan and China. The word gardenia, while seemingly taken from the garden itself, is actually botanist Carolus Linnaeus's nod to

Gardenia *(Gardenia)*

126

his longtime friend, amateur botanist Dr. Alexander Garden of Charleston, South Carolina. Many different forms of this plant have been found: some trail, some have larger flowers and leaves than others, some bloom for longer periods of time. For years each variation was treated as a new species and given a name such as *G. florida*, *G. grandiflora*, or *G. fortunei*. Now it's thought that all these variations belong to the same species, *G. jasminoides*, so named because of its unforgettable jasminelike scent. Hadley, McLellan 23, Belmont, and Mystery are all excellent selections of *G. jasminoides veitchii*. All four of these varieties bear great large white flowers, and many of them.

The crucial gardenia-pleasers are sunny days and cool nights. The more sun they have, the more flowers they produce. If they have less than 4 hours of sun a day, they form beautiful foliage but not a sign of a flower. The daytime temperatures aren't so important — around 70 is fine, but they'll tolerate any indoor temperature that's comfortable for people. The night temperatures are another matter. Gardenias don't set new buds if they're exposed to night temperatures over 60 to 62 degrees; even a few warm nights will ruin their chances for blooming.

The nearly opened flower of a gardenia

Gardenias need constant moisture, both in the air and in the soil, and a monthly feeding with an acid-type fertilizer. The soil should be very acid — a pH of 5.0 or 5.5 is ideal — and well drained. There are several mixes that are suitable. The simplest and most costly is a packaged soil made up specifically for acid-loving plants. Equal parts loam and peat moss is another choice, or equal parts loam, peat moss, and well-rotted manure. Or, lastly, 2 parts peat moss, 1 part packaged potting soil, and 1 part sharp sand or perlite.

When you buy or repot a gardenia, the soil will be properly acid, but in many sections of the country tap water eventually makes it alkaline. This causes a gardenia problem known as chlorosis, which shows up as pale green leaves with dark green veins. The solution is to give the plants ½ ounce of iron sulfate — available from the drugstore — in 1 gallon of water. (Iron chelate, sold at garden centers, will serve the same purpose.) Start the treatment as soon as you notice the problem, and repeat it once or twice a week for about a month. In fact, it's a good idea to treat your plants every 2 or 3 months as a preventive; in that way you can avoid chlorosis altogether. (If the leaves are pale throughout with no dark veins the problem is lack of nitrogen and the remedy more frequent fertilizing.)

There are some other problems that bedevil gardenias and their admirers. Bud drop can be caused by any number of factors, including dry air, too much water or too little, cold drafts, too much fertilizer, or a series of gloomy, sunless winter days. Newly bought plants sometimes suffer from bud drop in reaction to the sudden loss of greenhouse humidity; you can reduce this problem by setting the plant on a humidifying tray and then spraying the buds two or three times a day with tepid water until the plant adjusts. Loss of foliage — a far less common problem — is sometimes caused by underwatering; this can be hard to diagnose because it can occur as a delayed reaction, only showing up a week or so after the drought, even at a time when the soil is ideally moist again.

Gardenias can be propagated from stem cuttings of new growth at any time of the year. The cuttings should be about 5 inches long, and the cut taken halfway between two sets of leaves. Remove all but the 4 top leaves on the cutting, dip the stem in rooting hormone, and set it 2 inches deep in moist rooting medium. Set the pot into a plastic bag in a warm but sunless spot, and bottom-heat to about 75 degrees. After about 2 months, or when you notice new growth, the plant is ready to be potted in one of the soil mixtures suggested above.

One last point on gardenia care. They love a summer outdoors in very light shade. My routine is to trim off ungainly branches, repot the plant in a 2-inch-larger pot to allow for summer growth, and then plunge the pot into the ground after the danger of frost has passed. All summer long I see to the plants' needs for moisture and food, and then I bring them in before the weather turns cold in the fall.

A trailing lantana, with its gracefully pendant stems

Lantana *(Lantana)* The lantana is a flowering shrub native to tropical America, where it scoots along pathways and nudges into gardens with such determination that it is considered little more than a weed. Indoors, that energy level becomes an advantage. As a pot plant, the lantana is dense and full, with pungent rough-textured leaves and plentiful flat-topped clusters of tiny fragrant flowers. It's at its flowery best in the spring and summer, but it blossoms off and on for the rest of the year, too. And it's very easy to care for.

There are two types of lantana that can be grown indoors: those that grow in shrub form, and those that trail.

129

Common Lantana *(Lantana)*

The shrub types are varieties of the common lantana (*L. camara*). The colors include white, pink, yellow (sometimes these start out yellow and change to other colors as they mature), red, orange, or bicolored. Some gardeners train the shrub lantanas into tree shapes, letting one main stem grow to 2 or 3 feet tall, and then branch. Personally I prefer to pinch back the growth and have shorter, bushier, more densely flowering plants, no taller than 8 to 10 inches.

Though the flower shapes are the same, trailing lantanas are far more delicate looking than the shrub types, thanks to their long, graceful branches. *L. montevidensis* (sometimes called *L. sellowiana*) bears great numbers of 1-inch clusters of rosy lavender flowers, making this species an elegant plant for a hanging container. On old plants the branches grow to be as much as 4 feet long.

Both the shrub and the trailing lantanas need the same easy care: a minimum of 4 hours of daily sunlight, night temperatures around 60 and days around 70. They'll grow in almost any soil: I use commercial potting mix. Let the soil become slightly dry between deep waterings, and feed the plants every other week with any houseplant fertilizer. I'm not impressed with lantanas once they age — they become awkward and lose their lower leaves. I keep new plants coming from stem cuttings, which can be taken any time of the year. It's especially important, if you put your plant outside for the summer, to cut it back hard when you bring it inside in the fall. The plant will be far healthier than if you try to save the entire canopy of foliage that developed so beautifully through the warm months.

If there's a single problem with lantanas, it's that they are so prone to white flies. I have a friend who won't have them in his collection at all because they can encourage such a serious infestation. If you're buying a plant, look it over carefully. Shake the plant a bit to see if the white flies rise up out of the foliage. Then check under the leaves for the white fly nymphs. Don't buy a plant with any sign of these pests. And even if you buy a plant you think is clean, segregate it from your other plants for 10 days. If you don't spot any white flies by then, you should be all set. (For more about white flies, and other pests and plagues that threaten houseplants, see the July feature.)

🏠 **Leadwort** *(Plumbago)* The Cape leadwort, which also goes by the name Cape plumbago, is a frothy, airy evergreen plant that came originally from South Africa. It's too large a plant for the windowsill, but it does very well in a hanging container in an intermediate greenhouse. The one most often grown is *P. auriculata* (also known as *P. capen-*

sis). It sends out trailing branches that usually grow to be 3 to 4 feet long, with 2-inch-long leaves spaced along the length. The azure blue flowers, each about 1 inch across and borne in 3- to 5-inch phloxlike clusters, first appear in the summer, and continue until the onset of the winter dormancy. (*P. auriculata alba* bears white flowers.) Leadworts are not compact plants — some might call them straggly — but you just have to live with that as mature plants can't be kept pinched back without sacrificing flowers.

Leadworts need full sun all day long; if they're grown in too little light, the growth is really gangly. They do their best if the night temperatures are in the low 50s and the days around 70. They'll survive in cooler air, but they won't be quite as good-looking. I pot them in ordinary commercial

Leadwort (*Plumbago*)

The delicate azure-blue flowers of a leadwort

potting soil. Leadworts grow actively from spring through fall, so during those months I keep them evenly moist and feed them monthly. When they stop producing flowers, I omit fertilizer from their diet and water them only frequently enough to keep them from wilting. Then, just before the end of their winter sleep, sometime in early January, I cut them back by at least a third, sometimes as much as half. New plants are easy to come by, either by stem cuttings taken in the spring or by seeds. And this is one plant that grows at full tilt from seed, producing 4-foot plants by August from seeds planted the previous winter.

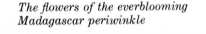 **Madagascar Periwinkle** *(Catharanthus)* This is a great little houseplant or summer annual that deserves more of a following. It stays in flower month after month, slowly growing larger but remaining fairly tidy as it ages. If it's set outside in the summer — still in its pot — and allowed to grow luxuriantly, it will produce handsome cut flowers, an unusual feature for a houseplant. As a bonus, the flowers have a long vase life because the buds continue to open even on the cut stems. Most varieties have pink

The flowers of the everblooming Madagascar periwinkle

132

blooms, but there are white and rose varieties as well.

Madagascar periwinkles can be started from seed but it's a slow process. The better idea is to buy a plant, enjoy it until it starts to become woody after a year or so, and start new plants from cuttings. (When you buy the plant, it may be identified as *Vinca rosea*, its former botanical name, rather than as *Catharanthus roseus*, which is its correct title.) Keep the young plants pinched back so they become full and bushy.

When they're grown outdoors as summer annuals, Madagascar periwinkles need shade, but indoors they do best in bright indirect light, with full sun in the winter. Pot them in commercial potting soil. Keep them consistently moist and feed them once a month. They can stand any amount of heat, but they stop producing flowers if the night temperatures drop below 60 degrees. Originally discovered in Madagascar, these lovely plants are now to be found throughout the tropics.

Madagascar Periwinkle
(Catharanthus)

■ **Maidenhair fern** *(Adiantum)* Dainty-looking maidenhair ferns are native to most parts of the world, but the tropical species are of most interest to us as houseplants. They have wispy clouds of ½-inch leaves — often pink as they unfold, a forthright pea-green as they mature — on stiff, wiry black stems. They would unquestionably be more popular still if their demand for humidity didn't make them so touchy. They can be grown indoors if the air is kept moist enough, but they're not easy. (If you're devoted to them but can't seem to please them, try a few small plants in a terrarium. For more on how to do this, see the September feature.)

The delta maidenhair fern (*A. raddianum*) is a little more tolerant of dry conditions than the other varieties, and the best choice for growing indoors; it's a relatively short plant at 6 to 15 inches tall. If you have a warm humid greenhouse you have a wider choice. The southern maidenhair fern (*A. capillus-veneris*) bears extremely delicate fronds, 6 to 20 inches tall. The brittle maidenhair fern, *A. tenerum*, is rarely grown as a basic species, but two of its varieties, both 15 to 24 inches tall, are often cultivated: Farleyense bears dense arching fronds with deeply cut segments and the fan maidenhair fern (*A. tenerum wrightii*) has fan-shaped leaflets.

The way to please maidenhair ferns is to use a soil high enough in organic matter to hold moisture efficiently. My mix is equal parts commercial potting soil and either leaf mold or peat moss, with 2 tablespoons of bone meal added for every gallon of the soil mix. During the spring, summer,

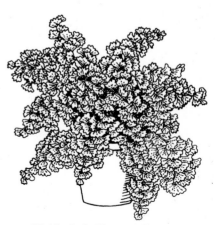

Maidenhair Fern *(Adiantum)*

The charming but somewhat difficult maidenhair fern

and fall I keep the soil mix constantly wet — unusual advice for a houseplant — and set the pots on humidifying trays. During the winter I let up on the water, giving them only enough to keep the fronds from wilting. If the new fronds come in curled and brown, lack of moisture is probably the problem. (If the fronds, new and old, turn brown at the edges, it's more apt to be the result of contact. Like the Boston fern, maidenhair ferns are very sensitive to touch.)

If their needs for moisture are met, their other requirements are fairly simple. The night temperatures should be in the 50s, the days in the 60s. They want the bright shade of a north window: the closer you can come to ideal moisture and humidity levels, the more light they can take, but never to the point of full sun. They'll live on 150 foot-candles of artificial light. For food, a single feeding of a half-strength fertilizer every 6 months is fine. They make a yearly flush of new growth in the spring, so if they need repotting it should be done just before this time, in late winter or early spring. That's also the best time to propagate them by cutting the fronds down to soil level and dividing the roots (see the April feature). Maidenhair ferns can also be

134

propagated by spores any time of the year. (See the January feature.) Young plants are very inexpensive, though, and they grow quickly.

■ **Passionflower** *(Passiflora)* Beginning this month and continuing through August, passionflowers send out some of the most unusual, intricate flowers known; there are never very many of them on a plant at one time, but each one is large and fascinating. Their ten petals (actually five petals plus five sepals that enclose the flower bud) surround several rings of thin filaments, and from the center projects a stalk that carries the plant's reproductive parts. (Legend has it that the parts of the flower symbolize Christ's passion and crucifixion, hence both the common and the botanical name.) Depending on the variety, the flowers are either purple, red, or white, or sometimes combinations of all three. In my experience, the red-flowered plants are the most difficult and the purple ones the easiest. Some varieties are fragrant as well. Passionflowers are among the few genera of popular houseplants that are native to the United States, growing wild from the southern reaches of this country into South America. However, it must be admitted that native species are rather weedy and seldom cultivated as compared to tropical ones.

Passionflower *(Passiflora)*

A red passionflower, dramatically colored but challenging

135

Passionflowers need a good 4 hours of sunlight every day, with night temperatures around 60 and days no cooler than 68 degrees. I use commercial potting soil. Under good conditions, these vines can grow to be an unwieldy 12 to 15 feet long. Ordinarily, vining plants are kept pinched to control the growth, but in the case of the passionflower, this would cost blossoms. Instead, train the plants around a circular wire mesh form — or any trellis arrangement — so they can continue to grow and flower without becoming unmanageably tall. (If you're growing the plants in a greenhouse, make sure to keep them in pots so they don't take over all your space.) Passionflowers grow actively and quickly from January through the fall, so keep the soil constantly moist and feed them lightly every other week during this period. Then in the fall, when the growth slows down, stop feeding them altogether and give them only water enough to prevent wilting. In January, cut them back to about 6 inches from the soil line to encourage branching and to get them off to a fresh start with new sturdy free-flowering growth for spring.

I usually propagate new passionflower plants from stem cuttings, which I take any time of the year. They can be started from seed, too, but the germination is unpredictable and apt to be disappointingly slow.

A rosemary plant in flower

Rosemary *(Rosmarinus)* Rosemary is usually thought of as an herb, dried and packaged on the kitchen shelf, but it's a handsome, rugged pot plant as well, providing fresh greens for seasoning and to add to a potpourri. It's one of the nicest herbs to grow indoors. From midwinter through early spring, it bears tiny lavender flowers among its needlelike foliage; the leaves are fragrant if they're touched. My favorite variety is known as prostrate rosemary *(Rosmarinus officinalis prostratus)* because of its creeping habit of growth. Its pinched tips, by the way, can go right into the pot on the stove if they're not used to start new plants.

Rosemary needs to be grown in dry soil; it helps concentrate the essence of the fragrance in the foliage. So I let the soil dry out a bit between thorough waterings, and I feed the plants every 2 or 3 months. Like most herbs, rosemary is sun-hungry, so I give it a spot where it sits in the direct sun for at least 4 hours every day; if it doesn't get enough light, the growth is pale, elongated, and weak, and the flavor poor. Night temperatures should be in the low 50s; day readings around 70 are fine. Rosemary plants are easily propagated any time of the year by cuttings. Seed-sown plants are very slow to mature.

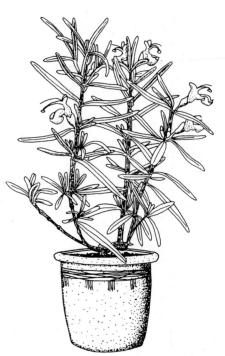

Upright Rosemary *(Rosmarinus)*

Star Jasmine *(Trachelospermum)* Star jasmines *(T. jasminoides)* are not jasmines at all, but they're so delightfully fragrant that they certainly deserve the title. The fragrance comes from the five-petaled starry white flowers that appear in clusters through the spring, with occasional tantalizing flowers intermittently through the summer too. The flowers are generally about 1 inch across, and the shiny, slender green leaves about 2 inches long. There's a variegated variety, *T. jasminoides variegatum,* with red-accented green-and-white leaves, but I don't think it holds a candle to the green-leaved variety. Star jasmines are evergreen vines native to China, and they can be trained on trellises and allowed to climb indoors, too. But they're slow-growing plants, and I prefer to keep them pinched back so they remain as short, compact bushes.

Star jasmines are not difficult houseplants. They do best if the night temperatures are in the low 50s and the days near 70; if they're given a warmer spot, they'll grow more quickly. Most of the year they need bright indirect light, but during the winter, half days of sunshine are helpful. Give the soil a chance to dry out slightly between thorough waterings, and feed the plants every 2 or 3 months. It's important to repot them when they're pot-bound, as the

Star Jasmine *(Trachelospermum)*

137

A star jasmine flower, with the skeletons of older flowers in the background

older leaves are apt to turn yellow if the soil is exhausted; commercial potting soil is fine.

Like most houseplants, star jasmines appreciate outdoor air, so when the summer comes I move my plants outside to a lightly shaded spot and plunge the pots into the ground so they won't tip over. When the weather cools in the fall I bring them back inside and start new plants from stem cuttings. The cuttings won't grow very quickly, but they can blossom when they're only 6 inches tall.

Q: I love snapdragons, and I've decided to grow them in my greenhouse this winter. Do you have any advice for me?

A: Yes, and it's important advice. Summer-flowering snapdragons are genetically different from the winter-flowering ones. If you try to sow summer-flowering snapdragon seeds for winter flowers, you'll see nothing but foliage. It isn't easy for the hobby greenhouse grower to find the winter-flowering snapdragon seeds, as they're usually sold only to the commercial market. But some seed houses do carry them, and identify them either as "greenhouse-type," or as "winter-flowering." You might also see them labeled as Group I or II snapdragons, which are early- and late-flowering winter snaps; Groups III and IV are summer-flowering. Sometimes seed houses offer a mix of seeds from Groups I and II, which include different colors. If you're able to find a more detailed selection, these varieties of Group II snapdragons make good choices: Maryland White, Snowman (white); Hercules, Maryland Pink, Pink Ice (pink); Maryland Lavender (lavender); Navajo (red); Golden Spike (yellow); and Gallant Fox (bronze). All in all it's a complicated business, and you might consider just asking your local commercial grower to sell you a few plants. By the way, sow snapdragon seeds in July for flowers during the winter months.

Q: I've been hearing so much about a new technique to grow houseplants in water. I travel a good deal, and I'm intrigued to know more about this, especially if it means my plants could stay healthy when I'm away for a couple of weeks.

A: You're talking about hydroponics, a technique that's been practiced in Europe for some time but has only recently come into the limelight here. Many plants, including African violets, philodendrons, dieffenbachias, and Chinese evergreens, will grow indefinitely in water, and do beautifully. If you've got it in mind to unpot your soil-grown plants and move them into water, do some research to make sure that each one is suitable to this type of culture. When you're making the transfer, wash every bit of soil from the plants' roots; if you don't, the soil will decay in the water, and that's not good for the plants. For the period of time (often a month or more) it takes the plant to adjust to the new medium and develop water roots, which are completely different from soil roots, treat it as a convalescent. But rest assured, it will adjust. Hydroponics is a new but promising technique that could be a boon to all indoor gardeners, especially to people like you, because plants growing in water can be left for 2 to 4 weeks without any attention at all. (For other ways to maintain your plants during a short absence, see the August feature.)

WATER AND FOOD

All plants, like all living creatures, need food and water. But most houseplants die because they get too much of one or both, the victims of the dangerous philosophy that if some is good, more must certainly be better. The important thing is to give plants the amount of food and nutrition they need, neither more nor less. That means understanding the needs of each plant, and seeing each one as an individual. If you treat your entire plant collection as a group of equals, watering and fertilizing all of them identically on a regular tour of your indoor garden, you'll be playing horticultural Russian roulette.

Water Overwatering is the number-one houseplant killer. Too much water drives the nutrients out of the soil, compacts the soil's structure, and leaves no room for air to circulate. Without air in the soil the roots suffocate and rot, the foliage yellows, and the plant dies. Not a handsome sight, but a common one.

The way to avoid this is by giving the plant the right amount of water. This will vary from species to species; for instance, plants that are native to the jungle rain forests are accustomed to, and therefore need, more water than do those whose ancestors grew in the deserts. Water needs even vary from plant to plant within a species, depending on the conditions in which the plant is growing. The closer the plant is to its natural conditions, the more contented it will be and the more water it will be able to put to use. Water needs are also related to a plant's life cycle. Plants expend far more energy when they're in active growth and flower than they do when they're dormant. And even plants whose activity is steady month to month throughout the year react to outside light conditions: weak winter sun or a string of dreary December days causes the plants' growth to slow down until warmer, sunnier weather. The container enters into this issue, too. A plastic pot holds water in the soil about three times longer than does a porous clay pot. And speaking of pots, if the container is too small for the plant, the soil's moisture will be called on more quickly than if the plant is in roomy quarters with plenty of soil. (If you're fond of extremes, the thirstiest plant is one that is native to a tropical rain forest, growing pot-bound in a clay container, in flower, enjoying perfect light conditions, and suffering through a dry day in August.)

The best way to diagnose your plants' water needs is by poking your finger into the soil and feeling for the degree of moisture. The terminology used in the alphabetical entries is based on finger testing, so I've defined the terms, below, according to how the soil would feel.

Allow soil to dry completely between thorough waterings: The soil 1 inch below the surface feels dry.

Allow soil to dry slightly between thorough waterings: The soil 1 inch below the surface feels slightly moist.

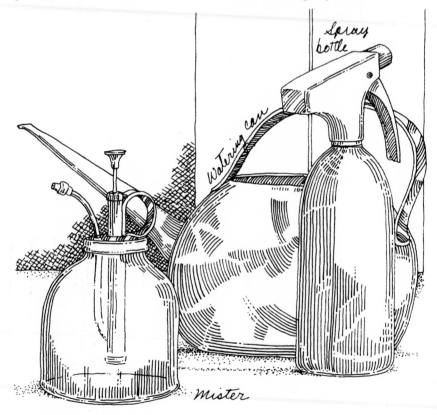

140

Keep soil barely moist: The surface of the soil never feels dry.

Keep soil wet: The plant is always kept in a saucer of water, and the surface of the soil looks and feels moist.

It's best to water plants in the morning; this gives them several hours of daylight to absorb the water and nutrients. If the soil surface is wet at night, the plants are apt to develop crown rot. Never use cold water on plants. Use water that's slightly warm to the touch. If there's any way for you to water your plants entirely with rainwater, do so; it's pure horticultural champagne. If you use tap water, let it stand overnight so it warms to room temperature and any chlorine in the water can evaporate. Softened tap water is fine as long as there's a deionizing element in the softener. There is some recent research to indicate that fluorides added to municipal water supplies make the foliage of some tropical plants, like spider plants, turn brown; the ultimate solution to this is to use rainwater. I don't use it myself because my municipal water supply is quite pure, but I know of greenhouse growers in hard-water areas who collect rainwater for their plants.

As to watering itself, there are three ways to moisten soil.

Top-watering is the way most gardeners water their houseplants. It means, simply, pouring water onto the surface of the soil, beneath the foliage and close to the center of the plant. This is best done on a

Top Watering

bright sunny morning, especially if the foliage is dense enough to shade the soil surface. Top-watering is quick and easy and has the advantage of flushing the soil of any fertilizer salts that have collected at the surface of the soil.

Bottom-watering involves setting the plant in a saucer of water so the roots can take up moisture through the drainage holes of the pot. When the surface of the soil is moist to the touch, empty the saucer of any leftover water so the soil doesn't absorb excess moisture. This is a very gentle watering technique, thorough, and easy

Bottom Watering

on delicate roots. But if fertilizer is added to the saucer water, bottom-watering will draw fertilizer salts to the surface of the soil, where they will appear as a chalky white residue caustic enough to do some plants real harm. To cure this, top-water the plants a few times to flush those collected salts away. To prevent it, top-water whenever you feed your plants. (In hard-water areas, bottom-watering can draw harmful minerals to the surface of the soil; top-watering with rainwater is much safer.)

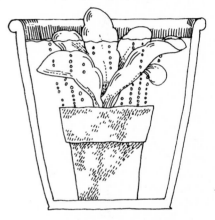

Submersion

Submersion is a messy affair, but just as most outdoor plants profit from a deep soaking rain now and then, most houseplants appreciate a plunge every couple of weeks in a pail of tepid water. The water has to be deep enough so the pot is entirely immersed and the surface of the soil flooded. You'll see and hear air bubbles rising from the soil; when they stop, take the plant out of the water and give it ½ hour to drain before setting it back in its place. Submersion is not only a good maintenance routine, but a life-saving remedy for a plant that's been allowed to become too dry.

141

Try to group plants according to their moisture needs.

Food Outdoor plants get all the nutrients they need from decaying organic debris or garden fertilizers. A potted plant indoors has no such ready food supply, and relies on the local attendant gardener for meals. Unfortunately most gardeners more than meet their responsibility, with the result that overfeeding is second only to flood in the list of houseplant killers. As with watering, the gardener has to understand the plant's needs. Remember that it's easier for a plant to live indoors on a lean diet than on a fat one because dim indoor light cuts back drastically on photosynthesis, the process carried on in the presence of light that enables plants to utilize nutrients.

Beyond water in the soil, most plants need moisture in the air, too. In the wild they get natural humidity, but indoors, especially in heated winter houses, the air is usually crackling dry. There are a number of ways to provide plants with the humidity they crave, though. The first is to group several plants together; all plants exhale moisture, and grouped together they help create a humid miniclimate for each other. Try to group the plants according to their moisture needs; if one plant that needs constant moisture is surrounded by succulents that go for days without water, its chances of being attended to are slim. Grouping not only makes for a healthier presentation, but a handsomer one as well. It's also helpful, even essential, to set many plants on humidifying trays. The goal here isn't to bottom-water the plants, but to make sure there's always water evaporating around the plants' foliage. I usually use plastic trays — rustproof metal ones or glazed waterproof ceramic ones are

fine, too — and add 1 inch of stones to the bottom, then water up to but not above the level of the stones. Finally, it's a good idea to mist the plants regularly with an atomizer that sends out a fine vapor spray of water; again, the idea is humidity in the air, not wet leaves, so spray around the plants, not at them. (Fuzzy-leaved plants, like African violets, should never be misted.)

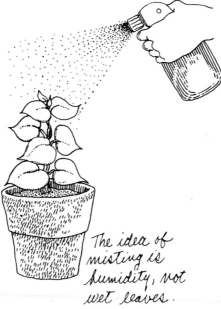

The idea of misting is humidity, not wet leaves.

There are two main classes of fertilizers, organic and chemical. As popular as organic fertilizers (like cow manure) are for outdoor vegetable gardens, they aren't always a practical solution indoors. For one thing, they may smell; for another, they work slowly. The chemical fertilizers are a better choice, so long as they're specifically labeled for use with houseplants, because their nutrients are immediately available and, incidentally, are chemically identical to those derived from organic sources.

Chemical fertilizers contain three nutrients essential to plant growth: nitrogen, which makes foliage rich and green; phosphorus, which encourages healthy root growth; and potassium, also known as potash, which helps the plants ward off disease. Fertilizers are usually identified by a series of three numbers that represent the ratio of these three nutrients, always in the nitrogen-phosphorus-potash sequence. In other words, 5-10-5 is 5 percent nitrogen, 10 percent phosphorus, and 5 percent potash; the remaining 80 percent is filler. Look for a composition with a ratio of 1:2:1, which provides most houseplants with a balanced diet. Some specialized fertilizers are designed to meet the needs of specific plants, like acid-type fertilizers for azaleas and gardenias.

Chemical fertilizers are available in a whole range of forms. Many slow-release fertilizers come as little beads or capsules that dissolve slowly so they don't burn the roots of the plant. They're timed to release a controlled amount of food slowly over a specified length of time, which may be as short as 2 or 3 months or as long as a year and a half. They're easy to use, of course, because they are initially mixed with the potting soil. They take care of the plant's food needs for long periods and can be replaced when the need arises by scattering more capsules on the soil surface where they will slowly dissolve with each watering. There are also fertilizer tablets and nutrient-impregnated "sticks" that can be pushed into the soil.

Quick-acting water-soluble fertilizers go to work immediately and begin to be incorporated into the plant's system within an hour or sometimes less. Some of these are in powder form, and are meant to be scratched into the soil surface. Others, in either powder or liquid form, are designed to be mixed with water; these are the easiest to use and the most popular by far. But be conservative, even stingy, with the proportions. As a rule, it's smart to use a solution only half as strong as the manufac-

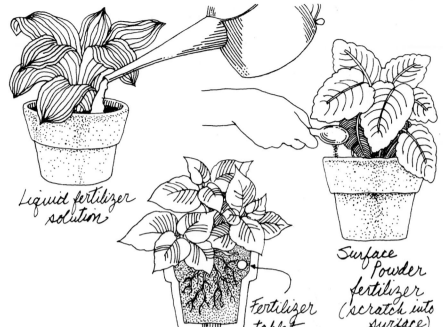

Liquid fertilizer solution

Fertilizer tablet

Surface Powder fertilizer (scratch into surface)

turer suggests. I sometimes suspect that fertilizer manufacturers, desirous of selling the maximum amount of their product, push their dosage recommendations to the utmost limit. Remember, overfeeding is the second most prevalent cause of houseplant fatality. The alphabetical entries indicate the specific food needs of the individual plants in this book.

When you buy a foliage plant from a garden center or florist, it has been given a feeding of slow-release fertilizer more than adequate to see it through the first 6 months in your house, so never feed a foliage plant until you've had it for half a year. (This isn't true of flowering plants. Assume that a new flowering plant was fed just before it was sold, then put it on its feeding

schedule according to the alphabetical entries.) Newly transplanted plants need about 2 weeks without food to give them a chance to become accustomed to new quarters. Give a young plant, whether seedling or cutting, a chance to grow 3 or 4 inches tall before putting it on its recommended fertilizer diet.

When you do feed a plant, be gentle. Fertilizers, even some organic ones, contain strong chemicals that can easily burn the roots of a plant. Don't try to cure a plant's ills or make up for bad growing conditions by overfeeding. In northern areas, in fact in most of the country, most nonflowering plants shouldn't be fed at all between November and February. Don't feed an obviously troubled plant, or one that's about to enter a rest period. Let me end by giving the fertilizer advice I've been giving for years: when in doubt, don't.

JUN

Flame Violet
Glory Bower
Golden Trumpet
Moses-in-the-Cradle
Orchid Cactus
Rex Begonia
Shrimp Plant
Wax Plant

Feature: Cactus!

Flame violet

JUN

In my part of the country, June brings warm nights, with temperatures of 55 degrees or higher, so this is the month when my houseplants take to the open air. Because I readied a place for them in May, I simply move them out to their lightly shaded trench for the summer. With the exception of African violets and other fuzzy-leaved plants, I put all my plants outdoors. If your outdoor summering area is limited, or if you can't bear to leave the house entirely plantless, be sure to set out at least the plants that respond best to a summer outdoors, such as gardenias, Madagascar periwinkles, star jasmines, wax plants, fuchsias, and princess flowers. Cyclamens will thrive in the summer air, too, but they should be repotted before they're set out. In fact, all these plants will make such dramatic growth while they're outside that you should be sure they have been repotted in the spring so they have room enough in their pots to grow without becoming crowded. When you set the pots into the trench, bury them just up to the rims. Every few days turn the pots so the plants don't have a chance to send down roots through the drainage holes.

If you have no area to set your plants outside, put them on a porch table for the summer; just make sure they're in a protected spot where they won't be blown over or drowned in the first soaking rain. If you leave your plants inside for the summer, put them in your coolest room; they're no more comfortable in the summer heat than we are. Air conditioning will help them enormously as long as they're not directly in line of a cold blast of air. Office plants will be fine through the summer, even if the building is air-conditioned only during the weekdays; they'll be far healthier than plants subjected to constant, overheated indoor air.

Looking ahead to later months, I make it a point to sow cyclamen seeds in June. They can, in fact, be sown at any time of the year, but this crop will be full-sized plants in 15 to 18 months, coming into their first blossom period in early autumn.

Flame Violet *(Episcia)* Flame violets are among the easiest to grow and prettiest of gesneriads, but few gardeners are as familiar with them as they are with African violets or gloxinias. Flame violets don't bloom freely all year as African violets do, but they do bear their white, pink, scarlet, or lavender flowers continuously from early spring through early fall. Most varieties have oddly textured and marked leaves that are far more interesting than those of their more popular relatives. Acajou, a particularly good-looking selection of the species *E. cupreata*, bears red flowers over dark mahogany and silver leaves.

Flame Violet *(Episcia)*

In their native habitat in the jungles of Central America, flame violets creep along the ground and send out runners like strawberry plants. When they're grown indoors they can be put in a regular pot, or they can be grown in a hanging container so the runners are allowed to trail over the edge. They need food monthly from early spring until they stop flowering. The stems of the leaves are susceptible to damage if they come into contact with caustic fertilizer salts that have collected on the surface of the soil. The way to avoid this is to feed the plants by top-watering, which will flush the salts down through the soil. (For more about this, see the May feature.)

Given their jungle heritage, it's little wonder that flame violets want warmth and humidity, and you may have trouble with them if you can't provide these two necessities. Keep them on humidifying trays (or in a terrarium) in a spot where the night temperatures will stay in the 60s. If the readings fall below 60, they'll start to lose their lower leaves and, like many other gesneriads, they'll stop growing or die at about 55 degrees. Give them bright indirect light, and keep the soil constantly moist, using tepid water, as cold water splashed on the leaves will blotch them, just as it does African violets. When they stop flowering, cut the plants back to encourage fresh new growth, and root the cut stems. The plants can also be propagated by planting the runners in commercial potting soil at any time of the year. (See the April feature for more information.)

Glory Bower *(Clerodendrum)* This is another uncommon tropical plant that does beautifully indoors. Where they grow wild, glory bowers are evergreen, twining, shrubby vines. Indoors they can be allowed to make their growth naturally, but they'll grow to the ceiling with a gawky, spindly shape. They're much better looking if they're kept 2 or 3 feet tall by pinching back. Because the flowers are borne only on the tips of the stems, the shorter, bushier plants are much more densely flowered.

Glory Bower *(Clerodendrum)*

Glory bowers are lovers of warmth; they want night temperatures of 60 degrees or warmer. The species *C. thomsoniae,* a native of tropical West Africa and sometimes called tropical bleeding-heart, sends out its scarlet-and-white flowers in the spring and summer, but if the warm temperatures can be maintained, it will continue to bloom right through the winter. I grow glory bowers in commercial potting soil and set them in a spot where they'll get bright indirect light. The soil should be kept constantly moist, and the water boosted with fertilizer every other week during the growing season. If you can keep them in flower all winter, continue to feed and water them normally all year long. If not, prune them back after they flower, keep the soil on the dry side,

148

and don't feed them at all. Then in the spring put them back on their growing-season regimen of moisture and fertilizer.

The best way to propagate them is from stem cuttings. (See the April feature.)

🪴 **Golden Trumpet** (*Allamanda*) Two factors stand in the way of this plant's commercial success: it grows slowly and it needs warmth. The professional grower has to keep golden trumpets in night temperatures above 60 degrees for nearly a year in order to have market-sized plants 1½ to 2 feet tall, and that is an expensive proposition. As a result most growers don't carry them at all, but those who do, sell them relatively inexpensively when they're small. In my opinion, that's just as well, because it gives the home gardener the chance to watch them grow.

Despite their commercial drawbacks, they're fine plants for the home gardener so long as they can be kept warm enough. They bear trumpet-shaped, primarily yellow flowers through the spring and summer. The best and most common of the indoor varieties is *A. cathartica hendersonii*, whose flowers are larger than the other varieties' at 3 to 5

Golden Trumpet *(Allamanda)*

A golden trumpet flower cluster

149

inches across. There's a violet-flowered variety (*A. violacea*), but it doesn't blossom as freely as the yellow-flowered plants.

Golden trumpets are natives of the South American tropics, and when they're grown indoors, they need at least half days of sunshine and warm temperatures, with night readings in the 60s. From April through September, when they're in flower, keep the soil constantly moist and fertilize them every other week. For the rest of the year, give them no food and let them dry out a bit before watering.

Golden trumpets are vines, and if they're provided a trellis they'll climb several feet high. As is often the case, though, they're better-looking — shorter, bushier, and more densely flowered — if they're kept pinched back while they're young. Keep transplanting them every spring before new growth starts to 1-inch-larger pots of commercial potting soil until they're about 3 feet tall; then move them only when they're jammed for space, as they seem to flower best when they're crowded. I've seen plants in blossom when they're less than 1 foot tall. Old plants appreciate a pruning in January to keep them 2 to 4 feet tall; the new growth comes in compact and bushy, and the pruned stem tips will root easily through the spring for a new generation of plants to share with friends.

Moses-in-the-Cradle *(Rhoeo)*

Moses-in-the-Cradle *(Rhoeo)* This plant is known by a whole string of odd, mostly cumbersome, common names, including Moses-in-the-cradle, Moses-in-the-bullrushes, man-in-a-boat, boat-lily, oyster plant, and several others. All these names are taken from the boat- or cradle-shaped configurations of bracts that nestle at the base of the foot-long swordshaped leaves (the bullrushes). Tiny white flowers (Moses, to complete the analogy) grow from the cradle/boat. But despite all the attention these names pay to the oddity in the crown of the plant, the dramatic element is the foliage, with its deep reddish-purple tinge.

Moses-in-the-cradle (*R. spathacea*) is native to Mexico, but the specimen that stands out most vividly in my memory is one I saw growing on the face of a volcanic rock wall in Hawaii; it was in full sun all day long, which made its growth compact and its color rich. When these plants are grown indoors, they'll live in either bright indirect light or full sun, but the more intense their light, the more colorful their foliage. They like night temperatures in the 50s and days close to 70, a feeding every 4 months, and soil that is always barely moist. They're slow growers, so they don't need repotting often, but when they do I put them in commercial potting soil.

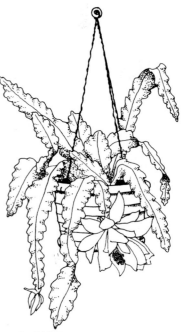

Orchid Cactus *(Epiphyllum)*

Eventually, as the plants age, the older leaves begin to look a bit ragged, and it's time to propagate new young plants. The quickest way to full-sized plants (about 18 inches tall) is either to repot the suckers that appear at the base of the plant, or, if the plant is old enough to have developed multiple stems, to divide the crown and roots. New plants can also be started from seed. Any of these propagation techniques can be done at any time of the year.

Orchid Cactus *(Epiphyllum)* Orchid cactuses aren't orchids at all. They're genuine cactuses, but they're native to the rain forests of Central America, and this has caused them to develop quite differently from their desert-

151

based relatives. They're epiphytes, growing naturally high in trees and feeding on decaying leaves and insects that collect in the nooks and crannies of the branches. They have no thorns, though some do have clusters of harmless hairs along the stems. They don't come from a dry climate, so they haven't evolved as much water-storing capacity as have desert cactuses; rather they have soft, waxy, flower-bearing stems that need moisture on a frequent, regular basis.

This is not to say that all orchid cactuses are alike. Most of the ones available today are hybrids that bloom off and on all year long and present the gardener with a huge selection. They come in nearly every imaginable color except blue; the flowers can range from 2½ inches across to a mighty 9 inches or more. The original species of orchid cactuses are still available, but the hybrids are far superior. (Christmas cactuses are an entirely different plant. See the December chapter.)

Orchid cactuses are at their best in bright indirect light with night temperatures in the 50s and days near 70. If the nights are too warm when the plants are trying to set buds, they'll develop foliage at the expense of flowers. I pot

An orchid cactus of the variety Rosetta

the plants in African violet soil, which is rich in organic matter. I keep the soil barely moist all the time and feed the plants with a low-nitrogen fertilizer, such as 5-10-5, every other week in the spring and summer. I omit fertilizer and give them less moisture during the fall and winter. I usually pot my plants in hanging containers and keep the stem length in control by pinching the tips back during a nonflowering period. If they're pot-bound, they should be repotted when the plant is not in flower.

Orchid cactuses are easily propagated from stem cuttings taken in the summer; I've seen cuttings only a few inches tall develop flowers as soon as their roots take hold. If you're interested in a wider selection of orchid cactuses than you can find at your local garden center, contact the California Epi Center, P.O. Box 2474, Van Nuys, California 91404. They grow nothing but *Epiphyllums*, and their stock is immense.

Rex Begonia *(Begonia)* To understand rex begonias, it helps to know that most if not all of the rex begonias grown today are complex hybrids, one of whose ancestors, however remote, was *B. rex*, a native of Assam. All begonias are flowering plants, and rex begonias are no exception. But they are not grown for their (usually pink) autumnal flowers; they are grown for their astonishing leaves, each uniquely splattered or zoned in red, pink, purple, brown, russet, bronze, olive green, maroon, red-black, plum, green-gold, white, or deep green, usually with silvery markings. In addition, the tops, edges, and bottoms of the leaves of most varieties are thick with long red hairs. You can see why such stunning plants are popular! Most of the rex begonias available today grow about 1 foot tall and have large, heart-shaped leaves that, on young plants especially, all tend to face in one direction.

Rex Begonia *(Begonia)*

Rex begonias are easy to grow indoors as long as they have shade, warmth, and humidity. By shade I mean bright indirect light; if you live in the north, where the winter sun is weak, give them half days of sunshine from October to January. The night temperatures shouldn't fall below 60 degrees. Set them on humidifying trays, and keep the soil barely moist all the time; so long as the air around them is humid, they're better off if the soil is a little too dry than a little too moist, so take care against overwatering them. They don't need much in the way of food — I feed my plants every month or two from midwinter through late fall, using a half-strength fertilizer. If the plants are squeezed for space I repot them in the spring in commercial potting soil. They have shallow roots that spread out rather than down as they

153

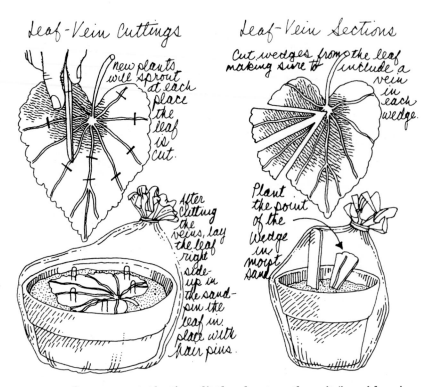

Leaf-Vein Cuttings

new plants will sprout at each place the leaf is cut.

After cutting the veins, lay the leaf right side up in the sand—pin the leaf in place with hair pins.

Leaf-Vein Sections

Cut wedges from the leaf making sure to include a vein in each wedge.

Plant the point of the Wedge in moist sand

grow, so I use a pot that's a little shorter than it is wide. A so-called azalea pot, three-quarters as tall as it is wide, is ideal.

Rex begonias are eager to multiply themselves, and can be propagated by several familiar techniques, including stem cuttings, which can be started anytime, and rhizome division, which is best done in the spring. Rex begonias also lend themselves to two unusual leaf cutting propagation techniques, both of which take advantage of the rex begonia's ability to sprout new plants from the veins of its leaves.

The first technique, called a leaf-vein cutting, involves nothing more complicated than severing some leaf veins and then pinning the entire leaf on moist rooting medium. Start by removing a leaf and its stem from the plant; pick a middle-aged leaf, neither the oldest nor the youngest on the plant. You'll be able to see a distinct vein pattern, with a large center vein and several smaller side veins. Turn the leaf upside down so you can see the veins clearly, and make several cuts through the center and side veins. Make sure that the side veins you select run from the point where the stem connects to the leaf all the way to the outside of the leaf. The center vein, being the largest, can support 2 or 3 cuts, but the side veins should be cut only once each. Distribute the cuts around the leaf; one new plant will grow at each cut, and if they're too close together they're hard to separate and transplant. Then find a pot large enough for

154

the entire leaf to lie flat, fill it with moist sand, and set the
leaf right side up on the sand. The leaf has to stay in close
contact with the moist medium through this entire process,
so pin it down with hairpins or opened paper clips; insert the
tip of the stem in the sand so it can continue to provide the
leaf with moisture. Then set the pot in a plastic bag and
keep it out of the sun; in the next 2 or 3 months new plants
will grow from the cuts. When they're about 2 inches tall,
separate the plants and pot each one individually in commercial potting soil.

    Leaf-vein sections, the second technique, have the
advantage over vein cuttings of producing individual plants
that don't need transplanting. Again, take a middle-aged leaf
off the plant and lay it upside down. Then cut the leaf into
wedges, making sure that each wedge contains one of the
side veins that extends from the base of the leaf, where the
petiole connects, out to the edge of the leaf. Usually it's possible to get 6 or 7 wedges from one leaf. You'll need as many
3-inch pots of moist sand as you have leaf wedges. Make a
hole in the sand and insert one wedge, pointed end down, at
a slight angle, about a quarter of the way into the sand. Slip

*The textured and colorful foliage
of the rex begonia*

155

the pots into plastic bags, with wooden labels as stakes to keep the plastic off the leaf wedges, and the shoots will appear in 2 or 3 months. When they're about 2 inches tall, remove the bags and transplant the young plants into commercial potting soil. When its work is completed, each leaf wedge will die back.

Shrimp Plant *(Justicia)* The shrimp plant *(J. brandegeana,* usually sold as *Beloperone guttata)* takes its common name from the bronze-red or yellow shrimp-shaped floral bracts that appear all year long at the tips of the stems. From among these bracts their true flowers, tiny and white, appear. In their Mexican homeland they can grow as tall as 3 feet, but they're usually kept pinched back to less than 2

Shrimp Plant *(Justicia)*

The floral bracts of the shrimp plant

156

feet tall when they're grown indoors. They have arched stems, so they're often potted in hanging pots, but they can be put into 6-inch standard pots too.

Shrimp plants are tropicals. If near-tropical conditions can be maintained in the home, they'll stay in bloom month after month; if not, they'll enter a rest period brought on by the lowered temperatures. Keep them where night temperatures are in the 60s, in a spot where they'll be in the sun for at least half the day. Let the soil dry out a bit between thorough waterings, and feed them every other week. If the plant enters a rest period, reduce the amount of water and eliminate food until warmer temperatures bring the plant back into active growth. A plant that has grown too large can be cut back in the spring. Root the stem tips in damp sand and pot them up in commercial potting soil for a whole new generation of plants.

Wax Plant (*Hoya*) Wax plants are old-time indoor favorites. They're a bit harder to manage now that fuel costs have resulted in cooler houses, but they still do fairly well indoors if night temperatures are in the 60s and the days are ten degrees or so warmer. If you can let them spend the summer outdoors in light shade, all the better. Their light needs indoors are more flexible: they're at their best with 4 or more hours of daily sun, but they'll also do well grown entirely in bright indirect light.

Wax Plant (*Hoya*)

The most common wax plant is *H. carnosa*, a vine native from Australia to southern China. Normally, its 3-inch leaves are dull green, but this plant has undergone several mutations, so there are several varieties available with different leaf colorations, such as pink and cream. One of its mutations is the odd plant called Hindu rope. I have rarely seen it blossom, but the true species and the other mutations all bear clusters of pale pink waxy blossoms through the summer and fall. There are many kinds of wax plants, but I particularly like the dwarf species, *H. bella*, that is native to India; it bears crimson-centered white flowers.

Wax plants do not flower freely when they're young. *Hoya carnosa* and its varieties usually don't begin to flower until their stems are about 3 feet long. The flowers, when they appear, grow year after year on leafless projections called spurs that protrude from the main stems. So gardeners who are intent on keeping their plants small, or in pruning away those apparently worthless spurs, will not see a sign of a blossom. Believe me, the flowers are worth waiting for: they're lovely, fragrant, and long-lasting.

While they're in flower, water the plants thoroughly but give them a chance to dry out moderately before water-

*The twisted foliage of a Hindu
rope wax plant*

ing them again. When they're too young to flower, and during their winter and spring rest periods, let the soil dry out almost completely between waterings. Feed them every month or two through the spring and summer only. Rather than pruning your plants every spring to encourage fuller growth, realize that they are vines and train them to a trellis or even a circular wire frame; this will keep them small while still allowing the stems to elongate. Stem tips root easily for a new collection of young wax plants.

Q: I've just noticed that my rosary vine has little purple blossoms. I've never seen them before, though I've had the plant for some time. Are the flowers unusual?

A: No, but they're so small that people tend to miss them. By the way, if you're scrutinizing your plant for the first time, you'll probably notice tiny bulbs, called bulbils, forming at the leaf joints. These can be used for propagating new generations of rosary vines, known botanically as *Ceropegia woodii.*

158

Q: I'm a country kid living in a city apartment, and now that summer's coming I can't help but remember my own fresh-picked vegetables from the backyard. Is there anything I can do to grow vegetables now, even though I'm five stories off the ground?

A: Sure. All you need is a spot, indoors or out, that's sunny for at least 6 hours a day. A sunny windowsill is all right, a place in the outdoor air a lot better. You can even use a window box and a balcony is perfect. (Don't use your fire escape for a garden; it's illegal and dangerous.) The easiest vegetables to grow in containers are those with small root systems, including peppers, eggplants, onions, cherry tomatoes, herbs, lettuce, and carrots. If you can provide a large tub, you'll have luck with cucumbers and sweet potatoes. In fact, all container-grown vegetables need large pots — plastic or metal are best. Add some drainage material at the bottom of the pot, and give each crop fresh new soil. Make absolutely certain that the soil doesn't dry out, even if it means watering the plants more than once a day.

Q: I know that most ferns grow well in shade, but what one would you recommend for a very dim spot in my house?

A: I suggest you try the holly fern, *Cyrtomium falcatum*. Its common name comes from the fact that its leaflets look very much like the leaves of English holly. This plant can indeed stand very deep shade, but be sure you don't overwater or overfeed it. Keep the soil just barely moist and feed it with half-strength fertilizer no more frequently than every 6 months.

Q: I have a small greenhouse, and would like to have a vine that will blossom all year long. Can you suggest one?

A: You're asking quite a bit from a plant, wanting it to stay in bloom without a rest period, but I think I have just the plant. It is a vine with large pink flowers that look very much like morning glories except that they last for several days, not just one. I've had this plant, *Dipladenia sanderi rosea*, in my own greenhouse for a number of years, and I'm delighted with it. It's not an easy plant to find, but a number of companies do sell young specimens. Sometimes it is listed as *Mandevilla*, its correct botanical name, but usually it's still called by its older name, *Dipladenia*.

Lettuce plant growing indoors on a windowsill

CACTUS !

One of many types of barrel cactus

All cactuses (or cacti) are native to the Western Hemisphere. They grow as far north as cool Canada, as far south as the moist tropics, and in great numbers in the deserts in between. (The northern cactuses aren't handsome candidates for growing indoors. Rain-forest cactuses are, but they have different needs from their desert relatives. See the June entry for orchid cactus and the December entry for Christmas cactus.)

There was a time — not so very long ago — when desert cactuses were dismissed as ugly, dangerous, snarly-tempered creatures. Now as a group they're probably the hottest item in the gardening business, partly because of their reputation for surviving even the blackest of thumbs. But their ruggedness indoors doesn't entirely explain their popularity; nobody, after all, wants an ugly plant simply because it refuses to die. I think that gardeners are coming to see cactuses for what they are: stubborn witnesses to the survival of life and beauty under adverse conditions.

Once, back in their evolutionary history, desert cactuses had leaves; as seedlings they still do, and a few do all through their lives. But as their homeland lost its vegetation and became desert, the leaves, which sacrificed too much of the plants' moisture, were gradually lost. Over time the plants evolved swollen stems capable of storing water for long periods of time. Some varieties can actually expand and contract those stems according to the amount of stored water. Most varieties also developed fearsome thorns to ward off thirsty marauders. (The thorns, as well as the plants' roots and flowers, grow from little bumps, known as areoles, on the surface of the stem; those areoles are the signal that the plant is a true cactus, and not some other spiny succulent.)

There are many varieties of desert cactuses, with different shapes, color intensities, and thorn patterns, but they all share a common heritage and can be cared for identically.

A type of opuntia cactus

160

They do best in a sunny window in the house. Spring and summer is their season of active growth, and winter, in general, is their rest period. Their watering needs vary with the season, so I've put together a watering calendar to help you keep your plants in shape.

January and February:

Give them only enough water to prevent the stems from shriveling. You may not need to water them at all for the entire first two months of the year.

Early March:

Give them very little water, and, throughout the month, spray them lightly now and then either in the evening or early morning, to remind them of the desert dew.

Late March through April:

This is their period of active growth, when they need more water than at any other time. Let the soil become nearly dry between waterings.

May through August:

Let them spend the summer outdoors in a spot protected from the rain and fiercest sun. (They can't take full outside sun when they've been growing for several months indoors; they're too weak for it.) Give them less water than you did in the spring so they'll have a chance to mature their season's growth.

September through December:

Water them about once a month, and spray them lightly every now and then so the stems don't dry out.

A cactus known as Sun Cup blooming in the greenhouse

Most cactus varieties produce splendid flowers in the spring if the light winter watering routine is combined with cool temperatures from November through February, in the low 40s at night and no warmer than the mid-60s during the day. If you've never seen a cactus flower, you're missing a great treat, but even if you have no interest in the blooms, keep your plants cool and dry through the winter. Otherwise you'll be depriving them not only of their flowers but of their dormancy, and their growth is apt to be weak and spindly as a result.

If you order a cactus through the mail, it will probably be shipped without roots, the reason for this is that the roots are very vulnerable to rot, so they're cut off before the cactus is packed for shipping. Don't let this worry you. Healthy new roots will form soon after you put the plant into soil. Cactuses are slow growers, and will live happily in the same pot for 3 or 4 years. Eventually they need repotting, a job best done in the early spring, when the new growth is getting started.

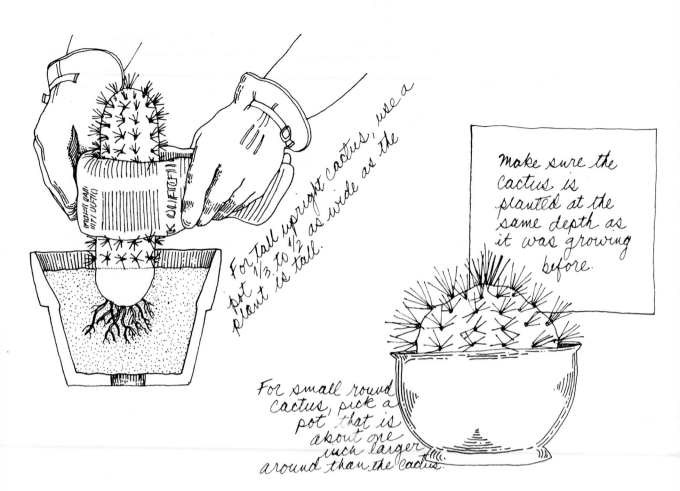

For tall upright cactus, use a pot 1/3 to 1/2 as wide as the plant is tall.

make sure the cactus is planted at the same depth as it was growing before.

For small round cactus, pick a pot that is about one inch larger around than the cactus.

Whether you're potting up a new cactus or repotting an old one, the procedure is the same, as I'll describe.

The great threat to desert cactuses is always excess moisture, so give them a rather small pot for their size, with relatively little soil to hold water on the roots. For a tall, upright-growing cactus, use a pot a third to a half as wide as the plant is tall. For one of the little round plants, pick a pot about 1 inch larger around than the cactus itself. Use clay pots, which will breathe out moisture, rather than plastic pots, which hold it in.

The soil should be nonacid, well-drained, and with relatively little organic matter. I use this recipe: 2 parts potting soil, 1 part sand, plus 1 tablespoon ground limestone (to help the thorns develop), and 1 tablespoon bone meal. The bone meal will keep the plant happily well nourished for about a year. In the early spring of years when the plant isn't being repotted, add one feeding of half-strength houseplant fertilizer.

Start off by filling a pot partially with the soil mix, deep enough so the cactus will be growing at the same depth that it had been previously. (There's no need for drainage stones on the bottom unless the pot is 6 inches or more across.) There is nothing difficult about setting the plant in so long as you have a good healthy respect for those thorns. Wear gloves, of course, but don't grasp the cactus even with a gloved hand, unless you want to find out just how sharp the thorns are. Take a few sheets of newspaper and fold them into a strap 2 or 3 inches wide; use the strap to hold the plant while you move it. Set the plant in at the same depth it grew previously and fill in around it with more soil mix. Don't firm the soil as much as you would other plants, but do tamp the soil lightly with a blunt tool. Give the cactus about a week without water, then moisten it and put it back on its regular watering routine.

Cactuses can be propagated from stem or leaf cuttings or from offsets, but I often start mine from seed because the seedlings are so fascinating to watch. Occasionally from a package of seeds there are a few tiny plants that emerge in bright colors, often some shade of red or gold. They owe their fancy colors to their lack of chlorophyll; they are doomed seedlings because no plant can survive without chlorophyll to help it manufacture its food. But they will live for a while, and if you act while they're young, you'll be able to save them by grafting them onto healthy green cactuses. The host will contribute its lifeline and the guest its color.

Any true cactus can be grafted to any other true cactus. The procedure is simple, and best done in the early spring. The necessary equipment includes the two cactuses, gloves, a sharp knife or a razor blade, a newspaper strap, kitchen tongs, and two lengths of light-weight chain or weighted twine.

The cactuses will grow together only if the exposed tissue of the scion is in touch with the exposed tissue of the understock. The first step is to slice off the tip of the understock. Then pare the edges slightly downward so that it forms a slight inverted bowl; the reason is that the cut will stretch a bit as it heals, and if the cut is straight, the understock is apt to push the scion out of place. Then cut off the root end of the scion and pare the top slightly upward; then set it onto the understock with the tongs. The scion should fit well. Maintain contact between the two by weight: cross the chains or weighted twine over the scion. Keep the new plant dry and out of the sun for about 2 weeks. When a gentle tug fails to dislodge the scion, remove the weight and give the new grafted plant its normal culture.

A display of grafted cactuses in the Victory Garden greenhouse

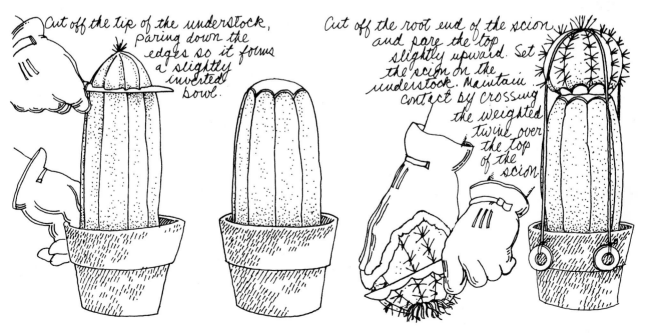

Cut off the tip of the understock, paring down the edges so it forms a slightly inverted bowl.

Cut off the root end of the scion and pare the top slightly upward. Set the scion on the understock. Maintain contact by crossing the weighted twine over the top of the scion.

JUL

Marguerites

JUL

July can be a hard month on houseplants. Not only is there heat to contend with, but gardeners tend to be more interested in vegetables and window boxes and perennial borders than in a regular quick check of the houseplant trench to make sure that the roots aren't drying out in the parching July heat. The pots should be turned every few days, too, so the roots don't work down through the drainage holes and try to establish themselves permanently in the summer location.

Some houseplants need special attention this month. Azaleas should be given the third of their yearly feedings in July. Monstera plants need their twice-yearly feeding now. And crotons should be taken off their fertilizer diet now to give them a chance to rest; the feedings should be resumed early next spring.

With an eye on later seasons, I sow petunia seeds in July so the plants are in blossom during the winter. These outdoor favorites are superb and uncommon houseplants, and easy to care for. This is also a good time of the year to root cuttings from gold-dust plants, as well as other plants that make their yearly flushes of growth in the early spring; by midsummer that new growth has had a chance to mature, but is not old enough to be so tough and woody that rooting would be difficult. If you want snapdragons in your greenhouse next winter, this is the time to sow the seeds. Be sure to plant a winter-flowering strain and watch carefully that the tiny seedlings don't dry out in hot weather.

Midsummer heat can be particularly damaging to greenhouse plants, because the glass intensifies the already withering heat. Make sure the ventilators are open and the shading system operative. Keep in mind that many of the ill effects of heat can be offset by raising the humidity, so keep the walks regularly wet down. If there are repairs to be made to the greenhouse or benches, or if you'd simply like to do some summer housekeeping, July is an ideal time to set the plants outside and tackle these chores.

Artillery Plant *(Pilea)* The apple-green foliage of the artillery plant is so profuse and wispy that it could easily be mistaken for a fern. In fact, it's a much easier plant to care for than most ferns, and more rugged. Artillery plants (*P. microphylla*, sometimes sold as *P. muscosa*) are related to aluminum plants and to the various panamigas (see the May chapter), and they share with their relatives both short growth — no taller than 12 inches — and interesting foliage. But the artillery plant has an odd trait. It sheds its pollen in an explosive puff: if you agitate a plant when the flowers are dry, you'll be able to see this happen, and even if you miss the fireworks, you'll see the pollen dusting the plant's leaves. Just for reasons of good housekeeping, you'll probably want to wash the plant with tepid water weekly so the leaves will glisten with health.

Artillery Plant *(Pilea)*

Artillery plants are low-growing natives of the Central and South American tropics, which means they need warmth, moisture, and humidity. I usually grow mine in bright indirect light, but they can take full sun if they're kept moist enough. The night temperatures shouldn't fall below 62 degrees. Keep the soil constantly moist, and the air

The fernlike foliage of a healthy artillery plant

Fuchsia *(Fuchsia)*

around them humid. (If you have trouble keeping them moist enough with a humidifying tray, try growing them in a terrarium.) Feed them every other month with a half-strength fertilizer. Cuttings root very easily, and can be potted up in commercial potting soil for full-sized plants in no time.

■ **Fuchsia** *(Fuchsia)* Given the popularity of these plants, I'd like to be able to say they're easy to care for indoors, but they're not. They require a combination of coolness and moisture that most gardeners find hard to provide. They're at their best if they're allowed to grow outdoors through the spring and summer, kept cool and moist the whole time. In much of the country the summers are too hot for this treatment; in fact, they're really happiest along the coastlines, especially in the Pacific northwest, where the air is always humid and the summers cool. My advice is to buy a plant in bloom in the spring, set it outside in a shady spot, where it will continue to bloom as long as the weather stays cool. Cut it back to within 6 inches of the soil line in the fall and bring it indoors. Keep it moist and cool through the winter, and set it back outside in the spring. In other words, consider it a porch plant. If you don't have a porch or shady outside spot for it, grow the plant in a cool bright window — fuchsias revel in winter sun when they're grown indoors.

Fuchsia blossoms, borne only at the tips of the stems

There's a controversy of sorts raging in the world of fuchsia devotees, the issue being the precise number of species currently known. Some say one hundred, and that is probably correct, but there are several thousand varieties with massive or subtle differences from plant to plant. For

168

the average gardener, the important information is that some fuchsias grow erect while others trail, and that most bloom only through the spring and summer, when days are at least 13 hours long. A few varieties are everblooming under lesser day length if they're given favorable growing conditions. Rufus is an upright everblooming variety with small turkey-red flowers. Abundance (double pink), Cascade (single dark pink-rose), and Mrs. Victor Reiter (single red and white) are all everblooming trailing fuchsias. The honeysuckle fuchsia, *F. triphylla,* is a bush type that blooms all year. The original species is red; the variety Gartenmeister Bohnstedt is salmon-rose combined with orange-scarlet; and Traudchen Bohnstedt is pale salmon-pink with white tips. Swanley Yellow, a variety that originated in England in 1900, is actually rather orange in overall effect. A point to remember is that nearly any fuchsia can be made to bloom out of season if it is given supplemental light of 1,000 footcandles to lengthen winter day length to 13 hours or more.

Fuchsias are at their best in very bright indirect light, with winter sun. I pot them in African violet soil, which I keep constantly moist; if the soil dries out, the leaves turn yellow and drop from the stems. I feed my plants once a month. They like night temperatures of 60 to 65 degrees when in active growth. In most parts of the country, as the summer wears on and the nights become hotter and the air drier, they begin to suffer. The bloom period will end quickly if the plants are allowed to set seed; so make sure to remove old faded flowers, and the single green berry behind each one (it turns purple when ripe); I usually groom the old blossoms at least once a week so that seed production doesn't sap the plants' energy. Propagate new plants from stem cuttings left over from the fall pruning — they produce flowering-sized plants by the next spring.

Fuchsias are susceptible to red spider mites, especially if they're grown in the sun; so it's a good idea to keep the foliage clean and pest-free with a regular forceful spray of cold water. Red spider mites or no, this is a good way to help meet the plants' need for moisture.

Marguerite *(Chrysanthemum)* If they can be given a cool, sunny spot, marguerites (*C. frutescens*), Canary Island natives, are among the easiest of flowering plants to grow. They bear 2- to 3-inch daisylike white, pink, or yellow flowers from early spring through late fall. They're most commonly available as potted plants in the spring, and can be transplanted into the garden, kept in pots outside, or grown as indoor plants. If you have trouble finding potted plants, buy some as cut flowers and root the side shoots.

Marguerite *(Chrysanthemum)*

A close-up of marguerites, often known simply as daisies

Marguerites do their best in full sunshine, but will do reasonably well with at least half days of sunshine; if they're given at least 4 hours of artificial light each night from October until April, they'll stay in bloom all year. They're cool-loving plants, and they don't thrive if the night temperatures rise much above the mid-50s. Keep the soil moist all the time, and feed the plants every other week. Marguerites grow extremely rapidly and fill the pot with roots in no time at all. By way of illustration, a 5- or 6-inch plant set into the garden in the spring will be 3 feet across and just as tall by the end of the summer, and dense with blossoms; a potted plant won't grow quite so dramatically, but it will develop quickly enough that it will be harder and harder to keep the plant supplied with sufficient moisture. When you notice the plant wilting despite your attempts to keep it watered, it's time to repot it into a larger container of commercial potting soil. As long as you keep up with the plant's growth, it will continue to thrive, but there's a practical limit to how large a houseplant can be. So my advice is to enjoy the spring-through-summer flowering period, and then take cuttings in late summer. I like bushy plants so I pinch them once when they're 6 to 8 inches tall, and again when the resulting side branches are 4 inches long. These fall cuttings grow through the winter and then come into bloom in the spring as the days become long (or immediately if given supplemental light as previously noted). However, cuttings of marguerites will root at any time of the year. If they're started in the spring, the plants will be in blossom within 1 month.

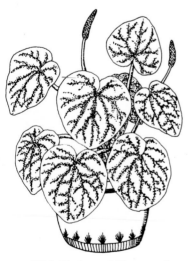

Wrinkle-leaved Peperomia
(Peperomia)

Peperomia *(Peperomia)* Nearly any plant that is native to the lower level of vegetation in a jungle is a good candidate for growing indoors because it can tolerate the twin plagues that beset plants in our homes — dim light and high temperatures. And of this tolerant group, the peperomia is one of the best. There are probably 1,000 different kinds of peperomias growing throughout South America and the islands of the Caribbean, and it's likely that many will find their way into indoor cultivation. For now, only a handful are available: the wrinkle-leaved peperomia, *P. caperata*, of which Emerald Ripple is the most frequently grown variety; the blunt-leaved peperomia, *P. obtusifolia*, most often seen in its variegated form; the ivy or platinum-leaved peperomia, *P. griseoargentea*, which looks like a small heart-leaved philodendron; and the watermelon peperomia, *P. argyreia* (it was once sold as *P. sandersii*), with silver-and-green striped leaves that resemble the markings on a watermelon rind. Any one of these easy-to-care-for plants is a good choice, and several together would be delightful.

A wrinkle-leaved peperomia, with the true blossoms projecting above the foliage

All peperomias are semisucculents, with thick, juicy stems and leaves that hold water in reserve. So the quickest way to kill a peperomia is to overwater it, especially to overwater it from the top. Some varieties have so dense a canopy of foliage that if the moisture doesn't have a chance to evaporate during the day, disease will claim the damp stems and the plants will be gone practically overnight. I put my plants in clay pots of commercial potting soil and let the soil become nearly dry between waterings. Every 3 or 4 months I boost the water with half-strength fertilizer. I keep my plants in a bright spot out of the sun; normal household temperatures are fine.

Peperomias are easy to multiply: propagate the ivy and blunt-leaved types by stem cuttings and the wrinkle-leaved and watermelon types by leaf cuttings.

Piggyback Plant *(Tolmiea)* These rugged foliage plants grow wild along the west coast of North America, from California all the way north into Canada and Alaska; they nestle in the cool, moist shade of the tall trees that grace that part of the world. Most plants from that climate

171

A piggyback plantlet riding at the base of a mature leaf

Piggyback Plant *(Tolmiea)*

do not do well as houseplants, but piggyback plants will thrive, provided they're kept in a spot that's cool and moist with partial shade. Their botanical name is *T. menziesii*, but they're sometimes sold as *Tiarella menziesii*, the *Tiarella* being a very similar plant that's native to the East Coast. Their most frequently used name, piggyback plant, is a reference to the peculiar way they grow and form new plants at the base of their leaves; one plantlet appears at the juncture of each leaf blade and petiole. Other common names are thousand-mothers and youth-on-age. These are excellent plants for hanging containers because as those little plants grow they weigh down the stems so the foliage curves over the rim of the pot.

Piggyback plants take very little effort. They like bright, indirect light, night temperatures in the 40s or low 50s, constantly moist soil, and a feeding every other month. They can be repotted in commercial potting soil at any time of the year. The easiest way to propagate them is to remove a leaf that has a little plant growing on it: take the plantlet, the leaf, and the leaf petiole. Cut off all but 2 inches of the leaf petiole, and insert it into damp sand so the leaf rests just at the soil line. The leaf and petiole will keep the little plant nourished during the few days it will take it to send down its own roots. As they become unnecessary, the old

172

leaf and the petiole will die, leaving behind the healthy, rooted plant.

⊟ **Rabbit's-Foot Fern** *(Davallia)* There are several species of *Davallia* that make good houseplants. Some of them have fine feathery fronds, and others are coarser and denser. But the foliage isn't the plant's main attraction — the rhizomes are. The rhizomes are peculiar in that they creep along the surface of the soil, and they're covered with coarse gray-brown hairs. They don't look like plant life at all, but like the feet of furry animals, and it's these rhizomes that have earned the plants their various common names: the deer's-foot fern (*D. canariensis*), the squirrel's-foot fern (*D. trichomanoides*), and the rabbit's-foot fern (*D. fejeensis*). Most of them grow to be about 1½ feet tall.

Rabbit's-Foot Fern *(Davallia)*

All the *Davallia* species do best in the warm, humid tropics; I once saw a rabbit's-foot fern growing in Hawaii that was 2 feet across and a solid mass of foliage. It's hard to replicate that, even in a greenhouse. But if you'll settle for a more modest but still handsome show of greenery, you'll find these species are easier to look after than most ferns, and less easily damaged by contact. The plants want bright north light, barely moist soil, and constant humidity. The days should be warm and the nights no cooler than the mid-50s. They're not big eaters, so I give my plants only a single feeding of half-strength fertilizer every 6 months.

All these species can be propagated by spores (see the January feature), but there are two quicker ways to produce large plants: by dividing the furry rhizomes and potting the divisions separately, or by cutting off a 2- to 3-inch sec-

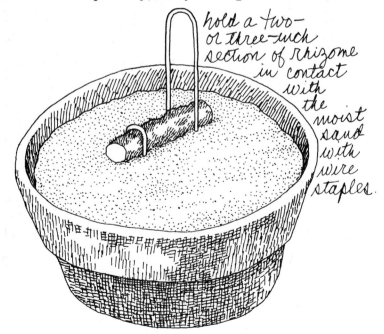

hold a two- or three-inch section of rhizome in contact with the moist sand with wire staples.

173

tion of one rhizome and securing it to moist potting soil until the roots form and the new growth shows. I pin the rhizome section to the medium with two 5-inch lengths of wire, bent to form simple staples, because if the rhizome loses contact with the moist soil, the roots won't form. If the plants are to be kept in pots, the simplest soil mix is equal parts potting soil and either peat moss or leaf mold. I've had a rabbit's-foot fern growing, wrapped around a clod of osmunda fiber, for over ten years; it's particularly nice grown this way, without a pot, because the rhizomes creep along and clasp at the osmunda fiber, and the whole network of furry rhizomes is visible.

Opposite: The furry rhizome, or foot, of a rabbit's-foot fern

Rieger Begonia *(Begonia)* We owe Rieger begonias to the genius of a German plant breeder, Otto Rieger, who gave us a great new series of begonia hybrids that are dense with red, white, pink, yellow, rose, or orange flowers month after month. They're among the most popular flowering houseplants in the country, even though as recently as 1971 there was only one greenhouse in the United States

A double-flowered, upright Rieger begonia, one of several types available

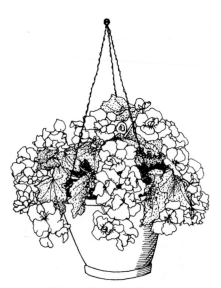

Rieger Begonia *(Begonia)*

that was growing them commercially. That's a rapid rise to fame, but they deserve it.

Most people buy Rieger begonia plants that are in, or about to, flower. A plant at that stage needs bright indirect light, supplemented with half days of sun during the winter months. Intermediate or warm temperatures are best, with nights in the 50s and days around 70 degrees. Keep the soil barely damp and feed the plants monthly.

The more contented they are, the longer Rieger begonias will stay in flower, often for 4 months or more. But eventually the flowers will fade and the plants will enter dormancy. When the last of the flowers fades, gradually reduce the amount of water; after about 10 days cut the stems down to about 3 inches from the pot. Use a clean sharp knife or razor blade, as scissors will bruise the stems. Clear away any diseased or decayed leaves from the remaining stems, and move the plant to a 1-inch-larger pot of commercial potting soil. Be sure to set the root ball a trifle higher than the new soil line so that the drainage is good and the chances of crown rot reduced. Continue to keep the soil on the dry side — and don't feed it at all — until new stems appear. Then put it back on its growing season routine, and the plant will produce another flush of blossoms again in 3 or 4 months.

Because of their complicated genetic background, Rieger begonias can't be propagated from seed, but new plants are easily started either by stem or leaf-bud cuttings. It should be noted, however, that most Rieger begonias are patented varieties whose reproduction asexually is prohibited except by permission of the patent holder.

Umbrella Plant *(Cyperus)* The slender, arched leaves of this plant, radiating from the tips of straight green stems, are a little reminiscent of the ribs of an umbrella, which is how the plant arrived at its common name. The full-sized species, *C. alternifolius,* is a native of the marshes of Madagascar, and grows to be about 4 feet tall. The Australian-born dwarf umbrella plant, *C. alternifolius gracilis,* is smaller, slimmer, and more graceful in all respects; it grows no taller than 18 inches or so.

Umbrella plants will grow in full sun or in bright reflected light. They do fine in normal house temperatures, with nights as low as the 50s. In fact, they're carefree in every respect but one: moisture. Umbrella plants grow naturally in bogs, where their roots are always in moist, spongy soil. So they're among that rare group of houseplants that needs constantly wet soil — I keep mine sitting in saucers of water day in and day out. If they're allowed to dry out, the tops will die within a day. The roots survive a day or so

Umbrella Plant *(Cyperus)*

176

longer than the foliage, so if you find your plant collapsed — there'll be no mistaking it, as the once-green foliage will look like hay — cut the stems back to the soil line, soak the soil well, and give the roots a chance to send up new growth. Luckily, the new foliage will grow quickly, provided the roots are still alive. Some persons grow umbrella plants in shallow water with goldfish darting in and out among the roots.

Umbrella plants do most of their growing between early spring and late summer, so once a week during those months I give them a feeding of half-strength fertilizer. If they need repotting it's best done in the early spring. They can be propagated any time, either from seed, by dividing the roots, or by setting one of the sprays of foliage, with 1 or 2 inches of stem, into a shallow dish of water or moist sand. I pot my plants in a mix of equal parts commercial potting soil and peat moss.

Foliage of an umbrella plant seen at close range

177

Q&A

Repotting a leathery-leaved earth star

Q: I have a friend with a plant called an earth star. Can you tell me anything about it?

A: The earth star is the name given to many bromeliads in the *Cryptanthus* genus. The name comes from the fact that its leaves spread closely to the ground in a starry shape. It has tiny white flowers and does best in bright indirect light. It's a most unusual plant, and very durable indoors.

Q: Some time ago I was given a handsome bouquet of gerbera daisies. They lasted well over 2 weeks. Can these wonderful flowers be grown indoors?

A: Only in an intermediate greenhouse, I'm afraid. These natives of South Africa will blossom year-round, with most of the flowers appearing between midwinter and early summer. You can buy plants or you can start your own from seed; the seed-grown plants take 6 months or more to reach flowering size. If you do start them from seed, buy the seeds of double-flowering forms, which will produce a smattering of single and semidouble flowers as well. They will all be perfectly delightful and stay beautiful for weeks. The plants live indefinitely and are best divided and reset in fresh soil in June.

Q: My cattleya orchid is doing so well that I've caught the orchid bug and am ready for a little more challenge. What other orchids can you suggest?

A: You should certainly try the moth orchid, *Phalaenopsis* (see the April chapter), and the *Paphiopedilum* (see the March chapter). Then try any one of the *Dendrobium* orchids. I especially like the one called *Dendrobium phalaenopsis*, which is rather large but blossoms for most of the year, and *Dendrobium nobile*, which blossoms after dropping all its leaves in midwinter. Another suggestion is a very small red-flowered orchid from Jamaica called *Broughtonia sanguinea*.

Q: I can remember as a child seeing a beautiful morning glory vine covering the porch of my grandmother's house. Can this plant be grown indoors?

178

A: Although they're seldom considered as houseplants, morning glories do rather well indoors. Plant 6 or 8
seeds in a 10-inch flowerpot in late summer in order to give
the plants time enough to grow to flowering size by winter.
When the seedlings appear, thin out all but the three strong-
est. Set the pot outside to take advantage of the last warm
days, but be sure to bring it in before frost. Give it your
sunniest windowsill, keep the soil barely moist all the time,
and feed the plants monthly with half-strength fertilizer.
They'll blossom best if they're given a trellis to climb upon.

Two double-flowered gerbera daisies

179

INDOOR PESTS AND PLAGUES

A regular trip to the showers keeps houseplants at their best

More houseplants die because they're improperly cared for than because of outside attack; nonetheless, indoor plants can fall prey to insects, and occasionally to diseases, and if they're not taken care of, a whole collection can be lost. There is nothing more devastating than finding your plants covered with bugs, but take heart, there is something you can do about it.

The goal is to prevent the arrival of insects and diseases if you can, or to conquer them immediately; your best allies in the battle are sanitation and watchfulness, and it's well to make them a part of your plant-care routine. First of all, always water your plants in the morning, or before midday, so the foliage and crown are dry by nightfall; root, crown, and leaf diseases run wild through plants that are damp all night, and insects breed happily in the moisture. Keep your plants clean with regular showers and baths — in the morning, again, so the plants are dry by evening. A weekly trip to the kitchen sink for a forceful tepid shower from the hand sprayer will send spider mites right down the drain, and will wash away other problems as well. Twice a month wash the foliage in warm sudsy water — I use a

few drops of a mild liquid dish detergent — and then rinse with the hand sprayer.

Make sure that your supplies are clean, too. Use sterilized soil; if you use garden soil, be sure to pasteurize it (see the January feature). Keep your tools clean. Before you re-use a flowerpot, scrub it clean, soak it for 10 minutes in a solution of 1 part household bleach to 9 parts water, then rinse it. Make sure your plants aren't grouped so closely together in a handsome arrangement that their leaves touch; plants are much healthier if there is fresh air circulating freely around them.

Keep your eye on your plants. Check them often for signs of trouble, and be sure to look along the stems and under the leaves, where insects congregate. Immediately isolate any plant that looks suspicious, so others aren't affected. (But don't make a hospital out of your plant collection; if you have a plant that's been hit badly, muster your courage and throw it away.) It's especially important, if you're given a plant from a friend's collec-

tion, or even a newly purchased plant, to keep it off by itself for a couple of weeks so you'll have an opportunity to spot problems before they spread. Professional growers are extremely meticulous, but they struggle with pest and disease problems far greater than the home gardener faces, and occasionally troubled plants make their way onto the market. So for safety's sake, quarantine a recently bought plant for 2 weeks or so. Put it in another room, or at least 10 feet from the rest of your collection.

These preventive measures will take care of a wide range of problems, but if the situation becomes serious, it's important to be able to pin down exactly the nature of your problem, and treat it specifically. Here's a list of the most common of the bugs and diseases that hit houseplants, and the care that will bring the plants back to health. You'll notice that the first line of defense is always nonchemical. If an infestation is severe, an insecticide that com-

180

bines pyrethrum and rotenone will probably eradicate it; this is the same material, in the same potency, that is sold for vegetable gardens, so you may already have some on hand. It will kill fish, so move the goldfish or aquarium to another room before using it. It is not at all harmful to humans. But it will kill most houseplant pests on contact, without penetrating the plant's system. Malathion is a very potent chemical that must never be used inside, and used outside only when other lines of defense have failed. Don't use malathion at all on maidenhair ferns, Boston ferns, table ferns, or on any of the crassula species. Systemic insecticides, which are applied either to the soil or to the foliage, are designed to be taken into the plant's system. I don't use them because I'm not convinced that the insecticide works its way back out of the plant's system, and when I throw old foliage on my compost, I don't want that worry.

Pests *Aphids:* These voracious eaters are soft-bodied sucking insects with a closetful of disguises. Some types are green, others black, yellow, brown, or pink. Most of them don't have wings, but some do. They're about ⅛ inch long. They go after both foliage and flowering plants, working toward the tips of the stems, on the undersides of the leaves, anywhere that the growth is soft enough for them to suck out the plant's juices. Aphids are quite visible, and so is their work. The foliage and stems will look unhealthy, the leaves will curl, and sometimes new buds will come in deformed. The weekly shower works wonders in keeping these insects at

bay; if the plant's too large to shower, regularly wipe the leaves and stems with a damp sponge. If the infestation gets out of hand, use an insecticide containing pyrethrum and rotenone, both safe, plant-derived insecticides.

White flies: Like aphids, these are sucking insects. The first sign of damage is pale leaves that finally yellow and fall off, the work of the white fly nymphs or larvae. The larvae are nearly too small to be

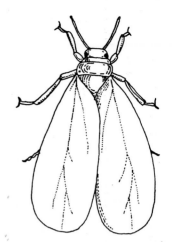

white Flies are tiny moths whose larvae suck plants, causing leaves to yellow.

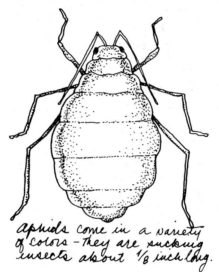

aphids come in a variety of colors - they are sucking insects about ⅛ inch long.

visible to the naked eye, but a magnifying glass will show them up all too clearly! As they mature into moths they can be seen rising in a cloud whenever the plant is disturbed. White flies are hard to control because they're relatively invulnerable to insecticides except in their nymph stage. They're also very destructive and will easily kill a plant given the chance. They're particularly attracted to some of the most popular flowering houseplants, including chrysanthemums, fuchsias, geraniums, poinsettias, and lantanas. The best control I know for white flies on ornamental plants is a syn-

thetic pyrethrum called Resmethrin or "white fly spray." You'll have to repeat the spraying program 4 or 5 times at weekly intervals to wipe out a whole population. Spray when temperatures are between 50 and 70 degrees and do not breathe the vapors.

Cyclamen mites: These head not only for cyclamens, but for gesneriads, too, as well as many outdoor plants such as strawberries and delphiniums. They're also sucking insects, and too small to see. They do their work in new buds and leaves. After a while the plant looks stunted, and the new foliage becomes malformed. Often flowering plants either don't form buds at all, or they produce a few disfigured blooms. I'll tell you what I do with plants infested with cyclamen mites: I throw them away, pots and all. These pernicious pests can be spread simply by handling infected plants. If you still want to "doctor" your plants, try immersing them, pots and

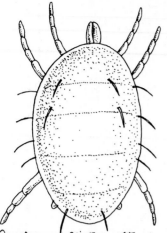

Cyclamen mites attack gesneriads, too. They are too small to see!

all, in 110-degree water for 30 minutes or use one of many available miticides. Good luck!

Scale: These don't sound like insects, but believe me, they are. They move around when they're young, but they're often too small or translucent to be noticed at that age. As they mature they band together in visible sta-

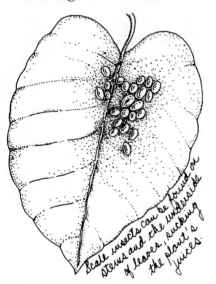

Scale insects can be found on stems and the undersides of leaves, sucking the plant's juices.

tionary clusters along the undersides of the leaves and on the stems. Sometimes an ugly black fungus develops in the honeydew secreted by the scale insects. If you're not on the lookout for the insects themselves, the first sign of a problem will probably be light-colored spots on the leaves; when you turn the leaf over, you'll find these little turtle-shaped insects, sucking the leaf's juices. The safest treatment is to go over the whole plant with a toothbrush and warm sudsy water; that should take care of both the old and the young scales. But keep the plant under close scrutiny for the next few weeks, because if you miss a few young scale on your first treatment, they'll mature and multiply. Scale is a very hard problem to conquer or stop if it gets out of hand, so if the infestation is severe, take the plant right out to the trash.

mealybugs are sucking insects too.

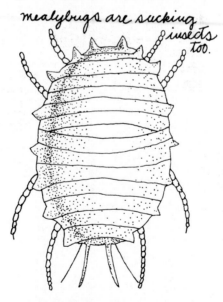

Mealybugs: These sucking insects look like little bits of cotton nestled down in the forks of stems, or in the crowns of plants — anywhere they are protected from bright light. Infested plants look stunted, and sometimes flower-

ing plants drop their buds. The best solution is to dip a cotton swab in rubbing alcohol and touch it to the colonies of the bugs. The insects will die and disappear from the plant. If the alcohol treatment doesn't work, take the plant outside and spray with malathion. In either case, rinse the plant after treatment.

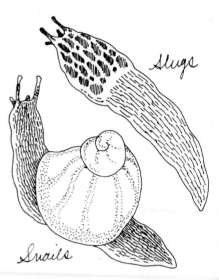

Slugs

Snails

Slugs and snails: These are the giants of the indoor bug world. They are neither dainty nor invisible. Nor are they as deplorable as the tiny sucking bugs. They can be from ½ inch to 4 inches long. They feed on the leaves at night, and leave a trail of silvery slime in their wake. During the daylight hours they seek cover at the base of the plant, or around the outside rim of the pot or even under it. The best preventive is good housekeeping — clear away old dead leaves so these creatures have to search for a dark hiding place. If you spot them on your plants, pick them off by hand and destroy them. If you can't bring yourself to touch them, set a saucer of beer or grape juice next to the plant; the insects will be drawn by the aroma, and will drown for their curiosity.

Plagues Diseases are rarely a problem for houseplants because they don't have much chance to spread in dry indoor air. But there are a few to be on the watch for. If it's necessary to use any of the fungicides, take the plants outside, providing the weather is mild, or spray them in an unused room.

Fungus leaf spot: The first sign of damage is blotches on the leaves, which later wither and die. It's an especially worrisome problem for greenhouse owners, whose plants grow in humid air. The first line of defense is to get rid of all the infected leaves. Make sure, when you water the plant, that water doesn't splash up onto the leaves. Space the plants so they have good air circulation and lower humidity. If the plants are badly hit, throw them away. Otherwise, treat them with zineb, maneb, or benomyl. These chemicals are really preventives; nothing can patch a hole in a leaf.

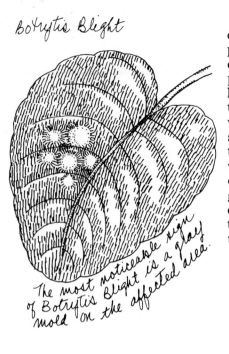

Botrytis Blight

The most noticeable sign of Botrytis Blight is a gray mold on the affected area

Botrytis blight: This also causes blotches on the leaves — either gray, reddish, brown, or yellow — that take on a slimy look. Sometimes the most noticeable sign of trouble is the gray mold that shows up in the affected areas. This fungus gets its start on wet foliage after several days of poor light and inadequate ventilation. It can spread rapidly, either by insects, or water, or the gardener's hands. Again, the cure is to make sure you remove any of the infected parts of the plant, provide the plants with better air circulation, and keep the foliage dry. If need be, treat them with zineb, maneb, benomyl, or captan.

Rot: Rot can affect the crown, stems, or roots of plants. The damaged area becomes mushy and usually the plant dies. Because the problem is related to poor drainage, the preventive is to bottom-water so the plants aren't oversaturated, and to make sure the plants aren't overfed, overwatered, overshaded, or overcrowded. If one of your plants gets hit, dust the soil with benomyl; if the problem persists, throw the plant away to save the rest of your collection.

Rot—
Stems and roots become mushy.

Blotches appear on leaves which will wither and die.

Fungus Leaf Spot

AUG

Staghorn fern

AUG

This is the month to start planning in earnest for next winter's houseplants. Tender narcissus bulbs sometimes come onto the market in August, and if they do they can be potted up immediately. I pot up a few bulbs every 10 days in order to guarantee a succession of flowers through most of the winter months. Cape cowslip bulbs are on the market at this time of the year, too, and should be potted up immediately; if you're new at growing bulb plants indoors, these easy-to-care-for plants make an ideal first choice. August is the best time of the year to take cuttings of firm new camellia growth; they won't root or grow quickly, but they can send out their beautiful blossoms when they're no more than 6 inches tall. I usually start marigold seeds this month, though they can be sown any time of the year; an August sowing brings the plants into flower by early winter. And there is still time this month to take cuttings of many houseplants that make yearly flushes of growth in the spring.

Calla lilies can be started into growth at any time of the year, but I've found that those started toward the end of the summer or early in the fall are especially nice. This is also a good month to take stem cuttings of flowering maples; they will root quickly and begin to blossom within 6 weeks. Browallia plants will begin to look straggly by late in the summer. They don't respond well to cutting back so I usually take cuttings for new plants and throw the older ones away.

If you have a greenhouse, August is a demanding month. I sow the seeds for my winter crop of calendulas now, along with my cinerarias, which will be in blossom in the early spring. Calceolarias started from seed this month or next will be in flower by early spring, too. Nasturtium seeds sown now will produce flowering-sized plants by winter. And poor man's orchids started from seed now will be ready to flower in mid-February. And if you have either a greenhouse or sunporch where you can keep them cool and sunny, August is the month to start potting up freesia corms; they'll send up the first of their fragrant flowers in December.

186

Euonymus *(Euonymus)* These plants are among the most forgiving, easygoing houseplants available. Their attractive shiny foliage clings to the plants for years whether they are grown in sun or bright indirect light, in the cool nights they prefer or in sultry summer weather.

Euonymus *(Euonymus)*

There are many species of euonymus, both deciduous and evergreen, but the best ones for growing indoors are varieties of *E. japonicus*, with well-proportioned oval foliage 1 to 1½ inches long, interestingly marked with yellow or white against shiny bright green.

Euonymus (yew-*on*-i-mus) plants make a flush of growth in the spring; if they're growing in ideal conditions, with bright indirect light, ample fertilizer, and night temperatures in the 40s or 50s, they may make as much as 12 inches of growth yearly. They'll grow more slowly if the conditions are less than ideal, or if they're pot-bound. Left on their own, indoor plants would become shrubs 3 or 4 feet tall, but they can be kept as small as 6 inches without suffering at all: this, along with their colorful foliage, is why they're often grown in dish gardens and terrariums. Because of their flush of growth, I think it's best to prune them once in the early spring, so that the new growth hides the cut branches; cut just above a leaf joint, and a new branch will grow from that spot. The stem tips will root practically overnight if they're set into moist rooting medium. Euonymus plants can be repotted at any time of the year except when their new growth is tender, in the spring. Pot them in commercial potting soil, keep them barely moist, and feed them every 3 or 4 months with a very mild (one-quarter strength) houseplant fertilizer. Euonymus plants tend to draw red spider mites if they are in a hot, dry location, so be sure to keep them regularly showered and bathed. (See the July feature.)

Variegated euonymus plant

187

Hawaiian Ti *(Cordyline)*

🪴 **Hawaiian Ti** *(Cordyline)* The durable, strap-shaped foliage of the Hawaiian ti plant is a staple in the traditional Hawaiian way of life. It's used in cooking, as thatched roofing, and is the "grass" of hula skirts. Incidentally, after each performance the dancers wrap their grass skirts in damp newspaper and put them in a refrigerator. That way they easily last a week or more! If you can provide the humidity they need, Hawaiian tis make fine houseplants, with sturdy, colorful leaves. *Cordyline terminalis bicolor* has green and pink leaves; *C. terminalis tricolor* combines green and pink with cream.

As natives of Polynesia, ti plants are accustomed to warmth, moisture, and humidity. They like their nights in

A particularly handsome Hawaiian ti plant

the high 60s, their soil always evenly moist, and a humidifying tray beneath; if the soil dries out, the ends of the leaves will turn brown. A feeding every 3 or 4 months will help them along. They do their best if they have sunshine at least half of each day; without adequate sunlight, their foliage isn't as colorful. But I can vouch for the fact that they survive with almost no light at all. I was given a ti log, the term used to describe a length of the stem, when I was in the Navy in Hawaii. I did nothing but insert it in water, and even though I kept it four decks down, where its only source of light was a weak incandescent bulb, it sent up leaves and flourished for the entire year and a half that I was aboard that ship; it continued to thrive beyond that time in the good care of my successor. Testimony enough to the plant's endurance.

I've seen Hawaiian ti plants that are as tall as I am, but it's more common to find them 1 to 3 feet tall when they're grown in the house, with their leaves a little more than 1 foot long. Like dracaenas, to which they're related, they keep growing up and up, and eventually they come to look like little palm trees, with all the leaves clustered at the top of tall, naked stems. Many gardeners like tall ti plants, but if you decide to prune your plant, you can do so at any time of the year; new sprouts will appear below the cut. Before pruning, I suggest that you air-layer the top of the plant and get yourself a youngster with leaves clear to the ground level; then prune back the stub as much as you desire. If you're interested in a generation of small plants, the ti is more than willing to cooperate. There are two ways to proceed. The first is to lay a stem on its side in damp rooting medium such as sand. Little plants will appear along the sides of the stem, and when these are about 2 inches tall, they can be cut off and rooted in damp medium. (See the

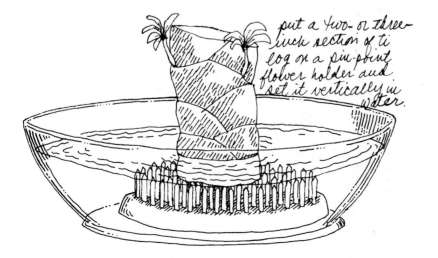

put a two- or three-inch section of ti log on a pin-point flower holder and set it vertically in water.

April feature for more about this technique and air-layering.) Or you can cut the stem into sections of any length and set each section vertically, bottom end down, either in damp sand or on a pin-point flower holder in shallow water. New shoots will break out near the tips of each section and roots will form at the bases. You can grow these plants permanently in water, or you can pot them up in commercial potting soil. Repot them as they need it, at any time.

If you don't have a plant to start with, the logs are available inexpensively through the mail; the specimens shipped are usually about 4 inches long and 1 inch or so in diameter.

Philodendron *(Philodendron)* Philodendrons comprise a huge family of houseplants. Over two hundred species have been found growing throughout Central and South America and the Caribbean Islands. Hundreds more have been created by plant breeders. There are so many different kinds of philodendron that if you were to put them all in a room together you'd be hard pressed to see the family resemblance between many of them.

Most philodendrons are vines, as is shown by the derivation of the name: *phileo,* to love, and *dendron,* tree, an apt description of the natural climbing habit of most species. The heart-leaf and fiddle-leaf types both fall into this category, and they're probably the best known of all philodendrons. The heart-leaf philodendron (*P. scandens,* sometimes sold as *P. oxycardium* or *P. cordatum*) is the biggest-selling foliage houseplant in the country. Oddly enough, we have Captain Bligh, of *Mutiny on the Bounty* fame, to thank for this plant — he was the first to bring wild specimens from Jamaica to England. The climbing, or vine-type, philodendrons bear small leaves if they're potted in hanging containers or allowed to trail along a surface; if they're given a vertical support to climb up, their leaves become gigantic. (The plant known as the split-leaved philodendron is in fact a *Monstera.* See the April chapter.)

A smaller category of philodendron includes the plants that branch from the ground, with all the growth coming from the crown of the plant. The saddle-leaved philodendron, Weber's self-heading, and Wendland's philodendron are all in this category, known as the self-heading philodendrons. They're all extremely slow-growing, and they practically stop altogether if they're neglected, but if they're given average care, they'll eventually become enormous. They don't get particularly tall, but a ten-year-old plant is apt to have a span of 8 or 9 feet. I usually give plants to the nearest school or hospital when they become oversized.

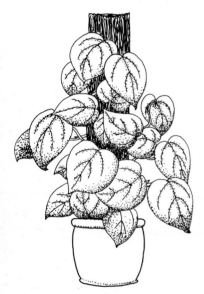

Heart-leaf Philodendron
(Philodendron)

Wendland's Philodendron
(Philodendron)

Regardless of their habit of growth, all philodendrons need the same care to keep them growing. They want bright indirect light without sun; the leaves are apt to burn in the sunlight. They withstand cool temperatures, but they don't grow much unless the night readings are in the high 60s. The soil should be barely moist all the time; feed them every 3 or 4 months with a standard houseplant fertilizer. (If you'd rather they didn't continue to grow, keep them cooler, let the soil dry out somewhat between waterings, and don't feed them.) Keep the foliage clean; this is especially important with large-leafed plants. I use plain tepid water and a damp rag or sponge.

Philodendrons will live for years growing in plain water. And they'll grow in nearly any other medium as well. I use a mix of equal parts commercial potting soil and peat moss. They can be repotted or propagated at any time of the year. Propagate the climbing plants by stem cuttings and the self-heading types such as saddle-leaved (*P. selloum*) and Wendland's (*P. wendlandi*) from seeds available from mail-order catalogues.

Staghorn Fern *(Platycerium)*

▬ **Staghorn Fern** *(Platycerium)* Staghorn ferns are epiphytic, which is a rarity among ferns. They grow naturally on the rough bark and branches of tropical trees, and feed on the decaying organic matter that collects along the trees' surfaces. They grasp the tree by means of their hard, smooth basal fronds; these fronds not only provide the plant's support, they also wrap around and protect the roots. The large, antler-shaped fronds originate at the base of the plant and are usually deeply pendant. There are many species of staghorn ferns growing wild in tropical regions of the world: *P. bifurcatum*, native to northern Australia, New Caledonia, and adjacent areas, is among the toughest of them all for indoor culture and is the one most often available from florists and garden centers.

Staghorn ferns have been grown indoors for more than a century, but their culture has mostly been confined to greenhouses or conservatories where humidity runs high. They weren't considered suitable for the home because the air wasn't thought to be moist enough for them. In actuality, staghorn ferns prefer less humidity than many common houseplants. The only real problem is that, because they are epiphytes, watering them without leaving a mess on the floor is difficult. Modern gardeners overcome this by drenching plants once or twice a week at the kitchen sink, then allowing them to drain thoroughly before hanging them in an airy place again. This takes a little effort, but healthy plants are so eye-catching that it's worth it.

Staghorn ferns are usually grown on wall-mounted slabs of wood. Between the plant roots and the slab is placed a 2-inch pad of long-fibered sphagnum moss, the whole thing tied in place with inconspicuous nylon fishline. The basal fronds hug the pad just as they do tree bark in the forest. They want a bright, well-ventilated spot out of the sun with night temperatures of 50 to 60 degrees.

The primary ingredient of good care is watering. Far too many gardeners overwater staghorn ferns: if moisture drips from the rooting medium when it is squeezed, it's too soon to add more water. Feed staghorn ferns with a liquid fertilizer diluted to half strength: from spring until late summer, feed them every 3 to 4 weeks; during the winter months stretch the feeding schedule to 6 weeks.

Like other ferns, staghorn ferns can be propagated from spores that grow underneath fertile fronds. But they can also, and more quickly, be reproduced vegetatively because the plant sends out new plants, known as pups, from among the basal fronds. When the pups are 2 or 3 inches tall they can be removed with a few roots and planted separately.

A large, well-grown staghorn fern

Strawberry Begonia *(Saxifraga)* This extremely tolerant houseplant is known variously as strawberry begonia, strawberry geranium, roving sailor, and mother-of-thousands. All of these names address the way the plant grows — by sending out runners just as a strawberry plant does. In fact, strawberry begonias are neither strawberries, begonias, nor geraniums. In China and Japan, where the plants grow wild, the runners creep along the ground, and the little plants at the end of the runners send down roots and put out runners of their own. Before long there's a mass of plants spreading in every direction. When it's grown in a hanging pot, the parent plant has to support the weight of the runner plants and keep them sufficiently fed and watered to withstand hanging out in the dry air. That's quite a bit to ask of a plant, but the strawberry begonia responds valiantly and becomes a delightful hanging plant. It will even send up a few airy white flowers, though it's grown primarily for its colorful foliage. The basic species (*S. stolonifera,* formerly *S. sarmentosa*) has hairy reddish-green leaves. *Saxifraga stolonifera tricolor* is a variegated variety with hairy leaves marked in red, green, and cream; if you have an extremely bright spot, you'll get the most color from the variegated plant, especially if it's a little pot-bound and not overfed.

Strawberry begonias are very adaptable to a wide range of growing conditions. They're best in bright indirect light, but they tolerate sunlight if they're kept moist enough. They'll withstand almost any night temperatures, from just

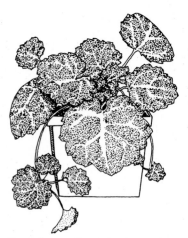

Strawberry Begonia *(Saxifraga)*

A strawberry begonia with the plantlets at the ends of the runners

above freezing to 60 degrees or more, but they're happiest just between those extremes. The soil should be given a chance to dry out just a bit between thorough waterings. Feed them lightly every 3 or 4 months; the foliage loses its color if the plants are overnourished.

The best way to propagate new plants is from the plantlets on the runners. Just pin a plantlet to moist commercial potting soil until it sends down its own roots. Then cut the runner. The new plant will grow rapidly, and will be of good size within a few months.

String-of-Beads *(Senecio)* The string-of-beads (*S. rowleyanus*) is fairly new to commerce, and not well known yet. It will be soon, though, as it's a great houseplant. It's

194

related both to the cineraria and to a fleshy-leaved trailing plant known as German ivy, but this is surely one of the oddest members of the family. Its leaves are globular in shape, ¼ inch in diameter, and succulent, with a narrow translucent "window-stripe" around each leaf. The leaves are lined up along wire-thin trailing stems, making this a fine plant for a small hanging container. The plant is sometimes known as string-of-peas, and in fact that's a fairly accurate image. The name *Senecio* comes from the Latin *senex*, which means old; it's a reference to the white, whiskery, hairy seedheads that appear after the tiny white flowers fade.

A native of the southwest African desert, the string-of-beads is very easy to manage as a houseplant. It does best in bright light without full sun. It rests during the fall and winter, when it would like night temperatures in the 40s, a feeding every 3 months, and only enough water to keep the leaves from shriveling. During the spring and sum-

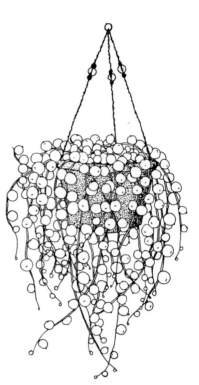

String-of-Beads *(Senecio)*

Several string-of-beads plants potted together in a hanging container

mer growing period, let the soil dry out slightly between waterings, and feed it every month. During its growing period, it can take night temperatures of 70 or more.

Cuttings of the stems root very easily directly in cactus soil; my own recipe for cactus soil is 2 parts potting soil, 1 part sand, plus 1 tablespoon ground limestone, and 1 tablespoon bone meal. If you root several cuttings in a hanging container, you'll have a fuller-looking plant than if you set in only one cutting to a pot.

🔺 **Tuberous-rooted Begonia** *(Begonia)* This is a spectacular plant for the cool or intermediate greenhouse, or for a shady summer porch or patio but it's not a candidate for growing in a home; it needs constant, high humidity and

195

Tuberous-rooted Begonia
(Begonia)

cool temperatures. Several wild species of tuberous-rooted begonias are native to Central and South America; they were hybridized over a century ago to give us the magnificent hybrids (*B. tuberhybrida*) available today. They come in either trailing or upright types; the large-flowered plants, with blooms up to 6 inches across, are uprights. Both types are exquisite, and produce summer flowers in every color except blue. In terms of flower shape, tuberous-rooted begonias are the mimics of the plant world, as each variation seems to favor another flower, such as a narcissus, carnation, camellia, or rose. This trait is responsible for their often being marketed with unfortunately fanciful names, like *B. narcissiflora*.

If you buy or are given a plant in flower, keep it in filtered sunlight and cool temperatures; the night temperatures should be in the 40s or 50s to help the flowers last as long as possible. (Tuberous-rooted begonias thrive along coastal areas where nights are cool and damp. It's nearly impossible to grow them in the hot central part of the country.) Keep the soil barely moist at all times and feed them every other week during the growing season with a standard houseplant fertilizer. In the fall, after the blossom period has ended, let the plants die back by eliminating fertilizer from their diet and gradually reducing the moisture supply until the foliage shrivels. Unpot the tubers and store them in a bag of dry peat moss or vermiculite in a cool, dry place at 40 to 50 degrees.

In March, bring the tubers out of storage and start them back into growth for the next season. If you are buying tubers, March is the month to look for them. Most other bulbs are sold by standard sizes but not these; their size is not only a function of their age, but of their genetic background. Buy from a dealer you trust, and buy for the traits of growth and color that you want.

Repotting the tubers is very simple. Start with a 4-inch pot filled with rooting medium; the medium can be either equal parts coarse sand and peat moss or leaf mold, or straight peat moss. Moisten the medium thoroughly and press the tuber, with the concave side up, into the mix so that it is just visible at the surface of the soil. Set the pot into a brightly lit spot out of the sun where the night temperatures will be in the low 60s. There will be top growth — one stem or several — within a matter of days. When the growth is 3 or 4 inches tall, move the plant to a 6-inch pot in a mixture of equal parts of commercial potting soil and peat moss or leaf mold. A handful of dried cow manure mixed into the soil of a 6-inch pot will help keep these plants well-fed and at their peak.

If your tuber has produced multiple stems, you can propagate the plant when you transplant, by cutting the stems and rooting them. (Leave at least one stem growing on the tuber to make new growth for the season.) Make the cut just flush with the surface of the tuber. Dip the end in rooting hormone and insert it 1 inch deep in moist coarse sand. Slip the whole pot into a plastic bag, and keep it in bright indirect light at about 65 degrees. These cuttings will be large enough to blossom in the summer.

There are several other ways to propagate tuberous-rooted begonias. You can take a 3- or 4-inch stem cutting at any time during the growing season. Select a stem low on the plant because it's apt to make vegetative growth rather than flowers, which would drain the young plant's energy. Make the cut about ¼ inch below a leaf, and remove the lower leaves on the cutting. Dip the end in rooting hormone and set it into moist sand. Seal the pot in a plastic bag, and keep it out of the sun at about 65 degrees. These plants will blossom in the summer, too.

The flowers of tuberous-rooted begonias are handsome on the plant or floating in a shallow dish of water

197

Cut a stem from the plant about ¼" below a leaf, remove the lower leaves and dip the end in rooting powder.

set the stem in moist sand and seal the pot in a plastic bag.

The tubers can also be divided. Start by initiating them into growth in March. As soon as the shoots appear, lift the tubers from the soil and divide them with a sharp knife into as many pieces as there are buds, or "eyes." Dust the cut surfaces of the tuber with sulfur, captan, or powdered charcoal, and let them dry in the air for a day or two. Then plant the divisions, eyes up, in coarse sand. When the new growth is 1 or 2 inches tall, transfer the divisions to regular soil mix. They'll blossom the first summer.

Press the tuber, concave side up, into rooting medium.

plant the tuber with the convex side down.

fill the pot with peat moss to 1½" below the rim.

Tuberous-rooted begonias can also be started from seed. They have to be started a little earlier in the year, in January, but the seed-grown plants make fine free-flowering plants the first season. In my opinion, starting from seed is the most interesting way to propagate these plants. It's also the cheapest and, because the hybrids are relatively stable, all of the plants will have lovely flowers.

The amount of moisture the seeds receive is crucial. If they're too wet, they're apt to be hit by damping-off fungus; and if they're too dry, of course, they won't germinate. So the soil mix is very important. I combine equal parts damp leaf mold and coarse sand. I sift about three-quarters of this mix through a ½-inch mesh screen and half fill a 2-inch-deep pot with the sifted mix. Then I sift more of the mix through ⅛-inch mesh, and put a ¼-inch layer of the finer mix in the pot. Then I bottom-water it, and after the soil has drained, I sow the minute, dustlike seeds. The seeds are so tiny, in fact, that I sometimes mix a bit of fine white sand in with them so I can see where they fall. The seeds shouldn't be covered after sowing. I just slip the pot into a plastic bag and set it out of the sun in a 65- to 70-degree spot. The seeds begin to germinate in a week or two; when they do I loosen the bag to give them more air. Seed-grown plants started in early winter indoors will start to blossom about the same time as tuber-grown ones started in March and, of course, will have developed good, healthy tubers by fall.

Sow seeds on the surface. Cover pot with a plastic bag.

Top layer: ¼" of soil mix sifted through ⅛" mesh.

soil mix made up of equal parts of coarse sand and damp leaf mold or peat moss.

Bottom layer: 1" of soil mix sifted through ½" mesh.

Venus Flytrap *(Dionaea)* Most of the world's plants live on the nutrients in the soil, fed by the decaying plant and animal life around them. Carnivorous plants, as a rule, are native to areas that are undersupplied with soil nutrients; so they have evolved ingenious methods to capture live insects and supplement their meager diet. Some of these plants are specially designed so that an insect, attracted by a sweet nectar, ventures deep into one of the traps and can't find a way out. Others combine a sticky nectar with a reflex action that closes partially and holds the insect in place. Some, like the Venus flytrap, simply snap shut.

Venus flytraps are small plants. Those grown indoors are usually only a few inches across, with six or seven traps at one time. The traps are really modified leaves about 1 inch long, and operate something like a clam shell with teeth. Their resting position is about a third of the way open. Insects are drawn to the traps by a sweet nectar; when the insect enters, it brushes against a series of extremely sensitive hairs. The trap doesn't respond to the first

Venus Flytrap *(Dionaea)*

199

A Venus flytrap, one trap poised to strike and another closed around its victim

signal, which might, after all, be nothing but dust, but on the second signal it closes instantly. The teeth, called cilia, mesh together and lock the victim in. Small insects, which would be more bother than they're worth, are able to escape through the spaces between the teeth. Larger insects, struggling to escape, continue to activate those sensitive hairs, which makes the trap close tighter and tighter. When it has closed completely, the trap cells exude a liquid enzyme that dissolves the insect's soft parts, which the plant digests; then the trap opens and the unusable remains fall out. When a trap has captured three or four insects, its work is done, and it falls off. New traps grow in its place.

Venus flytraps bring to mind dangerous, exotic jungles, but in fact they're native to North Carolina, where they grow in bogs. They're relatively simple plants to grow indoors, so long as they can be kept moist enough. The soil should always be wet, with the pots sitting in saucers of water, and the air as humid as you can make it; if the air is too dry, they won't be able to develop new traps. They're accustomed to full sun, and they continue to want it when they're grown indoors; if they're grown in too-dim light, the growth is elongated and the traps small. They like cool temperatures — in the wild they survive a light frost — with nights in the 40s and days in the high 50s. Pot them up in sphagnum moss, with sand added if you want. They don't grow during the winter; during the spring and summer they grow at the rate of about one new trap a week. If you set them outside for the warm months, they'll be able to find plenty of insects. Indoors you might want to apply a small amount of an organic fertilizer such as fish emulsion to the soil once every 4 or 5 weeks. Collected fertilizer salts would do them a great deal of damage, so top-water the plants regularly to flush the fertilizer through the soil. If you want, you can feed your Venus flytrap dead flies or tiny specks of ground meat. They don't need this to survive, but it is an intriguing procedure, especially for children.

Q: What's your opinion of the various products that can be used on plants' leaves to make them shiny?

A: I don't think much of them at all. Many of them clog the pores of the leaves and make it difficult for the plants to breathe. And they usually make the plant look too shiny to be real. I think it's much better just to wash plants' foliage regularly with a mild solution of water and a few drops of liquid dish-washing detergent, and then to rinse them. They'll be clean, healthy, and natural in appearance.

Q: Can you tell me anything about a plant known as the apple of Carthage?

A: Yes. This is the plant we know as the pomegranate. Standard varieties grow to be 10 or 12 feet tall, but there is a dwarf plant (*Punica granatum nana*) that rarely grows taller than about 1 foot. Like the larger plant it has handsome long-lasting brick-red flowers about 1 inch long; they appear mostly in the spring and summer, with occasional flowers blooming through the rest of the year. The blossoms are followed by edible fruit about 2 inches in diameter. The dwarf pomegranates make fine houseplants if they can be given full sunshine. Ordinary household temperatures suit their needs. The soil should be constantly moist, and the plants need a feeding every 3 or 4 months.

201

CARE WHILE YOU'RE AWAY

Though in varying degrees, all plants need warmth, food, light, and moisture. If you're only going away for the weekend, it's enough just to water all your plants thoroughly and set them on humidifying trays out of the sun. If you're planning to be away for a month or more, all the plants' needs will have to be attended, and the only way to do this is by enlisting the services of a plant-sitter. A neighbor who knows and loves plants is obviously the ideal choice; otherwise, try to hire a plant-sitting service.

If you're going to be away from three or four days to a month, the only real worry is moisture. Any plant can survive a month without fertilizer, and would welcome the rest. Warmth isn't a problem, even if you're taking a winter trip and you turn your thermostat down to the minimum. Most plants will do perfectly well if you move them away from the cold outside walls and windows and into the center of the warmest room provided it is well illuminated with natural light. If you have any plants that are particularly sensitive to the cold, like gesneriads, set them on top of the refrigerator where there is always heat from the motor. Light is important because it affects the amount of moisture available; it's best to move all your plants out of the direct sun and into bright indirect light while you're away. They can tolerate reduced light much more easily than drought.

There are several ways to see that your plants don't dry out in your absence. One is to put them in plastic pots, which hold moisture in, rather than in porous clay pots, which dry out three times as quickly as plastic. If you do have some plants in clay pots, and plan on being gone only three or four days, a technique known as double-potting will help. Start with a holeless urn or pot that's at least 2 inches larger than the clay pot. Line the bottom of the urn with clay shards, and then set in enough long-fibered sphagnum moss over the shards to raise the rim of the clay pot to the same level as the rim of the urn. Then fill in the space between the two pots with more of the sphagnum moss. Water the soil ball and the moss well, and the plants are all set for several days.

A simpler solution is to enclose the plants in plastic bags to create a mini-greenhouse effect. The secret is to arrange it

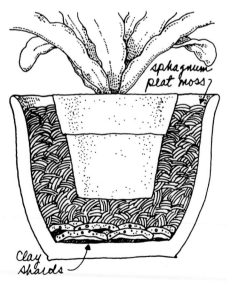

sphagnum peat moss

clay shards

so that water, condensing on the inside of the plastic, isn't allowed to escape, but is recirculated through the holes in the bottoms of the pots to replenish the plants' moisture supply. It's a sort of closed ecological system. Start by watering each plant well; then insert stakes into the soil to keep the plastic bag from collapsing onto the foliage; slip the plant and pot into the plastic bag, and seal it shut. It's imperative that the pots do not sit in saucers, but with their drainage holes right against the plastic; otherwise, the water can't be drawn up and used over and over again while you're away. (Make sure to keep the plants out of the direct sun because the bags will trap the sun's heat and literally cook the plants.) Large plants can be handled this way, too, using dry-cleaner bags. If you have a large awkward plant, you'll have some luck if you soak the soil, wrap the pot in plastic, and seal the plastic around the stem of the plant; this will hold some moisture in the soil ball, but of course the leaves will continue to transpire moisture, so it's not a reliable method for more than three days or so.

Wick-watering is a method that will also work with houseplants. Start by unpotting the plant and feeding one end of a moist glass-fiber wick — available from garden centers — through the bottom hole. Unravel the end of the fiber and splay it out on the bottom of the pot like a pinwheel. Let the unraveled end of the fiber hang down about 2 inches through the hole of the pot. Add a thin layer of fine, sifted soil — no drainage material should be used — on the bottom of the pot, and then set the plant back in. Set the pot above a container of water so that the free end of the wick is in

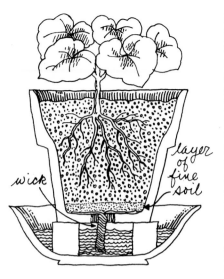

wick

layer of fine soil

water, but the pot isn't. Needless to say, this is a troublesome procedure, and not one for a large collection, but if you have only a few plants, it's perfectly satisfactory as long as the water supply holds out.

If you have a large collection, you'll want to work out a way to handle all your plants together. You can set several plants into your bathtub if the room is bright enough. Protect the surface of the tub with a few layers of newspaper, then set bricks in on top of the paper and put your plants down on top of the bricks. Plug the tub and run the tap until the water is deep enough to just cover the bricks. The absorbent bricks will carry water upward to the holes in the bottoms of the pots. Keep in mind that some tubs, especially in old houses, aren't level; you'll have to work out a way to adjust for this so that the pots are sitting just at the water level.

By far the best of the mechanical plant-sitters is a new device known as a capillary mat. It will work for one plant, or, if the mat is large enough, for dozens. The beauty of this

arrangement is that when the plants are set on the moistened mat — which looks like indoor-outdoor carpeting — the roots are able to take up just the amount of moisture they need. Even plants that normally require a period of drying out between waterings will do beautifully on a capillary mat because they take up such a modest supply of water. The mats work like sponges, and are kept constantly moist by an adjacent water supply. You can use a pan or humidifying tray to hold the water, or you can buy a capillary mat kit at a garden center; these kits usually come with some sort of a water-holding tank. Make sure you protect the floor or tabletop where you set up the capillary mats.

If you're going away for the summer and have a spot outdoors where you can set your plants, by all means do so. But be aware that plants face special threats outdoors: wind, flood, drought, and sunburn. My advice is to find a spot with dappled sunlight, and dig a trench; add drainage material at the bottom of the trench, set the plants in, and fill around them with soil. This will keep them from blowing over, from drowning, and also from drying out too quickly. But they'll still need watering, and if you're going away for more than a few days you'll have to find someone willing to look after them during dry spells.

Cover the bottom of the bathtub with newspaper, set bricks on the paper and the plants on the bricks. Barely cover the bricks with water.

capillary mat

water supply

203

SEP

Echeveria and aeonium

SEP

In September, the night temperatures are dropping and the houseplants that have spent the warm months outdoors should be brought inside. Before you do, hose down the foliage and scrub the pots to wash off insects. If there is a petunia or wax begonia in your garden that you're especially fond of, dig up the whole plant, slip it into a pot, cut the stems back somewhat, and bring it indoors. Other favorite outdoor plants, like impatiens and geraniums, are difficult to relocate successfully, so it's a better idea just to take cuttings to grow through the winter indoors.

Amaryllis bulbs usually enter their dormancy in the early fall; after a rest of at least a month they can be started back into growth. Bougainvilleas, which usually rest through the winter months when they're grown as houseplants, should be cut back when the flowers fade. Lantana plants should also be cut back severely in the late summer to make room for the new winter growth. And golden trumpets, which are nearing the end of their flowering cycle, should be put on a minimal diet to encourage them to rest until spring.

This is the time of the year to think ahead to some holiday plants. Flowering kalanchoes started from seed earlier in the year will come into flower in January unless they're hurried along with 14 hours of uninterrupted darkness daily from the first of September through the first week of October; this will bring them into bloom in December. To get house-grown poinsettias to blossom again, they need the same 14-hours-of-darkness schedule from the third week in September through the month of October. And starting early this month Christmas cactuses need the cool and/or dark location that will insure flowers in December. Remember to cut down on the water and eliminate the fertilizer when Christmas cactuses are forming their buds during the fall. For a holiday time further ahead, this is the month to pot up Easter lily bulbs, too. They'll come into bloom in the spring, but probably not right on schedule for Easter Sunday.

In the greenhouse, September is the month to attend to hydrangeas in order to bring them into flower again for the next spring. This is also the best time of the year to sow the seeds of painted tongues. They'll come into blossom the following May.

Boston Fern *(Nephrolepis)* No parlor in the Victorian era was considered furnished without a Boston fern. Overwhelmed by its own popularity early in this century, it was shunted aside only to be rediscovered lately by a new generation of indoor gardeners. A hundred years ago Boston ferns stood alone on 3-foot pedestals called fern stands, which allowed the foliage to cascade in a fountain of greenery that often reached to the floor. Fern stands went out of production when the popularity of the plants fell off, but now they're back on the market for contemporary gardeners. These stands make handsome objects, but the plants are a little happier potted in hanging containers where they're more visible, and the foliage is out of the way of passersby; this second point is particularly important because contact, especially an admiring stroke of the foliage, will cause the tender green of new foliage to turn brown.

The story behind the Boston fern is one of the classics of horticulture. The wild fern parent is the sword or ladder fern, *N. exaltata.* It's native to most of the tropics throughout the world, sending forth stiffly upright fronds about 5 feet tall. Because of the sword fern's long life indoors as a houseplant, growers propagated and sold great numbers of them during the latter part of the nineteenth century.

Boston Fern *(Nephrolepis)*

One of the growers serving that nineteenth-century market was the Robert Craig Company of Philadelphia. In the early 1890s this company sent a shipment to a grower in Massachusetts who found one fern that was different from all the others. Not only did it grow faster, but its fronds were wider and arched more gracefully than did those of the rest of the lot. For several years after this find, the plant was considered to be an entirely different kind of fern, but when a specimen was sent to the prestigious Kew Gardens in London it was determined that the maverick fern was a sport, or mutation, of *N. exaltata;* in honor of its first known location, Kew authorities named the plant Boston fern, *N. exaltata bostoniensis.* It so outperformed other ferns that it soon wiped out the competition and became the only type grown.

But nature had another surprise in store. About ten years after its introduction, the Boston fern itself began to mutate into other forms. The first was a type whose frond segments were divided into two leaflets, giving the plant thicker strands of foliage. By the time of the First World War there were cultivars — plants that originated and thrived in cultivation — whose foliage was mosslike, the result of repeated subdivisions. These ferns have fronds that are nearly round in profile in contrast with the flat fronds of

normal ferns. Even today growers are bringing out new varieties.

Small wonder then that the many and varied Boston ferns are sometimes confusingly similar in looks. Some authorities list forty-three named cultivars of the Boston fern, but only a few of these are generally available to the public at large. The dwarf Boston fern produces great numbers of bright green feathery arching fronds about 15 to 18 inches long. Elegantissima has double and triple overlapping leaves on arching 18- to 20-inch fronds. Fluffy Ruffles grows erect with rich dark green double-leaved fronds rarely longer than 12 inches. Mini-Ruffle is a well-named dwarf mutation whose spreading waxy dark green double-leaved fronds are only 6 or 8 inches long. Rooseveltii is close to the original Boston fern in size and appearance but the segments that line its arching 3-foot fronds are gracefully waved and oddly lobed. For the indoor gardener Verona is probably the best of the truly lacy-leaved types; its 10- to 12-inch arching fronds are triple-leaved, giving them a filmy look. Whitmanii is a dead ringer for Verona, but its fronds are half again as long.

Boston ferns often send out fronds atypical of the variety being grown, eager as they are to take on new identities. It's a good idea to remove these oddball fronds, particularly if they are similar to the plain fronds of the wild species. The plain wild frond is stronger-growing than the finer-textured foliage of the cultivated variety, and in this battle, the cultivated variety usually loses.

All Boston ferns are relatively easy to care for if they're kept beyond the reach of friendly fingers, whose touch they cannot tolerate. They do best in a moist soil that has an ample supply of organic material. Ordinary potting soil is fine, or you can mix your own soil from 1 part loam, 1 part peat moss or leaf mold, 1 part finely ground fir bark (usually available from orchid supply houses), and 1 part coarse sand, with 2 tablespoons of bone meal added to each gallon of this mix. Many successful growers pot their ferns in pure sphagnum peat moss. Since Boston ferns are native to tropical and subtropical regions, they do best in warm temperatures. Nights shouldn't fall below 55 degrees; daytime readings aren't important as long as the air is humid. They want neither full sun nor full shade; curtain-filtered or reflected light is ideal. (They thrive under artificial light provided they're given at least 400 foot-candles for 12 to 14 hours a day.) I feed them only twice a year, once in the early spring and again in midsummer, with a half-strength houseplant fertilizer. Sometimes the older fronds of Boston ferns turn brown. If this happens, just cut the frond off at the soil line.

Opposite. A table-top specimen of a nearly perfect Boston fern

The main problem that Boston ferns present to their owners is their astonishing rate of growth. In the space of a few months the roots will develop so quickly that they all but fill the pot. We had two massive Boston ferns hanging from the rafters of the Victory Garden that had to be dunk-watered a couple of times daily in order to meet the plants' need for moisture. Of course, what they needed was division. As a general rule, Boston ferns should be divided every year in the early spring, but if you find your plant with such dense roots that you can't get water into the soil, divide it at any time of the year. If the plant is so overgrown that the center foliage is dead and only the perimeter of the plant survives, make sure you cut the center out, and then divide the living section into fist-sized portions. Cut all the foliage right down to the soil line so that the new growth will come in unchallenged. Give each division the same-sized pot that the entire plant was in; the division will look a little lonely at first, but it will quickly make use of the extra space.

Unlike most other ferns, Boston fern mutations are essentially sterile and can't be propagated from spores. But the plants send out great numbers of wiry runners that produce plants in somewhat the same way that a strawberry plant does. So if you want a few new ferns, propagate them in the early spring by pinning the runners, still attached to the parent, onto pots of moist soil; when the young plants take root, cut the runners away. Or, when summer comes, plant the fern outdoors in an organic-rich soil in the shade, and let it propagate itself. In the fall, pot up as many young plants as you want and bring them indoors. This is the way that commercial growers propagate Boston ferns, though of course they use a greenhouse. Still more unique is the plant-tissue method of propagation, a system too exacting for the average home gardener.

Boxwood *(Buxus)*

⊔ **Boxwood** *(Buxus)* Boxwood has been an outdoor hedge plant for generations, but it's fairly recent to indoor culture. There are many different varieties, but they fall into two basic categories, both of which are handsome, with shiny foliage densely lined up along the stems. The Japanese boxwood (*B. microphylla*) has small, rather pale, yellowish-green leaves. The English boxwood (*B. sempervirens*) has larger, bluish-green leaves. Both types can grow to be 3 or 4 feet tall, but they're usually kept much smaller, often less than 6 to 8 inches tall; they're relatively slow growing indoors, so keeping them small isn't difficult. The dwarf English boxwood (*B. sempervirens suffruticosa*) is often seen in dish gardens or terrariums because of its smaller size and slower growth habits.

There are very few houseplants that are easier to care for or more tolerant than boxwood. They grow in either sun or bright indirect light. They're not bothered by cool temperatures or drafts; in fact they're best in a room where the night temperatures fall into the 40s or low 50s, though they'll live in warmer temperatures, too. The soil should be kept barely moist all the time.

Boxwoods only grow 2 to 4 inches a year, most of it coming in a flush of growth in the early spring. They should be fed once a year, just before the annual growth, and pruned lightly then too. The English boxwood will form new branches without further encouragement, but the Japanese boxwood may need an occasional pinching back to keep the foliage dense. The cuttings of either type will root easily if they're taken toward late summer or early fall, after the flush of growth has had time to mature. (If the cuttings were to be taken in the spring, the best time to propagate most plants, the growth would be so succulent that the cuttings would wilt and die.) After the cuttings have rooted, pot them up in commercial potting soil.

Calamondin Orange *(x Citrofortunella)* The calamondin orange, also known as the Panama orange, though it was discovered in the Philippines, is a delightful, easy-to-care-for houseplant that is widely available through florists and garden centers. It's a dwarf plant that rarely grows any taller than 2 feet; it bears fragrant white flowers from spring through fall, followed by fruit that is close to the size and shape of a small tangerine. The fruit is edible, tastes a little like a tangy orange, and makes a refreshing ade. It's not at all uncommon for a single plant to have blossoms, green

Calamondin Orange
(x Citrofortunella)

211

A calamondin orange in full fruit

fruit, and ripe fruit all at the same time. That is, if the flowers are pollinated. If the plant is put outside for the summer, the insects will see to that, but if it's kept indoors, the flowers can be pollinated by lightly rubbing a camel's hair brush from bloom to bloom as soon as they open.

For years the calamondin orange was thought to be a species of citrus, *C. mitis*. Very recent studies have shown that it is actually a bigeneric hybrid between a *Citrus* and a citrus-related plant called *Fortunella*. Its correct botanical name now is *x Citrofortunella mitis*. The "x" means it is a hybrid.

No citrus plant will live for long unless it has sunshine for a minimum of 4 hours a day, and the calamondin (kal-a-*mon*-din) orange is no exception. Otherwise, they're easy houseplants to please. They like moderate temperatures, with nights in the 50s; no amount of daytime warmth

212

disturbs them. Let the soil dry out slightly between waterings. Feed the plant once in the very early spring, again early in the summer, and a third time in late summer. Don't overlook the regular shower to keep the foliage clean and free of mealy bugs and red spider mites.

Calamondin orange plants grow fairly rapidly. Under ideal greenhouse conditions, they'll make 8 to 12 inches of new growth every year. That rate of growth requires that they be attended to so their roots don't become crowded. My advice is to prune lightly in midwinter, when the plant is initiating new growth; the pruning will shape the plant, and the new foliage will hide the cuts. Then repot the plant into a larger container, using African violet soil.

There are two ways to propagate calamondin oranges. The first is from stem cuttings of the mature current-season wood; the cuttings will root easily and bear their first flowers in about 18 months. This is the best method to multiply a good plant. They can also be started from seed produced by your own tree so long as you're sure to plant the seeds before they have a chance to dry out. Just push the seeds lightly into a pot of damp potting soil. Because the seedlings will be offspring of a hybrid, considerable variation can be expected. (Don't try to sow the seeds of a full-sized orange; you are apt to produce nothing but a thorny foliage plant with no fruit.)

There are, by the way, several citrus trees that do well indoors, as long as they're dwarf type. Oranges will do fairly well, but the easiest of the citrus trees, after the calamondin orange, is the lemon. They're much more rugged than one might expect and produce edible fruit. I had a winter heat failure in my home greenhouse once that claimed a discouraging number of my plants, including some I'd had for half my life. My lemon tree lost every leaf in the cold. But I pruned it back a little and it recovered beautifully, producing new buds and leaves in just a few weeks.

▭ **Cast-Iron Plant** (*Aspidistra*) Cast-iron is right. Back at the turn of the century every Victorian house, and every saloon and boardinghouse as well, had a cast-iron plant sitting off in some dark corner where it continued to grow year after year regardless of gross neglect. As time wore on, gardeners came to hold its perseverance against it and the cast-iron plant fell out of favor. Now it's being rediscovered after fifty years out in the horticultural cold.

A plant that tolerates the most abominable growing conditions may not seem to need special cultural attention, but while this plant stubbornly refuses to die if neglected, it is tough and handsome if it's treated well. It will grow to a

Cast-Iron Plant (*Aspidistra*)

A cast-iron plant, one leaf showing some variation in color

height of nearly 3 feet, with gracefully arching leaves some 30 inches long and 4 inches wide. The original species, *A. elatior,* is a native of China, with plain, solid green leaves. *Aspidistra elatior variegata* is a less rugged offspring of the original; the leaves have somewhat broad creamy white stripes against the dark green base color of the leaves. If the plant is overfed or grown under light that is too dim, the white coloration sometimes disappears.

Cast-iron plants do best in bright shadowless light, and do beautifully under 150 foot-candles of artificial light too. Nights in the low 50s and days around 75 is an ideal temperature range, but the plants put up with both warmer and colder readings. I keep the soil barely moist all the time and once a month from the spring until the fall I feed them with a houseplant fertilizer. During the winter months, when the light level is low, fertilizing isn't a good idea.

These plants are easily propagated by root division in the early spring. The roots are apt to break into small pieces during this operation, so plant several sections. It's important to plant several pieces of the rhizome together because each one is apt to produce only 1 or 2 leaves. It's a good idea to note where the buds are on the rhizome, and point the buds in the direction that you want the new growth to come. I think the plants are most attractive if the foliage is aimed toward the edge of the pot, and the leaves arch outward over the rim.

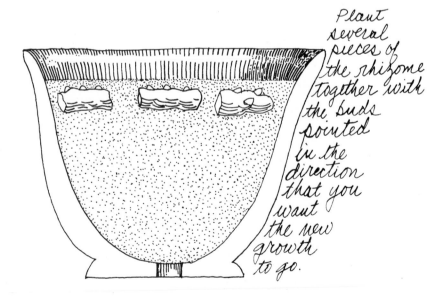

Plant several pieces of the rhizome together with the buds pointed in the direction that you want the new growth to go.

Early spring is the best time of the year to relocate a plant to a larger pot, but don't be too quick to do this, as cast-iron plants are slow-growing and can remain peacefully in the same pot for several years.

214

Echeveria *(Echeveria)* There are several species of echeveria, handsome succulents native to Mexico, that make good houseplants. They form tidy rosettes of leaves, often with red markings along the tips. The plush plant (*E. pulvinata*) is one of the sturdiest houseplants around, and is probably the best known of the echeverias; the green leaves are covered with pale hairs that turn red in cool temperatures.

Echeverias (ek-e-*vay*-ri-as) want as much sun as possible. They do best if the night temperatures are in the 50s and the days near 70. They're succulents, so the primary threat to their survival is overwatering. Make sure you let the soil become moderately dry between thorough waterings from spring through fall; in the winter, water them only enough to keep the leaves from shriveling. Feed them only once a year, in the spring, with a fertilizer diluted to half strength. Don't be quick to repot them, but if they need it, put them in a mix of equal parts potting soil and sand, lightly dusted with ground limestone and bone meal.

Young echeverias grow very close to the soil line, but as they age they develop a stem. With time, the stem

Echeveria *(Echeveria)*

A flat of young echeverias

215

grows taller and taller, the rosette of foliage always clustered at the top. As this process is taking place, the plant sends out new rosettes of foliage at the soil line. So eventually, an echeveria will have a large, gawky, stemmed rosette, with good-looking short young plants beneath it. Luckily the echeveria is so eager to root that the tall rosette can be cut from the plant and allowed to grow on as a short plant. Just cut the stem at the soil line, to leave the original plant looking neat; then cut off all but a 2-inch stub of stem on the rosette of foliage. Put the stem into a pot of moist soil mix, with the rosette resting just at the soil line. New roots will form within a couple of days.

Echeverias can also be propagated by setting a leaf cutting ½ inch deep in perlite.

Fatsia *(Fatsia)*

▭ **Fatsia** *(Fatsia)* Master gardeners that they are, the Japanese had been growing the plant we call Japanese fatsia (*F. japonica*) for generations when Western botanists, unfamiliar with the plant, arrived and "discovered" it. (The Chinese were equally familiar with the related species, *F. papyrifera*, whose inner stems have been used to make genuine rice paper since the earliest days of Chinese history; this plant is rarely seen in cultivation.) Fatsia is now a very popular plant in the West, as well as the East; here it's grown primarily as a houseplant, but it can live as an outdoor garden shrub in parts of the country where the winters are mild and the temperatures rarely fall below freezing.

The fatsia is a splendid houseplant, and very easy to care for. It will grow in full sun or bright indirect light. It will also grow under artificial light if provided with 800 or more foot-candles for 12 to 16 hours daily. Any commercial potting soil is fine: keep it constantly but barely moist. The plant does best in a cool room where the night temperatures don't rise much above 50 degrees. Feed it only twice a year, once in the early spring and again in early summer.

Fatsias can reach a height of 4 feet or more, with rich green leaves 1 foot across. But they can be kept at any size by pruning the stems just above a leaf. The pruning is best done in the spring. New plants can be started either from cuttings or from seeds.

The fatsia is one of the parents of an amazing offspring known variously as the fatshedera, the tree ivy, and botanical wonder. It's a bigeneric hybrid whose parents met in France in the Lizé greenhouse just before World War I. The mating between Moser's Japanese fatsia (*F. japonica moserii*) and the Irish ivy (*Hedera helix hibernica*) wasn't planned and might have gone undetected had not one of the Lizé brothers noticed and saved the maverick seedling, a

semi-erect plant that was shrubby like the fatsia, with lobed leaves like the ivy. In honor of its discoverer, the plant's botanical name is *Fatshedera lizei.* By nature, the fatshedera (fat-*shed*-er-a) grows upright, and if it's provided with a stake it'll grow to a height of 3 feet or more. But if the tips are pinched, the stems will grow short and bushy. It needs the same care that keeps the fatsia contented.

A fatsia plant, a good plant for a spot that needs a bold accent

🏠 **Freesia** *(Freesia)* Though it is now possible to buy specially stored freesia corms in the spring for blossoms in May and June, freesias are traditionally considered as winter and spring flowers. They're grown not only for their handsome long-lived blossoms, but for their incomparable spicy fragrance. The original orange- and yellow-flowered plants, which grow wild in South Africa, have been extensively hybridized and there are now freesias available, in addition to yellow and orange, in such hues as pink, lilac, blue, mauve, and white, plus some two-color combinations. The orange and yellow freesias are generally smaller but more fragrant than the newer hybrids; some of the large-flowered freesias have almost no fragrance at all.

Freesia *(Freesia)*

217

Freesias need constant sun and cool temperatures, limiting them to a greenhouse or a cool sunporch. They can be started as soon as the corms become available in the late summer or early fall. I usually pot up a few corms every couple of weeks between August and December, and have flowers from December to March. The corms are teardrop shaped, about 1 inch tall, and covered with a pale brown tunic; the top of the corm is the pointed tip. I use regular commercial potting soil, lightly dusted with ground limestone, and plant 8 or 10 large corms in a 6-inch pot, covering them with about an inch of soil. Until the growth gets started, I water the soil very lightly, keeping it as barely moist as possible. Then after the greenery appears, I keep the soil constantly moist to the touch; the foliage will turn brown if the soil dries out. I feed them monthly until the buds begin to show color. Freesias are cool-temperature plants, and do best if their night readings are in the 40- to 60-degree range. They will grow faster in the warmer end of

A single stem of fully opened freesia blossoms

that spectrum but their growth will be weaker and need support. In any event, once the flowers appear it's best to keep the plants where night temperatures are low, to help them hold their blossoms as long as possible. When they've finished flowering, give them less water and let the foliage gradually die back. Then unpot the corms and store them in a cool dark place until they're ready to be potted up again in the fall.

Freesia plants can also be grown from seeds planted in the spring; this is easy to do, inexpensive, and likely to produce disease-free plants. There's also more of a choice of varieties if you start from seed. Rub the seeds between your hands to remove the chaff and soak them for a day and a night before planting; then sow them in flats outdoors. Keep the plants moist and fertilized through the summer, and bring them indoors before frost in the fall. Then reduce the amount of water, and eliminate fertilizer entirely, so the foliage withers and dies. After about a month's wait, dig up the corms and replant them for flowers that winter.

Gold-Dust Plant (*Aucuba*)

Gold-Dust Plant (*Aucuba*) In parts of the country where winter temperatures remain above 5 to 10 degrees F., the gold-dust plant is favored as an outdoor shrub because of its evergreen foliage. It's not a common houseplant but it's relatively carefree indoors, and bold-looking enough to dress up a drab corner. The gold-speckled leaves are so shiny that they look varnished. The original plant, *A. japonica*, is native to Japan and other parts of southeast Asia; it has plain dark shiny leaves with saw-toothed edges on the portions of the leaves nearest the stems. The cultivated varieties are noticeably more colorful, with dramatic yellow markings.

The gold-dust plant is quite easy to please. It's happiest in bright indirect light, but will thrive with a minimum of 400 foot-candles of artificial light. If it's grown in sunlight it's apt to attract red spider mites. It does best when night temperatures are about 55 degrees and the days some ten degrees warmer, but it will tolerate cool drafts and hot rooms. The soil — any commercial potting soil is fine — should be moist all the time. I feed my plant every 3 or 4 months with an ordinary houseplant fertilizer, and I keep the plants showered regularly to control the spider mites.

Gold-dust plants are sold at almost any height, from 6 inches to 6 feet. They make a flush of growth in the spring, so if you're interested in controlling their size, prune them early in the spring — between mid-February and mid-March — just as the new growth starts. If a cut is made in the stem just above a leaf, a new branch will grow from that spot. Don't try to root the cuttings from the stem tips of the

219

early spring pruning, though, as they will be much too woody. Wait until midsummer, when the current season's foliage has had a chance to grow to full size, but before the stems become tough.

There are both male and female gold-dust plants and both bear tiny maroon flowers. If the female flowers are pollinated, they produce bright red berries along the stems. Most gardeners don't bother, but it's possible to pollinate the female plants by touching a camel's hair brush first to the male flowers, and then to the female; if the blossoms are pollinated in March, the berries ripen by October and stay bright and shiny red until about February of the following year.

Gold-dust plants do not do well when they're started from seeds; despite their colorful parents, the seedlings often have plain green leaves. As a result, they're propagated almost exclusively from stem cuttings.

Jade Plant *(Crassula)* There are as many as 300 species of *Crassula*, most of them succulents native to the dry areas of southern Africa. The jade plant (*C. argentea*) is probably the best known of the group and, in fact, is one of the most commonly grown of houseplants. It reaches a height of about 2 feet, with smooth, fleshy leaves 1 to 2 inches long. There is a miniature variety that grows to full height but bears leaves only ½ inch long. Jade plants live practically forever indoors, and grow so slowly that young plants are often used in dish gardens. When the plants are old or pot-bound they occasionally bear small, fragrant white flowers during the winter.

Jade plants need full sunshine; they'll survive in bright indirect light but the stems are apt to be weak and

Jade Plant *(Crassula)*

Standard-sized jade plants

pendulous, and the leaves lacking the reddish tinge that marks sun-grown plants. One of the reasons that jade plants do so well indoors is that they're very adaptable to temperature variations; they prefer nights in the 50s and days near 70, but they won't suffer if the readings are anywhere in the 40- to 100-degree range. The soil should be allowed to become nearly dry between thorough waterings; if the plant is growing in less than full sunlight, give it even less water. Jade plants should be fed every 3 or 4 months. Keep a sharp eye open for mealybug infestations on your jade plant, and treat them immediately with alcohol and a cotton swab if you spot problems. The mealybugs will lodge in the crevices where the leaves meet the stems, and if they're not eradicated they'll become an insurmountable problem.

Jade plants are so slow-growing that they can live pot-bound for years. When they do need repotting, it can be done at any time of the year. They can be propagated at any season, too, either by stem or leaf cuttings.

Narcissus *(Narcissus)* Most narcissus bulbs are hardy. They can be planted outdoors even in the northern

221

Paper White Narcissus
(Narcissus)

sections of the United States without suffering winter damage. They can also be forced to bloom indoors along with tulips, hyacinths, and other spring-flowering bulbs (see the October feature). But the narcissus plants that are usually seen as houseplants have very tender bulbs that will survive outdoors only in areas where the ground does not freeze. The most common of these is the paper white narcissus, which bears clusters of delicate, fragrant white flowers. There are also two yellow-flowered types, Soleil d'Or and the Chinese sacred lily. Because these tender plants are not accustomed to the winter's cold, they do not need a visit to the bulb trench or cold frame in order to bloom. They can simply be potted up as soon as they're on the market in the late summer or early fall. This brings them into bloom earlier than any of the other spring-flowering bulbs. I usually plant a new pot of bulbs every 10 days from August or September through November; the flowers appear by Christmas and continue coming for most of the winter.

For years, florists and home gardeners alike were advised to plant paper white narcissus bulbs in either sand or pebbles. Sometimes I still use this method, but often I plant them in soil, and I fertilize them lightly every month. I find that this produces superior plants because the bulbs are not forced to draw solely on their own stored nutrients. They're strong enough after their blossom period to be planted outdoors in mild regions. Although I haven't experimented with this, they might even be strong enough to bloom indoors a second year, which bulbs grown in sand or pebbles could never manage. It's fair to assume, though, that the flowers wouldn't be quite as nice the second season.

Most growers advise setting newly potted narcissus bulbs into darkness for 10 days, to give the root system a chance to become established. For both the Soleil d'Or and the Chinese sacred lily, this is a good idea. They are both rather slow to form their roots, and the few days in darkness gives them a chance to get started. The initial darkness will add height to the stems, but they're sturdy enough to carry it.

The paper whites are another story, as my daughter, Mary, discovered during a science project she conducted when she was in junior high school. Using our greenhouse at home, she tested to see whether an initial period of darkness actually improved the quality of the plants. It didn't. In fact, she found that the plants set immediately into bright sun after potting were only 12 inches tall when they flowered, about 6 inches shorter than those given early darkness. Because the plants were shorter, they were sturdier and able to support the weight of the flowers, in marked contrast to

222

Paper white narcissus flowers

the tall, floppy-stemmed plants that developed from bulbs set into darkness after potting. The results were so overwhelming that I've never set paper white narcissus bulbs into darkness since.

I simply fill a bulb pan with potting soil and plant several bulbs together, with their tips just at the soil line. Then I water the soil once. I set the paper whites into bright sunlight and the Soleil d'Or and Chinese sacred lily bulbs into darkness. All these bulbs do best in cool temperatures, so I give them 40-degree nights. They will, in fact, do well at any night reading under 55 degrees. I keep the soil moist throughout the growing period, and feed the plants monthly. When the flowers open I move the plants out of the sunlight and into bright indirect light with the coolest possible temperatures to help the flowers last as long as possible.

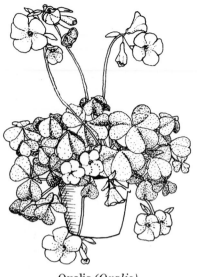

Oxalis *(Oxalis)*

▭ **Oxalis** *(Oxalis)* These are among the best of the indoor bulb plants. Not only are they easy to find and easy to grow, they have a long bloom period and come in a variety of colors, including pink, white, yellow, red, and purple. *Oxalis pes-caprae*, sometimes called the Bermuda buttercup though it's native to South Africa, is an especially nice yellow variety. Oxalis plants have rather slender flower stems and fairly low-growing foliage that looks like enormous clover leaves.

Oxalis plants can be brought into bloom anytime from fall through spring. They need to rest through the summer. I pot the bulbs in succession from September to March, setting them 1 inch deep in a mix of equal parts peat moss, packaged soil, and either sand or perlite, with a dusting of ground limestone added. The plants are small and look better in a group, so I set 6 bulbs together in a shallow 6-inch pan. Once they're planted I moisten the soil, and set the pot into the sun. (If oxalises don't have at least half days of sunshine, they are very disappointing plants because their growth is so weak. Their leaves and blooms are sensitive to light, and only open on sunny days; during darkness or cloudy weather the flowers close and the leaves fold up.)

Within 2 weeks of potting up, there is a healthy show of foliage from the bulbs, and flowers within a month. The flowers will last for about 2 months. During this growing period, the plants need night temperatures in the 50s, constantly moist soil, and a monthly feeding. At the end of the bloom period, when the flowers fade and the foliage starts to turn yellow, gradually reduce the amount of water and eliminate fertilizer altogether. Leave the bulbs in their pots until

Oxalis flowers, which open in the light and close in the darkness

fall, when they can be repotted and planted again. Take some care during this replanting operation. The bulbs will have produced a pot full of small bulblets, and even the tiniest of them — no larger than the head of a corsage pin — will produce a small plant and some flowers. Eventually all those little bulbs will grow to full size. So sift through the soil carefully, plant up all the bulbs, and you'll never need to buy another oxalis bulb.

Schefflera (*Brassaia*) The schefflera is a familiar, troublefree, leafy houseplant that will live for years indoors. It's sometimes known as the Australian umbrella tree because the glossy foot-long leaflets form umbrella-shaped rosettes 2 feet across. Its botanical name is *B. actinophylla*,

Schefflera *(Brassaia)*

A medium-sized schefflera plant

but the plants are occasionally sold as either *Schefflera actinophylla* or *S. macrostachya*.

In the wild in their native province of Queensland, Australia, scheffleras (sheff-*lee*-ra) can grow to be 40 feet tall, but indoors they're usually seen in the 2- to 6-foot range. In fact, one of their best characteristics is that they can be kept fairly small without suffering. I know a woman who kept her plant in a chilly sun room and only remembered to water it once a month or so; the plant lived for years, without apparently growing a bit and without losing any of its foliage or its good looks.

In order to grow, scheffleras need warmth, with nights in the high 60s and days ten degrees or so warmer. They're best in bright light but they'll tolerate sunlight if they're provided with enough moisture. Let the soil dry out a bit between thorough waterings, and feed the plants every 6 months. They can be repotted at any time of the year in commercial potting soil. If you would rather that your plant didn't grow, keep it cooler, drier, and a little pot-bound.

Scheffleras are very easily started from seeds and, in fact, that's the way commercial crops are begun. They grow fairly quickly if they're given enough food, moisture, light, and soil-room. I'd suggest that you set 3 or 4 young seedlings together in a pot so you'll have a good thick-foliaged specimen when they mature. Incidentally, seedlings show few leaflets to each leaf when young, producing larger leaves with more sections as they increase in age.

No discussion about scheffleras today would be complete without mention of the so-called dwarf schefflera. Among growers it is known as *Schefflera arboricola*, but it is still so new that it isn't listed in standard reference books, nor has its actual identity been established. Its leaves are composed of very smooth, small, oval leaflets and its habit of growth is restrained and exceedingly attractive. Care for it as for other scheffleras.

Swedish Ivy *(Plectranthus)* The Swedish ivy is an easy, well-liked plant that was popularized in Sweden, where it earned its common name; in fact, it is native to Australia, Africa, and India. The most familiar species, *P. australis*, has solid green leaves. *Plectranthus coleoides marginatus* is so named because its variegated green-and-white leaves resemble coleus foliage; this variety has a noticeable and, to me, unpleasant odor when the leaves are rubbed.

Swedish ivies are best in bright indirect light; sunlight, especially in the summer, is much too harsh for them. The night temperatures should be near 60. Keep the soil constantly moist and feed the plants every other month.

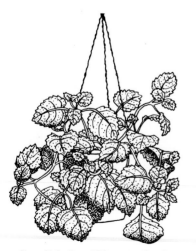

Swedish Ivy *(Plectranthus)*

226

Keep in mind though that Swedish ivies are very fast-growing plants, and if you feed them less often they will grow at a more relaxed pace. Even if you feed them very lightly, they'll need repotting in commercial potting soil regularly in order to guarantee that the roots have enough soil around them to provide moisture. Ultimately, even with the most

A well-grown Swedish ivy

conservative of care, the plants will be pot-bound, unable to hold water, too large to repot, and stalky. They don't take well to cutting back, so the best move at this point is to propagate new plants. Just root three or four tip cuttings and pot them together in a 6-inch hanging pot. Keep them pinched back as they grow so they'll come in full and bushy. You'll have a good-looking, showy plant very quickly.

Q&A

Q: I have a large corner that I'd like to fill with a big plant, 4 or 5 feet tall. The spot gets good light but no sun. Any suggestions?

A: There are several large plants that would do well, including weeping fig (*Ficus benjamina*), schefflera (*Brassaia actinophylla*), Massange's dracaena (*D. massangeana*), and the Norfolk Island pine (*Araucaria heterophylla*). Each has a different shape, and one will probably suit your purposes. They're all easy to care for.

By the way, when you buy a plant of this size, it may be pot-bound and, if so, it will need attentive watering. If you like the size of it, though, postpone repotting, as it will grow rapidly if the roots are given more room. Letting the soil become moderately dry between deep waterings will control the plant's growth, too.

You should expect the plant to lose a few leaves at first; it's nature's way of reducing the plant's burden during the stressful adjustment to new surroundings. Nurseries acclimate large plants to shade for a period of 6 to 8 weeks before putting them on the market, giving them a chance to drop their leaves in privacy and develop new foliage that is accustomed to lower light levels. If it were not for this practice, the problem for the home gardener would be much more upsetting.

Q: Sweet peas are my favorite flowers. Can I grow them indoors through the winter?

A: Only in a greenhouse I'm afraid. They need night temperatures in the 40s and sunshine all day long. If you can provide that, they'll do beautifully. Make sure that you buy the seeds of winter-flowering sweet peas, though, or you will only get foliage until springtime. I usually sow my winter-flowering sweet peas in 10- to 14-inch flowerpots in mid-July and then bring them into the greenhouse before freezing weather. They begin to flower in November and continue to bloom all winter long if the faded flowers are picked off before they set seeds. Sweet peas, of course, are climbing vines and they need strings or netting for support. Professional growers often have plants 12 feet tall or more by growing them in ground beds. I grow my plants in large flowerpots and they're seldom taller than 8 feet. And the flowers are so fragrant!

Opposite: A collection of large plants that do well in bright areas of the house

DISH GARDENS AND TERRARIUMS

Dish gardens and terrariums both involve grouping plants with similar needs in one container, creating a mini-environment appropriate for all of them. The primary difference between the two is that terrariums offer more enclosure and therefore higher humidity than can be offered plants in most homes. Dish gardens are open containers that present several small plants attractively in a miniature landscape.

Dish Gardens The most important step in putting together a dish garden is the first one, selecting the plants. Because they will be cared for as a unit, they must have the same water, sunlight, and temperature needs. Many of the best-looking and most carefree dish gardens contain only succulents or only cactuses. You don't want your dish garden to be crowded with plants — they won't be as healthy or as attractive as a few plants arranged with some imagination. Select a few slow-growing plants of different heights, textures, and shapes, but keep in mind that the goal is to create a natural-looking arrangement. Pick plants that are in proportion to each other's size, and to the dish. This doesn't mean that all the plants should be the *same* size, but that they should look as if they could coexist naturally together.

Any container can be used for a dish garden. Usually they're 2 or 3 inches deep, with no drainage holes so that they can be kept neatly on a tabletop. Plant them in whatever soil is recommended for the type of plants being grown. When you've decided on the placement of the plants, set them in and firm them down quite well. Some gardeners add a layer of fast-draining material, like pebbles or sand or charcoal chips, over the surface of the soil; this gives the plants a handsome, natural backdrop.

Dish gardens require very little care; in fact, the easiest way to ruin them is by overattention. Most dish garden plants do best in bright indirect light; a dish garden of cactuses or succulents needs sunlight at least half of each day. In either case, make sure you turn the container regularly so the plants share the light. The plants should not be fed at all or they'll grow too quickly. They do need water, but not often; both cactuses and succulents need relatively dry soil. I water these plants from above, using tepid water, whenever the soil has had a chance to dry out. Some dish gardens contain plants that need barely damp soil, and I treat these a little differently: I take them to the sink once a week and submerge the containers until the bubbles stop rising to the surface. Then I prop the container on its side for half an hour — the plants won't fall out — to let the excess water drain. With the plants kept fairly dry and unfertilized, they'll stay small for some time. Eventually, though, they'll be too big for the dish garden and should be lifted out and potted separately.

A dish garden

Terrariums When planting a terrarium, it's even more important to select the right plants than when planting a dish garden. Terrariums are humid places, so the succulents and cactuses that do so well in a dish garden would drown in a terrarium. Instead, pick high-humidity tropical plants that thrive under conditions of reduced light. Any plants in these genera would make good choices: *Fittonia, Episcia, Pilea, Saintpaulia, Maranta, Adiantum, Asplenium, Davallia, Buxus, Pteris.* Select a variety of plants that will present a range of colors and textures, and buy very small specimens: it's surprising how large they seem when you try to get them into a small terrarium.

Any number of containers can be used as terrariums, as long as the material is either clear glass or plastic. If the container has an opening large enough to put your hand through, you'll have an easier time arranging the plants; otherwise you'll have to use specialized equipment such as tongs. The container should have a top so you can control humidity. The easiest to plant and most available choice is a ten-gallon fish tank; these don't have covers but you can make one from a sheet of glass or plastic.

Before you start to arrange your terrarium, clean the container and the tools you'll be using and make sure that the soil is sterile and the plants healthy. Then design your arrangement while the plants are still potted. It's much easier to move them around on the tabletop than to lift the plants in and out of the terrarium soil.

The procedure itself isn't complicated, but you'll have a much cleaner, neater final product if you work slowly and carefully. First of all, put a 1-inch layer of planting medium in the bottom of the container; I use 3 parts commercial potting soil to 1 part crushed charcoal, as the charcoal helps to keep the circulating moisture clean. The soil will splatter up on the sides of the container if you just pour it in, so I use a funnel, with a paper tube extender if need be, to feed the soil in. Before you set the plants in, unpot them, and pull away about half of the soil around the roots. If you can fit your hands into the container, just set the plants according to your design and firm the soil around them. If the container has a small opening, you will need to use long, narrow tools. Garden centers sell tools specially designed for this purpose, but I've found that very satisfactory alternatives can be cheaply made or borrowed from the kitchen. A wooden label taped to the bottom of a long stick will work as a trowel. You can handle and set the plants in with kitchen tongs. And any blunt-ended object can be used to firm the soil around the plants' roots. Once the plants are in, put down a layer of ground fir bark to provide a handsome soil surface. Then mist the plants lightly and set the terrarium in bright indirect light; if you put it in the sun, the container will concentrate the sun's heat and scorch the plants in no time.

Terrariums are designed to need little or no care. The plants shouldn't be fertilized at all or they'll grow too quickly.

A terrarium

If the container is kept covered all the time, it won't be necessary to add water, either, beyond an initial light spraying after the plants are set in; the moisture will stay in circulation because the system is closed. The problem with covered terrariums is that the moisture condenses on the inner surface of the container, making it very difficult to see the plants. I much prefer to leave the containers uncovered. I do have to add water occasionally, but I'd rather work a little than have a carefree arrangement that I can't see. There's no quicker way to kill terrarium plants than by overwatering, so I only add moisture when the soil is dry and the plants are near wilting; then I simply mist them and the soil with an atomizer.

If I'm going away for a month or so, I put the top on the container and let the plants attend to their own moisture needs.

OCT

Calla lilies

OCT

With the arrival of fall, many houseplants grow at a slower pace. Coffee plants and false aralias both slow down considerably in response to the weaker sunlight. Flame violets will stop flowering in the early fall, at which point they should be cut back, and the stem tips rooted for a new generation of plants; they will all come back into flower in the early spring. Shrimp plants and geraniums, both of which are everblooming in a greenhouse, are likely to stop producing flowers with the coming of the cooler, dimmer months. On the other hand, some plants come into their own in the fall. Spider plants will produce most of their runners as the days become shorter. Chrysanthemums come into bloom normally at this time of the year. And camellias send out the first of their exquisite flowers.

October is often chilly enough to require turning on the house heat. Remember that this dries out the soil and the air. Make sure that your plants are adequately moistened, and try to make up for the lost humidity by misting around the plants with an atomizer, and by setting the plants on a tray of pebbles and water. Grouping houseplants together helps create a humid atmosphere, too, and is far healthier than isolating plants off by themselves.

Looking ahead to later months, amaryllis bulbs have enjoyed their brief rest and are ready to be started back into growth. This is the month to pot up such spring-flowering bulbs as tulips, hyacinths, and hardy narcissus and set them into a trench or cold frame for their short winter. In the greenhouse, October is the last chance to sow cineraria seeds for winter flowering. Rat-tail statice seeds sown this month will produce plants large enough to flower in midwinter and continue through late spring.

This is the time of the year when indoor gardeners like to shop for new plants to add to their collections, especially if they've been away for the summer and return to find their older plants in less than top condition. Flowering plants in particular make good indoor companions when the winter winds begin to pile the snow in drifts in the outdoor garden. And in response to the increased interest, your local florist or garden center will have a healthy supply of new plants to choose from.

Browallia (*Browallia*) Browallias are often grown as annuals in shady outdoor flower gardens, but they are truly perennials that will live on and stay in constant bloom if they're not subjected to frost. I have had browallias in my home greenhouse that flowered on and on for more than a year and a half; when they grew straggly I threw the plants away, but not before rooting cuttings from the stem tips. Browallias come in several shades of blue as well as white: I'm partial to the blue ones because it's such an unusual flower color. The flowers are 1 to 1½ inches across and shaped like petunia blossoms; in fact, the two plants are related.

Browallia (*Browallia*)

Browallias (brow-*all*-ia) are at their best when given bright reflected light in the summer and sun in the winter. (If they're grown in too much summer sun they'll attract spider mites and develop sunburned flowers.) They thrive when the night temperatures are in the upper 50s: they'll live through cooler temperatures, but they won't grow very quickly. Keep the soil barely moist. Feed the plants monthly through the winter, every other week during the warmer months.

A purple/blue-flowered browallia

Browallias become straggly with age and if they're cut back the new growth is poor and thin. So the best way to manage a collection is to start the plants by seed in February. I set 6 seedlings together in a 10-inch hanging container, and put the pot out on a cool porch in the summer. They'll become straggly toward late summer or fall. At that point, take cuttings and throw the large plant away. The cuttings will start to blossom immediately and can be kept through the winter, then given their own summer outdoors. A young plant, whether seedling or cutting, is inclined to branch on its own, and doesn't need to be pinched back to encourage fullness.

Calla Lily (*Zantedeschia*)

Calla Lily (*Zantedeschia*) In South Africa these sweetly fragrant plants are wildflowers so plentiful that they all but carpet huge open fields, stretching as far as the eye can see. They're so common, in fact, that in some areas of their homeland they're called pig lilies because wild pigs dig for their roots in roadside ditches. In warm areas of the United States, south of 35 degrees north latitude, they'll grow successfully as garden plants, but elsewhere they're strictly house or greenhouse plants.

The most common of the calla lilies is the incomparable white one, *Zantedeschia aethiopica* (zan-tee-*desh*-ia ee-thi-*o*-pik-a), sometimes listed as *Richardia aethiopica*. The wild species can grow 3 or 4 feet tall, but most of the varieties sold as houseplants mature at a more manageable 18 inches in height. *Zantedeschia aethiopica minor* and Godefreyana are both good choices. There was a time when January was the peak of the white calla lily growing season, which lasted from September to June. They were allowed a dry dormant period during the summer half of the year because it was commonly believed that the roots needed a rest. Now it's known that white calla lilies don't need a dormant period at all; they'll blossom throughout the year if they're given the right growing conditions, which means full sunshine from September until June, and partial shade (about half the sunshine available on a sunny day) the rest of the year.

There are colored calla lilies too. *Zantedeschia elliottiana* has golden yellow blossoms and rich dark green leaves with white spots. The flowers of *Z. rehmannii* are pink or rose colored. And there's a good-looking group called Apricot Sunrise Hybrids, whose colors are subtle shades of pink, red, and yellow.

Dormant roots of calla lilies are available throughout the year, but they're generally planted by greenhouse and houseplant growers toward the end of the summer, usually

August or September. This gets them growing nicely and producing their first flowers before the arrival of the dull, short days of late autumn. And it allows them to miss the heat and bright sun of midsummer. They're at their best if the night temperatures fall between 55 degrees and 65 degrees, with the days in the mid 70s.

The calla lily is one of the few plants that actually does its best if the pots are set in saucers partially filled with water at all times; if the roots dry out, the plant is apt to become dormant. The soil should be highly organic: mix 3 parts commercial potting soil with 1 part sphagnum peat moss. And since the plants need a good amount of phosphorus, I usually add about 2 cups of bone meal to every bushel of potting soil, or about 1 tablespoon to a quart of soil mix. Once a month I feed them with a standard houseplant fertilizer.

The yellow spadix in the center of the calla lily carries the plant's true flowers

Calla lilies can be grown easily in ground-level beds in a greenhouse, which is the way they're often grown commercially, but few amateurs want to devote this much space to a single crop. Hobby greenhouse owners, and many of the commercial growers too, are better off growing their calla lilies in separate flowerpots. The roots of the white calla are large, so they're generally started in 6-inch pots and then gradually shifted up until they're finally in pots some 12 or 14 inches in diameter. White calla lilies often grow so dramatically that their roots soon crowd even the largest flowerpots, so I divide them in late August or early September, using a large butcher knife to slice the crown into several sections, each of which I repot separately.

The colored varieties are much less luxuriant in growth than the white, and do best if they're grown in 5- to 6-inch pots. They come into blossom any time of the year about 60 days after they're potted if they're given night temperatures in the low 60s and days in the upper 70s. After the flowering season ends, I allow the foliage of the colored callas to die down, a process that takes 3 or 4 weeks. During this period I give them only enough water to keep the foliage from wilting, letting the soil become moderately dry before watering. This causes the bulbs to go into dormancy. After a 2- or 3-month rest without water they can be started into new growth again by repotting in fresh soil and resuming their watering routine.

Century Plant *(Agave)* The common name of these succulents is a bit exaggerated. A plant growing in the wild will blossom after about seventeen years; indoors, where the conditions are less than perfect, they may wait as long as fifty years to send up a flower. When it finally does appear,

Century Plant *(Agave)*

the flower grows on a spike from a rosette of sword-shaped leaves, each one of which is lined along both edges with tough, pointed teeth. When the flower dies, so does its supporting rosette, but a few young plants are left alive and healthy at the soil line. The plants' growth is as slow as the blossoming schedule, which is just as well. Ultimately, even indoor century plants can be 3 feet across; so the slow-poke pace works in the gardener's favor. It means that the plant can be bought when it's 4 or 5 inches tall and enjoyed for years before the furniture has to be moved. The prettiest and tidiest of the indoor species is the Queen Victoria agave (*A. victoriae-reginae*), an odd name in view of its Mexican heritage. If it's kept on a Spartan diet, it will stay less than 1 foot across for 10 years or so.

To thrive and grow indoors, century plants like sunlight and nights in the 40s or 50s; in the warm months water

A landscape of Queen Victoria century plants and other succulents

them when the soil is dry, and in the winter let the plants nearly shrivel before watering. Give them a feeding of half-strength fertilizer once a year. They can be repotted at any time of the year in a well-drained soil. I use a mix of either equal parts potting soil and sharp sand, or 1 part loam, 1 part leaf mold, 1 part sharp sand, and ½ part crushed charcoal. Regardless of which mix you use, dust the soil with ground limestone and bone meal. Don't forget the plants' teeth when you're repotting. Handle them as you would a cactus. (See the June feature.) If you would prefer to slow your plant's growth, keep it pot-bound, thirsty, and skip the yearly feeding.

Century plants can be started from seed as well as from offsets; surprisingly enough, they grow rather rapidly,

238

and can be 3 inches across when they're only 2 years old. That may sound small, but it's a good-sized, full plant. Century plants can be propagated at any time of the year.

Chrysanthemum
(*Chrysanthemum*)

🪴 **Chrysanthemum** (*Chrysanthemum*) Few plants will dress up a room as brightly or quickly as a pot of chrysanthemums. There are several kinds of chrysanthemums, including feverfew and marguerites, both of which are daisy-flowered. The most familiar type is known as the florists' chrysanthemum (*C. morifolium*, sometimes sold as *C. hortorum*), a large category that includes the football, cascade, pompon, and spider mums, among others. The florists' chrysanthemums are available in every bright floral color except blue.

When I was a boy, mums were only available in the fall. Now they are sold year-round, and bought eagerly.

A kitchen windowsill arrangement, a pot of chrysanthemums to the left

Most people, though, don't get their money's worth because they buy a plant whose flowers are completely open. Unless you need an immediate splash of color, it's much smarter to buy a plant dense with buds so you can enjoy the full life span of the blossoms. When you buy, look for short, compact plants. And most important of all, inspect a plant for aphids before you put your money down. Many of the potted mums on the market are infested with these devils and you don't want to introduce them to your healthy houseplants. Even if you find a plant that seems to be pest-free, quarantine it for a few days, if possible, so that any unseen aphids don't spread to your other plants.

A plant in bud will last for 3 or 4 weeks in the home if it's given cool temperatures — the cooler the better — and at least half days of sunshine. If it's kept in too dark a spot, the leaves will turn yellow and fall off within two or three days. The blossoms will live on but the plant won't be good-looking. Keep the soil moist all the time. Some growers pot their mums in a very lightweight, well-drained mix that dries out quickly; you may find yourself watering your mums once or twice a day.

For the most part, home gardeners are best advised to throw their plant away after the flowering period. But if you've bought your plant in the spring, you can put it into the outdoor garden. Cut the foliage back first, divide the crown, and set out single plants. They may bloom and they may even be hardy and survive the winter. Even if they don't flower, you haven't lost anything.

If you have an intermediate or cool greenhouse, you can grow chrysanthemum plants very easily, as long as you let them blossom in the fall according to their own schedule. Chrysanthemums make vegetative growth when there are more hours of daylight than darkness; and they form flower buds when the periods of daily darkness are longer than the periods of light. So their natural inclination is to grow during

Close-up of chrysanthemum blossoms

the summer and set buds in the fall. Commercial growers learned how they could take advantage of this fact some thirty years ago. They found that if they artificially manipulated the levels of light, they could bring them into flower at any time of the year. It's a fairly exacting procedure and not worth the effort for the hobby gardener.

Instead, start with rooted cuttings in the spring. Either take cuttings of a known greenhouse variety or buy rooted cuttings through the mail. They can be bought from several mail-order houses, many of which advertise regularly in horticultural literature. Plant single cuttings in 4- to 6-inch pots. I usually use a soil that's 3 parts potting soil to 1 part peat moss. Keep the soil moist and feed the plants every 2 or 3 weeks; mums respond especially well to a foliar fertilizer. When the plants are about 5 inches tall, pinch the tip back. Pinch them again when the resulting branches are about 4 inches long. They are rather sensitive to temperature when their flower buds are forming; commercial growers find that the buds set most evenly when the night temperature is 60 degrees, but they'll do fine anywhere in the 55- to 62-degree range. Chrysanthemums treated in this manner come into blossom in the fall. There are early, midseason, and late varieties with an enormous selection of flower shapes, sizes, and colors.

Copperleaf *(Acalypha)* The copperleaf, also known as the beefsteak plant, is a native of the South Sea Islands. It bears a few inconspicuous flowers in the winter, but it's valued more for its mottled red, copper, and pink leaves; I've never seen two leaves that were marked identically. The copperleaf is a good plant to add to a primarily green collection because it provides such a colorful contrast.

Copperleaf *(Acalypha)*

The copperleaf (*A. wilkesiana*) is at its best when grown in full sunlight; it will live in bright indirect light but its coloration will be duller. It's a true tropical plant that wants warmth, with nights in the low 60s at least; it will die in cool temperatures. It also needs high humidity, so it does best in a collection of plants set on a humidifying tray. It will suffer if it's left off by itself in a dry room. Keep the soil barely moist all the time and feed the plants every 3 or 4 months.

When copperleaf plants grow in the tropics, they can reach a height of 8 or 10 feet; they can be kept at any size indoors, though. Most of the houseplants I've seen were a foot tall or less. If the plants start to look straggly, they can be given a new lease on life by cutting all the stems back to a height of 4 to 8 inches. Strong new growth will soon appear and, of course, the pruned stems make good cuttings

A copperleaf, brightly colored from growing in full sun

Opposite: A handsome red-margined dracaena dominating a collection of smaller houseplants

Dracaena *(Dracaena)*

for a new generation of plants. Overcrowded plants should be given a larger container of commercial potting soil in the spring.

Dracaena *(Dracaena)* There are so many common and popular variations of this plant that, collected together, they would make a fair-sized indoor jungle. The most common of them is the red-margined dracaena, *D. marginata;* it's a very durable houseplant that will grow to ceiling height if allowed. The dragon tree dracaena, *D. draco,* has stiff swordlike blue-green leaves as much as 2 feet long; when the plant is grown in the sun the edges of the leaves turn bright red. (The dragon tree has the distinction of being one of the

longest-lived of all forms of vegetation. In 1868 in the Canary Islands, a gale blew over a specimen calculated to be over 6,000 years old. It was 70 feet tall with a trunk 15 feet in diameter.) The wild species, *D. deremensis*, isn't grown often itself, but two of its varieties are: Janet Craig, which has long shiny leaves, and Warneck's dracaena, whose leaves have prominent white stripes. Massange's dracaena, the most popular variety of *D. fragrans*, is sometimes referred to as a corn plant because of its resemblance to corn foliage. Sander's dracaena, *D. sanderiana*, has green leaves edged with white; it is so eager to grow that it will even do so in plain water. Each of these plants will become very tall but they're usually sold as small specimens. The gold-dust dracaena, *D. godseffiana*, is a shrubby plant with handsome white-spotted leaves; it reaches maturity at 30 inches or less, but it grows so slowly that it is often used in dish gardens and terrariums.

All dracaenas (dra-*see*-na) are rugged, carefree houseplants. They do best in bright indirect light with the night temperatures in the high 60s. They're very susceptible to light levels; if a plant that has been growing in dim light is moved to a brighter spot, the new stem growth will be noticeably larger. Some gardeners take advantage of this attraction for light by laying a young plant on its side until the stem begins to bend upward toward the light, and then righting the plant; this gives the plant an eccentric, crooked stem. Keep dracaenas in soil that is always constantly moist and feed the plants every 6 months with any houseplant fertilizer. They can be repotted any time of the year in commercial potting soil.

Although dracaenas are relatively slow-growing plants, many of the taller varieties eventually become unwieldy; under ideal conditions they can hold about 1 foot of foliage, so as the plants age and lose their lower leaves, they come to look more and more like palm trees. When a plant gets to that point, air-layer the top of the plant, and then cut the stem down to within 2 inches of the soil line. New growth will appear quickly from that stem stub, and you'll have two plants for your efforts. (For more on these propagation techniques, see the April feature.)

▽ **Natal Plum** *(Carissa)* The Natal plum is an easy-to-care-for evergreen with shiny, small, dark green leaves; it's named for Natal, its native home. The original species, *C. macrocarpa*, isn't grown often, but the dwarf varieties, which grow to a maximum height of about 2½ feet, make fine houseplants; Boxwood Beauty and a variety known as *C. macrocarpa nana* are both good dwarf choices. The Natal

Natal Plum *(Carissa)*

plum sends up occasional fragrant white blossoms about 2 inches across; if the flowers are pollinated, the plants will bear edible fruit, also some 2 inches across, that look like plums and taste like cranberries.

A dwarf Natal plum, with its normal, broad-spreading habit of growth

Natal plums need at least half days of sunshine and fairly warm temperatures, with nights in the low 60s. Keep the soil moist all the time and feed the plants every 3 or 4 months. They grow very slowly and don't need repotting often, but when they do, pot them in commercial potting soil. The dwarf varieties can be propagated by stem cuttings at any time of the year.

Panda Plant *(Kalanchoe)* The panda plant is an extremely even-tempered succulent houseplant. It grows very slowly, making it a good candidate for a dish garden. Its leaves are pale green edged with brown spots that some-one has said look like cigarette burns. But this handsome plant does not deserve such a degrading status symbol. The botanical name, *K. tomentosa,* means woolly, in reference to the white hairs that grow on the surfaces of the leaves.

Panda Plant *(Kalanchoe)*

245

Sometimes, in the winter, the panda plant sends up a few yellowish-purple flowers. (The panda plant is related to the flowering kalanchoe, though there isn't much resemblance between the two. For the flowering kalanchoe, see the December chapter.)

Panda plants are native to Malagasy, where they grow in full sunlight. Indoor plants will live in bright indirect light, but they develop full color only if they're in sun all day long. The night temperatures should be in the low 50s. Like other succulents, they're vulnerable to overwatering; so let the soil become moderately dry between good, thorough waterings. Feed the plants every 6 months. They can be repotted anytime in a mix of equal parts potting soil and sharp sand, with a dusting of ground limestone and bone meal added. They can also be propagated at any time of the year, from leaf or stem cuttings, or by separating and planting the basal offsets.

246

Sanseveria *(Sanseveria)* Sanseverias have been grown as houseplants for years, but the early gardeners had very little choice in the plants they bought. Only the original, wild African species, *S. trifasciata*, was available, with its 2½-foot growth and slender striped leaves; this is the very plant that's said to be gourmet food to elephants. Mutations began to appear in cultivation and now there are plants that never grow any taller than an African violet. Most of the popular varieties are still the taller-growing ones, peaking at 18 to 30 inches, with leaves that are about 2 inches across and marked with horizontal stripes. Unfortunately, most of the sanseverias the public sees are mistreated in one way or another and dreadful-looking. Let me reassure you that a well-grown plant is very good-looking; older plants may even send out small, white, sweetly fragrant flowers.

Sanseveria *(Sanseveria)*

Sometimes known as snake plants, sanseverias (sanse-*vay*-ria) will tolerate any level of light, and parching drought. They will not do well if they're overwatered or chilled. The soil should be allowed to become fairly dry between thorough waterings from the early spring through late fall; during the winter months, water them only frequently enough to keep them from shriveling. The dimmer the light they grow in, the less water they will need. The night temperatures should be 65 or higher as the foliage will develop brown edges if the plants are too cool. Sanseverias grow slowly and can go 3 or 4 years without needing larger quarters. When they do, repot them at any time of the year in commercial potting soil.

Sanseverias can be propagated at any time of the year, either by dividing the rhizomes or by leaf cuttings. Don't try to root an entire leaf. Cut it into sections about 3 inches long, and insert them in sand, bottom side down.

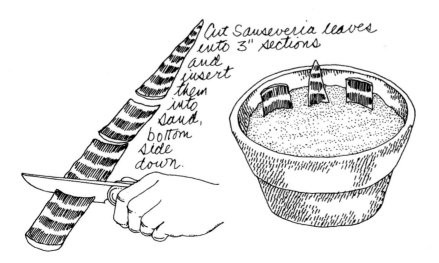

Cut Sanseveria leaves into 3" sections and insert them into sand, bottom side down.

247

(One variety, known as Laurentii, can't be propagated by leaf cuttings because it will lose the broad yellow markings that distinguish the foliage; instead, grow it by root division.)

This sanseveria, one of many types available, is full-grown at 8 inches tall

Screw-Pine *(Pandanus)*

Screw-Pine *(Pandanus)* Screw-pines grow wild along the beaches of the islands of Polynesia. When they're young, they grow close to the ground from a rosette of foliage, but as they mature they develop a central stem and their straplike leaves grow from the stem in a spiral arrangement. Screw-pines bear a fruit that resembles a cone and this, along with the spiral configuration, is responsible for its common name. (Hawaiians, looking for an analogy closer to home, have dubbed this plant the tourist pineapple.) As the plants grow they send out sturdy aerial roots at a sharp angle from the stem; the function of the roots is to help anchor the plant against the strong winds

A dwarf variegated screw-pine

that come off the water. Unless you live in a wind tunnel, these aerial roots are unnecessary for indoor plants; either let them hang over the edge of the pot or train them into the soil.

There are two varieties of screw-pine grown as houseplants. *Pandanus veitchii* is the standard-sized plant; it grows 3 to 4 feet tall, with 2-foot by 2-inch green leaves lightly striped with cream. It's a tall plant, but its width is the more significant dimension — even young plants can be 3 feet wide. The dwarf variegated variety, *P. veitchii compacta*, grows to the same height but its leaves are smaller at 12 to 18 inches long and about 1 inch wide. Because the curved leaves are shorter, the dwarf variety is narrower than its full-sized relative; it's also more attractive. Both varieties have vicious spines along the edges of the leaves, as

249

does the wild version (which is why the plant was the scourge of World War II servicemen who battled for the beaches of the South Pacific).

For all its unfriendly sound the screw-pine is a rugged and easy-to-grow houseplant. It does best in full sun, but will tolerate bright indirect light (or 400 or more foot-candles of artificial light). True to its tropical heritage it wants night temperatures no lower than 65 degrees and days well into the 70s. The soil should be allowed to dry out some between waterings. If they're fed too often they grow too quickly, so I feed my plants no more frequently than every 3 or 4 months. This way they can go on for years without repotting. When they're crowded, repot them in commercial potting soil; handle them as you would cactuses, with gloves and a newspaper strap, or you're apt to be severely scratched by the jagged spines. It's a good idea, too, to make sure the foliage is up off the floor; as the plant grows and the foliage begins to curve downward, this may require setting the pot up on a stool. New plants can be propagated any time from the offshoots that grow from the base of the plant.

Wax Begonia *(Begonia)*

Wax Begonia *(Begonia)* The wax begonia is a familiar houseplant and a fine one. It blooms all year long, as its botanical name, *B. semperflorens,* suggests, producing single, semidouble, or double white, pink, rose, or red flowers. (Known for generations as *B. semperflorens,* wax begonias are now considered by taxonomists as hybrids involving several South American species. The new name suggested is *B. x semperflorens-cultorum,* but my guess is that the old name will be around forever.) The blossoms are borne in clusters, but only a few flowers in each cluster are open. The foliage is either green or a shade of red, depending on the variety. The calla begonia, a type of wax begonia, has white-spotted leaves; it grows more slowly because it has less chlorophyll than the other varieties.

Wax begonias are often thought of as shade plants, but they can take any amount of sunlight; the red-leaved varieties actually need sun in order to develop their full color. All wax begonias are best if the night temperatures are in the 50s. Let the soil dry out slightly between thorough waterings and feed the plants every other week. The dead flowers drop off rather cleanly, but an occasional shake helps to dislodge any faded blooms. If the plant becomes overgrown, cut all the stems down to the soil line; the new growth will come in very quickly. If you wish, you can divide the roots at the same time and plant each new section in a pot of its own.

I find that wax begonias flower best when they're young; so it's a good idea to keep new plants coming along. Stem cuttings, heated from the bottom to 65 to 70 degrees, will root easily. But commercial growers rely almost entirely on seeds for new plants and the home gardener can, too. This is an especially good idea if you want many plants to set outside for the summer. The seeds are tiny, but their germination rate is high. Sow them sparingly over a seedbed of commercial potting soil which has been covered with a thin layer of milled sphagnum moss; bottom-water with warm water. Don't let the seedbed become saturated or damping-off disease is apt to set in. Bottom-heat the seedbed to 65 to 70 degrees and give it bright light. When the seedlings are ¼ inch tall, separate them into individual pots or six-packs. Seed-grown plants, despite their tiny beginnings, are large enough for 2- or 3-inch pots in about 5 months. (If you're starting a crop for your outdoor garden, sow the seeds in January. In the fall, these garden annuals can be lifted out, potted, and grown indoors through the winter.)

A wax begonia plant with several buds waiting to follow the lead of the opened flower

Zebra Plant *(Aphelandra)* The zebra plant is a showy beauty that blooms for about 6 weeks in the fall.

Zebra Plant *(Aphelandra)*

251

The flower of a zebra plant, seen against the brightly striped leaves

There is a scarlet variety, *A. aurantiaca*, but it's not very common; the most familiar variety is *A. squarrosa*, and its varieties, which produce spikes of dramatic yellow bracts, 5 or 6 inches tall, over prominently veined deep black-green leaves. The name "zebra plant" alludes to the nearly black leaves with their conspicuous white veins. The plant's tiny yellow true flowers appear from between the scales of the bracts.

Zebra plants need bright indirect light, night temperatures in the low 60s, and the benefit of a humidifying tray. From March through October, keep the soil constantly moist; during the rest of the year, give the soil a chance to dry out somewhat before watering again. Feed them only when they're in active growth at 2-week intervals with any houseplant fertilizer.

The big problem with zebra plants is always leaf drop. It's a normal occurrence in their cycle, but disheartening to gardeners unfamiliar with them. There is no way to prevent this, but there is a solution for it. About a month after the flowers fade, when several of the bottom leaves have fallen off, cut the stem back to just above the second lowest node, the little bump on the stem where leaves once grew. Repot the plant in commercial potting soil in a 1-inch-larger pot and continue to pinch the stem back each time it has made 6 inches of growth until the middle of July. By the following fall blossom time, the plant will have developed several stems, which will mean more blossoms than it had when you first bought it.

The plants can be propagated in the spring by rooting stem cuttings; remove all but one set of leaves before you set the cutting into the rooting medium. These cutting-grown plants will be ready to blossom in October.

About a month after the flowers fade, cut the stem back to just above the 2nd lowest node — the bumps on the stem where the first leaves grew.

Q&A

Q: I have a friend who's delighted with her urn plant and would like to put together a collection of various types of bromeliads. Do you have any advice?

A: I can understand your friend's interest in bromeliads — they make fine houseplants. Here are the names of a few other genera she might like to grow: *Guzmania, Neoregelia, Nidularium, Quesnelia,* and *Tillandsia.* Most bromeliads are epiphytes, growing naturally above the ground on the branches of trees. If you have a spot large enough to devote to them, they can be grown on a tree branch indoors, too. Begin by anchoring a limb with mortar or concrete in a heavy container that won't tip over. Wrap the roots with moist, long-fibered sphagnum moss, and secure the moss to the tree branch with plastic-covered green wire. Keep the moss moist and the central cups formed by the foliage full of water. They'll do fine in bright indirect light.

Q: I've been searching for a plant that would bloom pretty much all the time indoors and bear orange flowers. I had no idea I'd have so much trouble finding one. Do you have any suggestions?

A: You're after a rare combination, but see if you can find a firecracker flower (*Crossandra infundibuliformis*). It bears loose, soft, tangerine-colored flowers all year long, provided it's given at least half days of sunshine and nights with temperatures in the 60s. If you can't find a plant, you can grow one from seed.

Q: When I was in Europe last summer I saw a beautiful pink flowering plant which I understand is known as a godetia. I'd love to know more about it.

A: Strangely enough, the godetia, or satinflower, is a native American wildflower from the West. It makes a handsome annual in the summer garden and can also be grown in a cool or intermediate greenhouse. Anyone whose interest in flowers goes beyond the ubiquitous petunia or marigold would no doubt be fascinated by a plant that's as easy to grow and as exotic-looking as the godetia. It likes bright sunshine and rather dry soil. It will blossom 4 or 5 months after the seeds are sown.

FORCING BULBS

Hardy narcissus forced to bloom indoors in the winter

There is no quicker way to bring spring indoors, even while the snow swirls outside, than with a pot of spring bulbs. Many different bulbs can be forced, including tulips, hardy narcissus, hyacinths, squill, and crocuses. These are all hardy bulbs that need a 15-week pre-rooting period before they can be brought into active growth. That period of enforced cold convinces them that winter is at hand; when they're brought indoors to a warm spot, they assume that spring has arrived, and they bloom.

The spring-flowering bulbs come onto the market in September and October; some of these are large enough to be forced, and others not. Make sure that you buy large bulbs, marked either "for forcing," or "exhibition size." The largest-sized bulbs often vary in size according to the characteristics of the variety. Since you must trust the integrity of your bulb dealer, my advice is to be prepared to pay a fair price and, in any event, steer clear of so-called bargains. They bring only disappointment.

Any kind of pot can be used, but I usually pot several bulbs together in a 6-inch bulb pan. Hyacinths, which are large-flowered, look handsome planted as singles in regular 4-inch flowerpots.

Bulbs store all the nutrients that the plant actually needs to bloom, so they do not

need to be potted in rich, nutritious soil; all they need, in fact, is support. Yet, because I envision my potted bulbs as someday flowering in my outdoor garden, I give them more than mere support. I try to replenish rather than drain away their energy. For that reason, I generally use either bone meal–enriched garden soil or potting soil. Since I plan to set the bulbs outdoors in the garden, I also add a dusting of 5-10-5 fertilizer to the soil so they will have additional nutrients. When they're planted in the pots, the tips of the bulbs should just peek above the soil line, which should itself be about ½ inch below the rim of the pot. Then moisten the soil and they're ready for winter. Plan to keep the soil moist from that time forward until

the faded flowers and yellowed foliage signal the end of a growth cycle.

Tulip bulbs need some special attention when they're potted up. Unlike most bulbs, tulip bulbs are asymmetrical, having a curved side and a flat side. The largest of the leaves will grow from the flat side. I think a pot of tulips looks best if those large leaves all arch out over the rim of the pot, so I always put the flat side of the bulb against the outer rim of the pot.

There are several different ways to work out the winter storage of bulbs; the purpose is simply to keep the bulbs at a constant 40 degrees or so. They can't be allowed to dry out or freeze. A bulkhead or

254

cool cellar is fine for storing bulbs, as long as the temperatures are constant and the bulbs are kept moist and safe from severe weather. So is a refrigerator, if you can sacrifice the space; the air in a self-defrosting refrigerator is dry, so be sure to check the soil regularly to see that it's always moist. If you have a cold frame that you can mulch carefully so the interior won't freeze, you can set the bulbs inside for the winter period. Or you can do what gardeners have been doing for ages — dig a bulb trench. Dig the trench 3 inches deeper than the depth of the pots. Line the bottom of the trench with 1 inch of gravel or straw so the pots won't freeze to the ground. Set the pots in and cover them with 1 inch of sand. Before the ground freezes hard in the fall, cover the bulbs with at least 1 foot of dry leaves and a tarp or piece of heavy plastic to keep the leaves dry. They will provide insulation only as long as they're not allowed to get wet.

After 15 weeks, the first of the bulbs can be brought indoors. I usually bring in only a pot or two at a time, which gives me a sequence of flowering plants through most of the late winter and early spring. Put the pots on a bright but cool windowsill until the shoots are about 4 inches tall. Then move them into bright sun until the flower buds start to show color, at which point move them out of the sun and back into bright indirect light. While bulb plants are growing and in flower, they do best with night temperatures in the low 40s and days no warmer than 60 degrees. Keep the soil constantly moist but don't feed them.

Most bulb plants can't be forced a second time; it's too exhausting a routine. But if you have an outdoor garden, you can save the bulbs and plant them outside. They may not blossom extensively the first season, but they will regain their strength and eventually produce fine outdoor spring flowers. If you want to save your forced bulbs, you must allow them to ripen after they flower. Remove the flower stem, but leave the foliage as is, continuing to water as usual. When the leaves begin to turn yellow, reduce the amount of water and give them only enough to keep the leaves from wilting. By the time the leaves have withered entirely, the soil should be dry. The bulbs can be stored in their pots until the fall, or they can be taken from their pots and stored in a cool dry place. Mice will go after the bulbs if they're given the chance, so store them in a protected spot. Make sure there's air circulating, though, as bulb decay is another potential problem. If you spot mold on the soil of still-potted bulbs, dust the soil with benomyl.

Pots of forced hardy dwarf narcissus plants flanked by purple crocuses and red tulips

NOV

Clivia
Croton
Cyclamen
Devil's Ivy
Flamingo Flower
Grape Ivy
Jerusalem Cherry
Nasturtium
Ornamental Pepper
Pittosporum
Princess Flower
Spathiphyllum
Spider Plant
Weeping Fig

Feature: Greenhouses

Nasturtiums

NOV

Sometimes amaryllis bulbs send up the first of their flowers in November, but these are unpredictable plants that are just as apt to wait several more weeks before sending up their commanding flower stalks. Speaking of bulb plants, November is the last opportunity to pot up tender narcissus plants, including paper whites, Soleil d'Or, and Chinese sacred lilies.

During these months when the winter sun is so pale, set your sun-loving plants, especially the succulents, in the sunniest spot you can provide. Try to see that they get at least half days of sun, or their growth will be weak and pendulous. Many other plants, such as fuchsias, that need protection from brilliant summer sunlight appreciate all the sunlight that winter days can bring.

Because most plants respond to weaker sunlight and shorter days by slowing their growth, it's up to the gardener to take precautions against overwatering and overfeeding at a time when the plants can't put a rich diet to use. It's always important to water your houseplants in the morning, but it's especially so through the winter months, when the sun is so dull that the soil stays moist for hours. There are many plants that shouldn't be fed at all during the months between November and February. Too much fertilizer during the winter causes plants to make soft, leafy growth with weak stems and relatively few flowers. By contrast, though, some winter-flowering plants, like cyclamen, need more food and water through the winter than they do at the warmer, brighter times of the year because they are at their most active growth period during cool weather.

This is the month when the holiday plants start to appear on the market, including poinsettias and Jerusalem cherries and other plants commonly associated with Thanksgiving and Christmas. Most of them are not permanent plants because they are hard to bring back into flower again a second year. But they are colorful and greatly appreciated at this season; they can last indoors for weeks or even months without special attention.

Clivia (*Clivia*) The clivia is a South African plant named for Lady Clive, Duchess of Northumberland and granddaughter of Baron Robert Clive, who founded the British Empire in India in the eighteenth century. Sometimes called the Kafir lily, Lady Clive's namesake looks like a child's drawing of a flower, come to life: it's simple, symmetrical, colorful, and optimistic. Several straplike evergreen leaves, as long as 2 feet each, grow from the base of the plant and arch over the rim of the pot. In the early spring, leafless stems appear from the center of the base, each stem topped by a cluster of 3-inch orange or red-orange lilylike flowers. The flowers are followed by scarlet seedpods that can last on the plant most of the year; I usually remove these when they appear, to save the plant's strength for a heavier flower production the next time around.

Clivias (*kly*-via) are excellent and trouble-free houseplants. They need no more than bright indirect light and attention to their growing and rest cycles. They are most active from very early spring through fall, so during these months, keep them in a spot where the night temperatures

Clivia (*Clivia*)

Clivia flowers and buds against the background of the arching leaves

are in the 50s and the days 70 degrees or warmer. Feed them every month and water them regularly, giving the soil a chance to dry out slightly between deep waterings. Then in November or December, help them take a short rest by withholding fertilizer and watering them only frequently enough to keep them from wilting. During their rest, keep them in a spot where the night temperatures are close to 40 degrees. Toward the end of February or early in March, when the days are longer and the sun is warming, start feeding and watering them regularly again, and move them to a warmer location.

The best way to start a clivia collection is to buy a plant, sold either as *C. cyrtanthiflora* or as *C. miniata.* Young plants will be less expensive, but keep in mind that clivias need to have at least two or three crowns of foliage before they can bloom, and they can be several years growing to that size. (Even if you buy a plant that isn't old enough to bloom, make sure to allow it a yearly dormancy, just as you would an older specimen.) Clivias do not like to have their roots disturbed, so repot them only when they're very squeezed for space. They seem to flower best when they're a little pot-bound, too. I usually repot clivias about every third year — no more frequently — waiting until after the flowers have faded and the plants have begun their new vegetative cycle. They do best in gritty soil, so I use a combination of 3 parts commercial potting soil and 1 part coarse sand, liberally dusting the whole mix with ground bone meal. Clivias will grow to be large plants that need big pots or tubs to grow in, and as long as you can provide them with a container that suits their size, they will continue to improve, sending out more and more flowers every year. They don't require periodic division of the roots to stay healthy, but if you would like to increase your collection, divide the roots when you repot. If each division has two or three crowns of foliage, they should all bloom again the following year.

Croton (*Codiaeum*) The croton is a foliage plant from the tropics of southern India, Sri Lanka, and Malaysia that is every bit as colorful as many flowering plants. It's also a plant of many disguises. Depending on the variety, and there are hundreds of them, the leaves may be wide and short or long and slender, curled, wavy, or flat. The range of colors includes yellow, green, copper, red, pink, orange, brown, or ivory; the leaves may be one solid color, but usually they are marked with bizarre color combinations.

Crotons (*C. variegatum pictum*) are happiest in full sunshine; they'll survive in bright indirect light, but their

Croton (*Codiaeum*)

260

The new green foliage of this otherwise well-colored croton is a sign of poor light

colorful leaves revert to plain green if they get too little sun. They are not at all fond of cool breezes, and they prove it by dropping their leaves when subjected to a draft. The night temperatures should be in the high 60s and the days around 80 degrees. I use a commercial potting soil, which I keep moist at all times, and I feed the plants every 2 months, beginning in early spring and continuing through midsummer. During the rest of the year I give them no food at all, and of course, I give newly potted or purchased plants no fertilizer for at least half a year before I start them on the regular routine. Crotons are particularly vulnerable to mealybugs, so keep your eyes open and treat them right away if you spot any of these pests.

261

If you like action from your houseplants, this is a good choice for you. A plant that is a modest 10 inches tall now could be waist-high in three years (that is, unless it's pruned and generally kept in control). I repot and prune at this time every year, so later growth comes in dense and bushy. Good sturdy cuttings will root easily from now through summer. The plant can also be propagated by air-layering.

Cyclamen (*Cyclamen*)

■ **Cyclamen** (*Cyclamen*) Three centuries ago, Europeans considered cyclamens to be helpful for a variety of problems, including baldness, jaundice, snake bites, and for the arousal of romantic passion. Now they're known primarily as one of the longest-lasting and most beautiful of flowering houseplants. Standard cyclamens grow to be about 12 inches tall, miniature variations reach about half that size; both produce their white, pink, red, or lavender flowers from October through late March or April. They'll live year after year with just a minimum of attention.

Provident gardeners buy a plant early in the fall as the blooming season commences. At this stage, it needs good ventilation, a feeding of houseplant fertilizer every other week, as much sunlight as you can provide it, though it will also do fine in bright indirect light, and constant moisture; if the plant dries out when it's in bloom, the young flower buds are apt to die. It also needs cool temperatures, and this is where most gardeners have problems. Ideally, a cyclamen should have night readings in the 40s or low 50s, just as it would have in its native Near East habitat, where it would be shaded and cooled by taller vegetation. It will tolerate night temperatures as high as 65, but it won't do as well. I have a friend who keeps her cyclamen in an unheated bedroom, and only brings it out when she wants to dress up her living room for a party; hers is a happy and beautiful plant.

Cyclamens (*C. persicum*) are very easy to keep from year to year, as long as they're given some attention during the summer. When they stop flowering, reduce the amount of moisture they receive to the point where the soil is allowed to dry out moderately before watering again. Keep them in partial shade, out of the sun. When the weather is warm enough, with night temperatures predictably above 55 degrees, unpot them, shake off the old soil, and repot the corm, the beetlike root from which the plant grows, in a 1-inch-larger pot with commercial potting soil. Make sure that the corm is not set more deeply than it had been before repotting. As the corm ages, more and more of it will grow above the soil line; ideally, it will be a third to halfway out of the soil. Set the plant outside for the summer in a shady

262

spot and keep the soil barely moist. The old leaves will stay on the plant while the new ones grow in; during the summer the previous season's leaves will drop off. (If the corm is allowed to dry out entirely, it will lose all its foliage. But even a bare corm will usually produce new growth again if given moisture.)

Once you have fallen under the spell of florists' cyclamens, you may be tempted, as I have, to grow some of the wild species either in a shady garden or on a windowsill. Among the ones I like best are these: *C. coum*, a European species known as sowbread because wild boars savor the roots; *C. europaeum*, called alpine violet by the Swiss; and *C. neapolitanum*, the Neapolitan cyclamen. Each grows less than 6 inches tall and bears pink or, occasionally, white flowers about the size of large violets.

Cyclamens are started from seeds; they are not fast growing, usually needing some 15 to 18 months to grow to flowering size. But they don't need much attention during this period. I usually sow seeds in June so they're ready to blossom a year and a half later, right at the beginning of

Beneath these dazzling white cyclamen flowers are scores of buds that will open in the months ahead

263

their normal bloom period. I put just one seed into single peat pellets, and set the pellets into total darkness for 40 days. As the seeds sprout, toward the end of that period, I move them into bright light. Every day I check the seedlings to make sure they're moist. When the roots begin to show along the outside of the peat pellets, I move them, pellets and all, to individual 3-inch pots, taking care not to set them in any deeper than they had been growing. Throughout the growing period they need the same care that they get while they're in bloom.

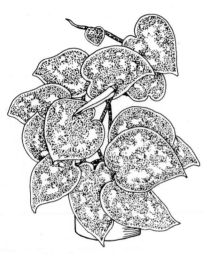

Devil's Ivy *(Scindapsus)*

Devil's Ivy *(Scindapsus)* In their native location in the Solomon Islands, devil's ivies are enormous plants with leaves as much as 2 feet across. Luckily, plants grown indoors never reach that size; they're sometimes identified as juveniles because the leaves are so much smaller. If they're grown in hanging containers, or allowed to trail along a tabletop, the leaves are only 1½ to 2 inches across and 2½ to 4 inches long. If they're sold with a totem-pole support, the leaves will be larger as the plant grows, but the biggest of them probably won't be more than 6 or 7 inches long. (Devil's ivies are sometimes confused with heart-leaf philodendrons, partly because of their superficially similar leaf shapes and partly because of their tendency to develop larger leaves when given a support upon which to climb.) There are several varieties of devil's ivies available; as far as an indoor gardener is concerned, they are different only in the coloration of their leaves. *Scindapsus aureus* has green leaves marked with yellow. Marble Queen's green leaves are marked with white. The leaves of Tricolor are green with cream, yellow, and pale green markings. (Both Marble Queen and Tricolor are varieties of *S. aureus*.) Silver pothos (*S. pictus argyraeus*) is a native of Borneo; its leaves are small, bluish-green, and edged with silver.

Given warmth, humidity, and partial shade, all of these plants are easy to grow. They should be set on a humidifying tray in a room where the night temperatures won't fall below 65 degrees. Bright indirect light is best; they will lose their distinctive coloration if they're not given enough light. (This is true of many variegated plants. In dim light, they are forced to put all their available chlorophyll to use in order to take full advantage of the light they receive, and the chlorophyll causes the leaves to be green. Variegated foliage is a luxury afforded only to plants growing in suitable light.) It is possible though to provide plenty of light for them to grow with their full coloration under 400 or more foot-candles of artificial light; we have a plant growing in plain water under lights in the windowless Victory Garden

264

office and it's doing beautifully. If they're grown in commercial potting soil, give them a chance to become nearly dry between thorough waterings. Silver pothos soil should be kept barely moist all the time. Every 3 or 4 months, give the plants a feeding with houseplant fertilizer. Keep them pinched back for fullness and root the pinched tips to keep young plants coming.

A devil's ivy growing in a hanging pot in the Victory Garden greenhouse

Flamingo Flower (*Anthurium*) The flamingo flower, sometimes known also as the pigtail plant, is a native of Colombia. It's related to the spathiphyllum and the calla lily and, like them, it bears a large colorful bract called a spathe. In the center of each spathe there is a long, curved appendage called a spadix, which carries the plant's tiny true flowers. The spathes of the wild species are red and measure 4 to 5 inches long. By selection and hybridization, we now have plants whose flowers are 6 inches or more long, varying in color from deep, dark red to scarlet, pink, rose, salmon, white, and white with red dots. The spathes, as shiny as though varnished and with the texture of leather, last for 2

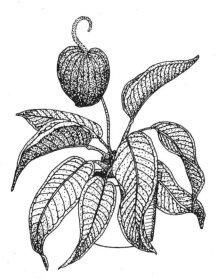

Flamingo Flower (*Anthurium*)

265

or 3 months on the plant, and if they're cut and added to a floral arrangement or vase, they'll still look beautiful several weeks later. The plants bloom all year long. Once the plant reaches maturity it sends out a flower with every new leaf. It also builds up a crown above the surface of the soil. The new leaves will grow from the crown, as will, eventually, some offsets.

The flamingo flower is an excellent plant if it's in a humid environment. It does especially well in a greenhouse, conservatory, or plant room or, when it's small, in a terrarium. (If you can't provide it with these ideally humid conditions, grow it on a large saucer or a humidifying tray.) It should be kept in a bright spot, out of the sun, where the night temperatures won't fall below 65 degrees. Flamingo flowers should be potted in highly organic soil: I generally use a mix of equal parts fir bark and coarse long-fibered sphagnum moss. Keep the potting mixture moist constantly and feed the plant every other week. As the crown begins to develop above the soil level, it's a good idea to wrap moist long-fibered sphagnum moss around it. Keep the moss damp by wetting it regularly with warm water as you water the plant.

266

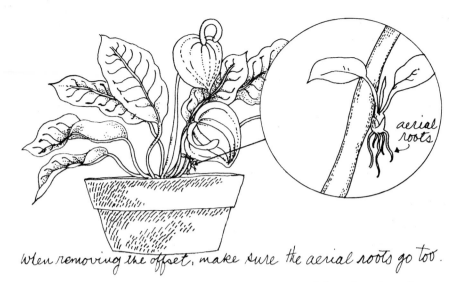

aerial roots

When removing the offset, make sure the aerial roots go too.

Flamingo flowers can be propagated by planting the offsets that develop from the crown; make sure when you remove the offset that it takes its fat, aerial roots with it. You can also start new plants from seeds sown in the spring in a mixture of equal parts damp sand and sphagnum moss and bottom-heated to 75 or 80 degrees. Seed-grown plants will start to flower in about three years.

Grape Ivy (*Cissus*) Time was when all members of the *Cissus* family were thought to be types of grapes, because their flowers and tendrils were so similar. In fact they are related to one another, but they are of different genera. The confusion hangs on in the common names of some of the *Cissus* family though. The term grape ivy is part of it, as is the grape ivy's former botanical name, *Vitis rhombifolia, Vitis* denoting the grape family. (The accurate botanical name is *C. rhombifolia.*) Their titles aside, the members of the *Cissus* family make up some of the best of the small indoor vines. The grape ivy and its dwarf relative, *C. striata*, are the most familiar of them, but the kangaroo vine, *C. antarctica*, is another handsome member of the family. They all thrive on the same easy care.

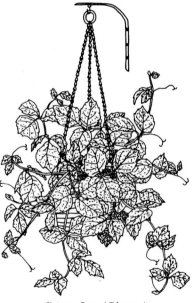

Grape Ivy *(Cissus)*

The grape ivy has rich green three-part leaves that remind me of poison ivy (without the itch). Its buds are a brownish color, with a halo of soft fuzz; the mature leaves still have a fuzzy underside. To grow quickly, grape ivies need very bright light, warmth, constantly moist soil, and frequent feedings. Most gardeners, though, buy a plant the size they want it to be, and don't want to encourage growth. So to keep a plant in control, give it bright indirect light, or 400 or more foot-candles of artificial light; night temperatures in the high 50s; moisture only when the soil has become moderately dry; and food every 4 months or so using

267

any houseplant fertilizer. These plants have no intrinsic timetables for repotting or propagating, so whenever they are crowded I move them into larger pots filled with commercial potting soil, and I propagate them from stem cuttings whenever the mood strikes. They have a tendency to shoot stems off in odd directions, so I keep them pinched back, especially when they are young, to encourage a bushy habit of growth. Although these ivies can be grown as ordinary pot plants, they are much more attractive when displayed in hanging containers so that their graceful new growth can cascade over the edges.

A healthy grape ivy plant

Jerusalem Cherry *(Solanum)* Jerusalem cherries are colorful and popular plants during the November and December holidays, the time of the year that they ripen their bright yellow or orange, marble-sized fruit. It's important to note that though the fruit is reputed to be poisonous, it has been grown as a houseplant for generations. According to a recent government report, no person has died from eating any plant sold by florists in the United States. Although they're perennials in their native Madeira Islands, they are

268

usually treated as annuals when they're grown as house-plants and thrown away after their fruiting period is over. You might be tempted, if your plant is healthy and full, to try cutting it back to encourage rich new growth, but you're apt to find that the inner stems of the branches are bare, and any pruning effort is almost bound to leave a straggly, unattractive plant without much of a future.

So rather than try to hold a plant over for another year, sow the seeds for a new generation in January or February. Either buy the seeds or harvest them from the ripe fruit. Keep the seedlings pinched back as they grow; by late

Jerusalem Cherry *(Solanum)*

The brightly colored but inedible fruit of a Jerusalem cherry

May or June, they should be 5 or 6 inches tall. At that point, repot them into a larger container and set them outdoors in a sunny spot, where they will benefit from the light and their white summer flowers will be followed by fruit. By the time you bring the plants inside before the cool weather, they will probably have some flowers remaining, some green fruit, and some fruit that's nearly ripe.

All through their growing season, including while they're in fruit, Jerusalem cherries *(S. pseudocapsicum)*

need sun for at least half the day. They also need relatively cool temperatures, with night readings in the low 50s; if they're kept too warm the leaves turn yellow. Keep the soil — commercial potting soil is fine — constantly moist; be attentive about this, as Jerusalem cherries are great consumers of moisture. Fertilize the plants every month. Finally, keep your eyes open for white fly infestations; if you're given a plant, quarantine it for 10 days until you're sure it's free from these pests, and if you grow the plants yourself, watch for them all along their growing period, especially during and after their summer outdoors.

⌂ **Nasturtium** *(Tropaeolum)* Nasturtiums are common garden annuals and fine cool greenhouse plants; they're unlikely houseplants, but possible if they can be given a cool sunny spot. They will stay in blossom for most of the winter, producing their soft, fragrant flowers in white, yellow, pink, red, orange, scarlet, and deep reddish-brown. The original species, *T. majus*, is a tall-growing plant that produces mostly single flowers; if it's offered a vertical netting, it will

A single-flowered nasturtium, a fragrant cut flower for a short-stemmed bouquet

clamber eagerly. The dwarf varieties, which grow to be about 1 foot tall, bear both single and double flowers. They have sufficient growth to overhang a pot edge handsomely and, as a result, they make good trailing plants. I especially like Jewel and Whirly Bird, both dwarf varieties that hold their flowers well above the foliage, unlike some of the old-fashioned varieties whose flowers are often hidden beneath the canopy of leaves.

These South American plants from the foothills of the Andes need constant sun. They also need good ventilation and low temperatures, with night readings in the 40s or low 50s. If the plants receive too much nitrogen, they will produce leaves at the expense of flowers, so at their monthly feeding I give a half-strength low-nitrogen fertilizer. If you can find it in liquid form, 5-10-10 is a good choice; otherwise look for any liquid fertilizer sold as a flower booster. Keep the soil under nasturtiums moist all the time. And be on your guard against aphids. They'll be noticeable first right at the junction of the stem and the leaf; left unchecked they'll attack the flower buds next, and they'll be well established on the flowers by the time they open.

Nasturtium *(Tropaeolum)*

Nasturtiums stay in flower for about 3 or 4 months, sometimes longer; they're annuals and should be discarded at the end of their blossom period. They can be grown outdoors year-round where the summer and winter temperatures are cool enough, such as in coastal Southern California. For my part, I'm interested in a greenhouse crop during the winter; so I sow the seeds in commercial potting soil in late summer or early fall and they begin to blossom within 6 weeks.

■ **Ornamental Pepper** *(Capsicum)* The ornamental pepper is one among several interesting pot plants on the market at this holiday time of the year that make fine if short-lived houseplants. Although some are of a perennial nature, they are treated as though they were annuals because they are difficult or impossible for the home gardener to bring to fruit or flower a second time. But for the weeks or months that they live they add bright spots of color and a change of pace. Most of them are inexpensive and help to enliven windowsills when outdoor gardens are drab and disheveled.

Ornamental peppers grow to be about 12 inches tall; they bear many tiny inconspicuous white flowers that are followed by handsome colorful fruit held well above the foliage. There are several different shapes of fruit, depending on the variety, but they all go through the same color changes: they start out green, and turn white, yellow, and purple in succession. Eventually they all turn brilliant red or orange.

Ornamental Pepper *(Capsicum)*

One of many types of ornamental
peppers, these having slimmer
pods than some of the others

The plants are related to garden peppers, and like their relatives, their fruit is edible; very hot, but edible. They're great for chili!

Ornamental peppers (*C. annuum*) are native to South America and they crave sunshine throughout their lifetime; the more sun, the better. They also need warmth, with night temperatures in the low 60s. Keep the soil moist, but don't feed the plants when they're in flower or fruit. The plants will hold their fruit for months; when they're no longer attractive, discard them.

If you can provide sunshine and warmth, you can start new plants from seeds. Plant them in commercial potting soil in early spring. After the seedlings have been given individual pots and are about 3 inches tall, begin feeding them monthly. Keep the soil moist and be sure the plants have full sunshine; you can set them outdoors, still in their pots, during the summer months. Stop their monthly feedings about the time the fruit appears.

Pittosporum (*Pittosporum*) Several pittosporums are native to eastern Asia, from Japan to Australia. The Japanese pittosporum, *P. tobira*, does very well as an evergreen shrub in mild parts of this country, and as a handsome houseplant elsewhere. Its tongue-shaped, 3- to 4-inch leaves are a handsome deep green, and tough enough to stand up to dryness, drafts, and chills. Pittosporums are woody shrubs that live indefinitely and may grow to be 3 or more feet tall and just as wide if they're not pruned occasionally. In the spring mature plants bear clusters of ½-inch white or lemon-yellow flowers that have the sweet fragrance of orange blossoms. The original species is a fast-paced plant that will

Pittosporum (*Pittosporum*)

grow 1½ feet a season if given enough food, water, and sunshine; Wheeler's pittosporum is a relatively new variety with smaller foliage and a compact habit of growth.

Pittosporums are very tolerant houseplants. They do well in either bright indirect light or full sun; they grow more quickly in full sun, but they're more apt to attract red spider mites. Their ideal night temperature is in the 40s or low 50s, but they'll stand much warmer temperatures, and again, they'll grow more quickly. Let the soil become moderately dry between thorough waterings, and feed the plants twice a year, once in the very early spring and again early in the summer. Pittosporums often go for years without needing repotting, but when it is necessary, it can be done at any time of the year, using any commercial potting soil. If your plant grows too large for its space, it can be pruned all the way down to within a few inches of the soil line; it will revive even if all the foliage is pruned away. The best way to propagate pittosporums is by stem cuttings started in late summer, or by air-layering at any time of the year. When the plants are young, keep the tips pinched back so growth will be as compact as possible.

Wheeler's pittosporum, with its especially compact, dark foliage

Princess Flower *(Tibouchina)*

🏠 **Princess Flower** *(Tibouchina)* This dazzling Brazilian shrub, sometimes called glory bush, is a seldom-grown gem that needs a press agent. It's heavy with Phoenician purple flowers nearly as big as your hand during the summer, fall, and into the early winter. The flowers begin as red buds, and as they open, display long wavy brown stamens that look like the legs of a huge spider. Each flower only lasts a day or so but new ones are always on the way. The plant's one drawback is its rank growth if given too much fertilizer. Its elliptical leaves, in pairs along the stems, are 2 to 3 inches long, deeply veined and covered with silvery hairs. As the leaves age they turn red before falling off, but the plant is always in foliage because there's a constant supply of new young leaves. The princess flower is usually sold as *T. urvilleana,* or sometimes as *T. semidecandra.*

The plant's growing season is from the spring through the early winter; during the rest of the winter the plant is dormant. The care of the plant varies according to each part of its annual cycle. During the growing season the plants need the protection of dappled shade; I usually leave them outside in a partially shaded spot in the Victory Garden for the summer and they respond beautifully. I make sure the soil is constantly moist, and every 3 or 4 weeks during the growing season I feed them with a standard houseplant fertilizer. Because princess flowers are fast growers that can easily get leggy, I pinch back the stem tips repeatedly until midsummer, which makes the plants bushy and provides many flower-bearing stems for the blooming season to follow. They like warmth, with days around 80 degrees and nights 55 degrees or higher; if the temperature is too cool, they stop blossoming until things warm up.

When they finish blooming, I withhold fertilizer and reduce moisture so that the soil becomes moderately dry between light waterings. They do best if given full sun during the winter months. As soon as the plants begin new vegetative growth I cut back all the stems at least halfway, often to within 6 inches of the soil, to curb their tendency to grow too tall. If the roots are crowded, I repot them at the time of pruning. When new buds swell along the cut-back stems I resume the richer diet of the growing season.

When princess flowers are grown outdoors in the nearly frost-free areas of southern California and Florida, they can become 10- to 15-foot shrubs. Potted versions are easily kept to a manageable 3 feet or less by pruning, but there's a limit to how long this pruning can continue; in my experience the best-looking plants are no older than 3 or 4 years. After that they begin to look gawky. Gardeners with large greenhouses can take advantage of this tendency to

Opposite: A princess flower with its prominent spidery anthers

straggliness and support the plant like a vine. I prefer to throw an old plant away after taking 3- to 4-inch cuttings in the early spring. I dip the cuttings in rooting powder and then set them into damp sand, perlite, or vermiculite. They root rather easily, but they're particularly quick-rooting if they're heated from the bottom to about 70 degrees. When the roots are still less than 1 inch long, I move them to their own pots in any commercial potting soil. They often bear flowers when they're less than 12 inches tall.

Spathiphyllum (*Spathiphyllum*) The spathiphyllum, sometimes called the peace lily, is a combination foliage and flowering plant. Each fragrant white blossom, often more than 6 inches long and 4 inches across, is composed of two parts: the snowy spathe, shaped much like a gently rolled napkin, and, from its base, a sticklike white spadix upon which its tiny true flowers are closely set. It does, in fact, look much like its relative, the calla lily. There are never many open flowers at one time, perhaps a dozen, sometimes only half that number. As they age, the flowers turn green; that's when I remove them. If spathiphyllums

Spathiphyllum (*Spathiphyllum*)

The blossom of the spathiphyllum shows the similarity to its relatives, calla lilies and flamingo flowers

276

(spath-i-*fie*-lum) are given a good growing environment, they stay in nearly constant bloom; if ideal conditions can't be maintained, they still make handsome foliage plants. The leaves are shiny, slow growing, and long lasting. The best of the varieties is Mauna Loa; it blooms all year long, and has larger flowers and leaves than its most common competitor, *S. clevelandii*.

Spathiphyllums are cousins to philodendrons and share with them the ability to grow in poor light month after month. They actually prefer shade, with some pale filtered sun in the winter. They are tropical plants native to the warm jungles of Central and South America and they grow best when the weather is hot and humid. Night temperatures shouldn't fall below 65 degrees. I pot them in a soil mix composed of 2 parts peat moss, 1 part potting soil, and 1 part either sharp sand or perlite and I keep this mix quite moist at all times. Every 2 or 3 months I give the plants a bit of houseplant fertilizer. They can be propagated any time of the year by division.

Spider Plant *(Chlorophytum)* The spider plant is one of the most common houseplants in this country. The variety that is seen most often is the variegated one, *C. comosum variegatum*, which has foot-long leaves striped with creamy white. The original species, *C. comosum*, has slender all-green leaves. Spider plants, also known as ribbon plants or spider ivies, are responsive to the length of the day; they produce most of their plantlets, or spiders, when the days shorten in the fall, although they are apt to send out a few at other times of the year, too.

As is obvious from their popularity, anybody can grow a spider plant; as is also obvious, very few gardeners can grow a good one. When the plants are in perfect health they're beautiful, but if conditions are less than ideal they develop the brown foliage that seems to curse most of the specimens one sees. The most important preventive of browning foliage is moisture. Keep the soil moist all the time, and try to use rainwater; it's been recently discovered that fluorides present in tap water, even in minute proportions, will turn the foliage tips brown. Brown tips will probably continue to be a problem, though. The best advice I can offer is to prune the tips away with scissors; if you give each leaf a new pointed tip the operation will barely be visible.

Spider Plant *(Chlorophytum)*

Beyond moisture, spider plants need bright indirect natural light or 400 or more foot-candles of artificial light. Keep night temperatures in the 50s and feed the plants every 3 or 4 months with any houseplant fertilizer. They don't need repotting often, but when they do, use commer-

cial potting soil. The plants can be propagated any time of the year by root division or by pinning the spiders to moist soil.

Weeping Fig *(Ficus)*

Weeping Fig *(Ficus)* The weeping fig is native to India and Malaysia. It's a kind of rubber tree, but the family resemblance is not obvious. Weeping figs (*F. benjamina*) grow to be forest giants in their native habitat and specimens 20 to 30 feet tall are often used in atrium plantings in modern hotels and office buildings. In the home they can be of any size to suit the location because they can be pruned to limit growth as desired. Their mature foliage is a shiny deep green, while new leaves are pale by contrast. A healthy plant is dense with foliage that clings to pendant branches that account for its common name, weeping fig. It is sometimes confused with the stiffer-branched species, *F. retusa nitida*, called Indian laurel.

Weeping figs are certainly among the best of the indoor trees, and their popularity shows it. Their primary problem in life is that gardeners are unprepared for the leaf drop that is normal for plants adjusting to new surroundings. If the plant is acclimated to shade by the grower before it is sold, it will have an easier time of it than if it is taken directly from a full-sun greenhouse and put into the dim light of the average home. The leaves that develop in greenhouse sun will be too thick to survive in low light; the plant will shed them to insure its survival, and the new leaves, born in dim light, will be thinner and able to thrive in the home. The period of leaf drop may go on for months, but the plant will eventually stabilize on its own. It should

278

This weeping fig, some 20 feet tall, dominates the lobby of the WGBH studios, where Crockett's Victory Garden *originates*

also be noted that the leaves of tropical evergreen trees go through a constant aging process; old leaves eventually fall, but not before new ones have grown at the tips of the stems. It's nature's way of maintaining a balanced growth; so don't become upset about a few falling leaves now and then.

Both during and after this period of adjustment, weeping figs can take either sun or bright indirect light; they will grow more quickly in sunlight, but they will dry out more quickly, and the combination of dryness and sunlight makes them more vulnerable to red spider mites. Keep the soil constantly moist; most weeping figs are large plants in big pots, so make sure you moisten the soil ball thoroughly. They're happiest if the night temperatures are in the upper

279

60s — they're native to warm climates — and if they're fed every 6 months with any mild houseplant fertilizer. Keep the foliage clean with regular showers and baths. I never use anything stronger than mild sudsy tepid water on my plants' leaves and I rinse them with plain water.

A weeping fig can often go for several years in the same container. Eventually, though, it becomes pot-bound; you can tell because it's harder and harder to provide enough water. At that point, repot it into a larger container, using commercial potting soil. If your plant is too large for your purposes, you can prune it back as far as you wish, all the way to within a few inches of the soil line if necessary, and fresh growth will arise to rejuvenate the plant. If you'd like to make fresh young plants from the old one, air-layer it before pruning.

Q&A

Q: Not too long ago a neighbor moved out of town and left me with her sizable plant collection. One of them, labeled "apostle plant," seems to be in trouble already. What should I be doing for it?

A: The apostle plant, also known as the twelve apostles, is so named because each fan of foliage usually contains twelve leaves. It's also sometimes called a walking iris because of its irislike leaves and the fact that its flowering stems bend over to the ground and a new plant takes root at that point. Actually, several species of *Neomarica* are known by these common names. The blossoms look like those of irises. The three lower petals are white, often with yellow or brown markings, and the three upper petals are blue. The flowers are fragrant, beautiful, and short-lived, lasting only one day each. But these plants blossom for many weeks during the midwinter and early spring if given bright indirect light and night temperatures in the low 50s, with daytime readings as high as 75. If your plant is in trouble, you're probably not giving the soil enough moisture; keep it wet at all times. Feed the plant every month with a houseplant fertilizer.

Q: My jungle geranium is showing clear signs of stress, so presumably I'm doing something wrong. What care should I be giving it?

A: The plant is probably chilled. The jungle geranium (a name given to several species of *Ixora*) is a tropical plant. It makes a fine houseplant if the night temperatures can be kept above 60 degrees. Keep the soil barely moist and feed the plant every other week from early spring to fall; the rest of the year, feed it only monthly. Give it at least half days of sunlight. It should blossom continuously.

Q: When I was buying my bulbs this fall I ran across one that was called a veltheimia. It was expensive and unfamiliar so I didn't buy any of the bulbs, but the display photograph of the plant looked intriguing. Is it a good houseplant?

A: It certainly is. It's a native of South Africa that sends up exquisite, shiny green leaves and spikes of handsome pink flowers in midwinter. Pot the bulbs in the fall and set them in a spot where there is sun for at least half the day. Night temperatures anywhere in the 40- to 60-degree range are fine. Keep the soil moist while the plant is growing, and feed it monthly. Move the plant out of the direct sun when it's in flower. When the blossom season has passed, allow the foliage to continue growing on a sunny windowsill until it eventually turns brown and withers, an indication that it is about to enter its rest period. Let it rest without food or water until early in the following autumn. Veltheimias do not need repotting every year, but it's a good idea to wash away some of the surface soil around the bulb and replenish with fresh soil. As for the expense of the bulbs, it's justifiable; an old bulb sends out many offsets from its base; soon you'll find yourself with a large collection to share with friends.

Q: I'd like to grow some herbs indoors. Do they make good houseplants?

A: Some do, if they're given enough sunlight and cool enough temperatures. Rosemary is the easiest (see the May chapter). Basil, mint, parsley, thyme, chives, and bay will do fairly well, too. In fact, you can lift many garden herbs before frost in the fall, keep them potted indoors over the winter, and set them back out in the spring.

GREEN-HOUSES

A lean-to greenhouse

Most flower lovers long for a greenhouse; they want their own opportunity to challenge winter. Until recently, only the very wealthy could indulge this longing. Greenhouses were designed and constructed individually, and maintained manually. The stoves had to be stoked and the vents opened and shut whenever the temperatures varied, which meant that someone had to be on hand at all times. Very few could afford either to build or staff a private greenhouse.

Now, thanks to prefabrication and automated heating and cooling mechanisms, many thousands of gardeners are finding greenhouses affordable. They're available at almost any price, from a few hundred dollars to several thousand, but even with a modest budget it's perfectly possible to provide your plants with an environment far superior to an indoor room.

Buying a greenhouse of any size requires thought and planning. Don't spend a penny until you've studied the market, talked with people who own greenhouses, considered the amount of time that maintaining greenhouse plants demands, and calculated the additional construction costs of the foundation, temperature control systems, and interior structures. Keep in mind when you're considering your budget that plants do better in a large greenhouse than a small one; a small volume of air heats up rapidly in the sun, and then cools just as rapidly. Of course,

small and large are relative terms and you can only buy what you can afford. Plants will do better in even a small greenhouse than in a bright indoor room. The best idea is to select a modular-designed greenhouse that you can expand later if the need arises. If you have no experience with greenhouse culture at all, you may want to start with a window greenhouse, which is essentially a glass box that fits on the outside of a window. This is the least expensive first step. Window greenhouses are heated by house heat and by the sun, and cooled by manual vents. Humidity is provided by trays of pebbles which the gardener keeps moistened. If you enjoy the window greenhouse, then you've surely got the bug

and are ready to consider moving on.

Types There are two basic types of greenhouses: lean-to and free-standing. There are advantages and disadvantages to each. Free-standing greenhouses can, as their name implies, stand on their own on the best site available. They allow in maximum light through all four walls. They are easy to cool in the summer because the breezes can pass through them quickly. If there's an insect infestation, the gardener can simply leave a smoke-type insecticide, even a potent one, at work in the closed greenhouse, without worrying about the powerful gases seeping into a house full of people. Free-standing greenhouses can be attached to a house at one end, with the loss of some light, but they still allow more light to penetrate than is possible in a dwelling because three sides are glass. On the other hand, free-standing greenhouses are expensive to build, expensive to heat, and they usually segregate the plants at some distance from the house, where they can't be readily appreciated, especially if shoveling a snowy path precedes direct entry into the greenhouse.

A lean-to greenhouse is simply half a free-standing greenhouse, and must be built against an existing building. They are somewhat less expensive to build, not only because there are relatively fewer greenhouse parts, but because the heat, wiring, and plumbing can be extended from the house. Less heat escapes because one side rests against the warm wall of the house and often they're protected from the wind. I have a friend who built a lean-to greenhouse along one wall of his large, high-ceilinged family room. On a sunny day, when he opens the sliding glass doors that separate the house from the greenhouse, the sun-heated greenhouse air warms the entire room. Everyone in the house can enjoy the plants, even if they don't share in their care. And the gardener can tend to the plants without putting on boots and heavy clothing and trudging through snow. On the other hand, treating pests in a lean-to greenhouse can be a problem because fumes from the insecticides will enter the house no matter how tight-fitting the door. And, of course, the light level is lower than in a free-standing greenhouse because the house shades one side.

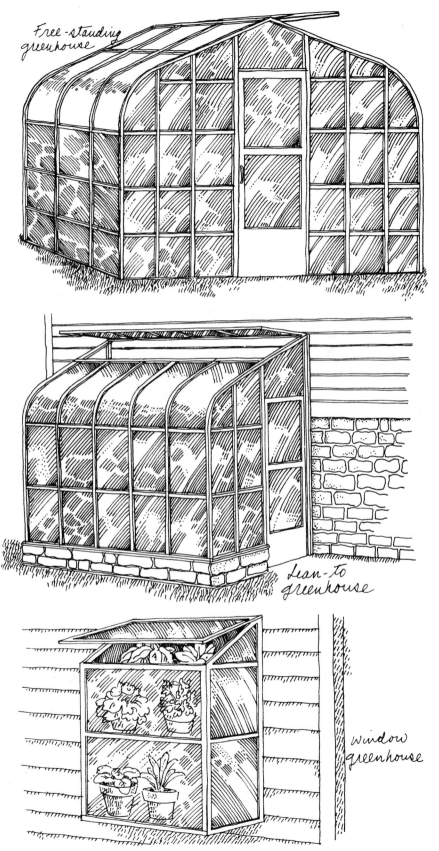

Free-standing greenhouse

Lean-to greenhouse

window greenhouse

Tending and admiring the greenhouse plants

Siting People generally assume that greenhouses have to be situated in constant sun, but this isn't so. I'd build a greenhouse even in a shady area; the amount of light the plants would receive would be far greater in a shady greenhouse than in even a bright room. A shady greenhouse is perfect for orchids and gesneriads and bromeliads. I would never *select* a shady spot over a sunny one though; I can shade sections of a sunny greenhouse, but there's no way to bring the sun into a shady one.

A satisfactory greenhouse can be built facing any direction, but in order of preference I would list south, east, west, and north of your site. Make sure that you use a compass to learn the true orientation. The sun rises in the northeast and sets in the northwest in the summer. During the winter months it rises in the southeast and sets in the southwest and its rays are weak and wan and the days are short when you need light most of all.

Construction Prefabricated greenhouses are the best and least expensive. Even if you aren't handy enough to construct the entire kit yourself, you can hire local carpenters, masons, and electricians to help you. Don't try to design and construct your own greenhouse; it may look just the way you want it to, but the chances of it being water- and airtight are slim. What so often happens with a homemade greenhouse is that provision is seldom made to carry off condensation. Cold water dripping on plants ruins them in short order. Professional greenhouse manufacturers have invented designs to carry the water away harmlessly.

Materials Until fairly recently, greenhouses were framed in wood, either heart redwood or cypress. Now the framing material is nearly always aluminum. It is lightweight and inexpensive. It doesn't require maintenance and doesn't deteriorate. It's also a stronger material, so the framing members can be smaller without a loss of strength, which means that more light reaches the plants.

As they have for generations, most gardeners still opt for glass greenhouses. Glass lasts for fifty or even a hundred years and lets in the most light. And, because it is double-thick, there is remarkably little breakage. High-grade rigid plastic is often flammable and costs as much or more than glass; manufacturers sometimes offer a ten-year guarantee. Rigid plastic rarely breaks, but it is translucent rather than transparent, so less light reaches the plants. On the other hand, the need for shading is often eliminated because the sun's rays are diffused by the translucence of the plastic. And, of course, in greenhouses made of rigid plastic the plants can't be clearly seen from outside, nor can the person inside a rigid plastic house see outdoors. Rigid plastic costs about the same as glass to install. The cheapest material is polyethylene, but it often has to be replaced twice a year. Some flexible plastics are both clear and long-lasting; how long, no one yet knows for certain. One thing that is known about flexible plastic greenhouses is that they are very noisy on a windy day as the plastic bellows and shakes in the breeze.

Some greenhouses are being built with double walls to save heat. It's a good idea with a serious drawback: if there is any moisture between the walls, fungus will start growing and ultimately spread across the glass or plastic, blocking light.

Light and Shade

Greenhouses are designed to give plants the maximum amount of light, and sometimes, especially in the summer, more light reaches the plants than they are accustomed to in their native environments. For this reason, most hobby greenhouses need shading devices during the summer. There are many ways to shade a greenhouse. Rolled coverings, such as plastic, aluminum, or woven saran, can be applied to the outside of the glass and rolled and unrolled as the light intensity requires. The disadvantage to these exterior coverings is that they have to be operated from the outside. They also have to be

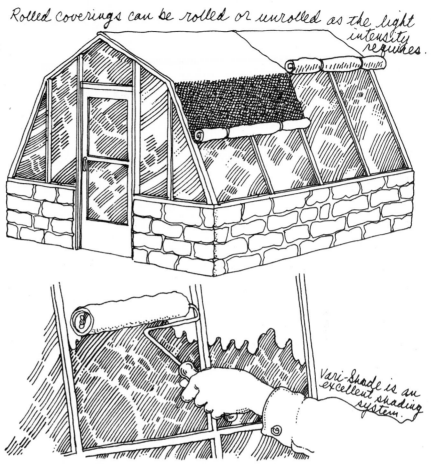

Rolled coverings can be rolled or unrolled as the light intensity requires.

Vari-Shade is an excellent shading system.

removed during the winter months because they provide too much shade and because they're apt to hold snow, which will block the light and add too much weight to the roof of the greenhouse. Commercial greenhouses use various shading compounds, usually sprayed on the glass in the spring. They last for several months, protecting the plants all summer and wearing off by fall. The one-time application makes their use fairly easy, but their shading qualities are constant, even on cloudy summer days when the plants need more light.

Other shading systems are applied to the inner surfaces of the glass, and operated from inside the greenhouse. Woven saran, which is a dark green or black flexible plastic, can be

used indoors, as well as out. But the best of the shading systems that I've found is a white, water-soluble material known as Vari-Shade. It is uniquely sensitive to humidity. When the greenhouse humidity is high, as during the winter months, the material is translucent, allowing the plants to receive most of the light's value. In the summer, when the heat and brighter light reduce humidity, the Vari-Shade becomes opaque, blocking the most intense rays of the sun. Vari-Shade is applied only once and lasts for years, but can be scrubbed off at any time with plain water.

Temperature Control

Greenhouses respond very quickly to changes in outdoor weather: varying temperature, wind, clouds, and the sun combine to heat up or cool down the interior so rapidly that heating and cooling systems are needed to maintain ideal temperatures for the plants being grown.

Most modern greenhouses are cooled by evaporative cooling; that is, lowering air temperatures by drawing outside air through pads of wet excelsior. This method usually lowers readings by about 20 degrees. Some rely solely on vents, operated automatically, to let cool air into the greenhouse when the temperatures rise.

Heat can be provided by gas, oil, or electricity, either directly or through forced hot water systems. Although research is ongoing, solar energy at this point is best used only for supplementary heat.

Because plants have ideal temperature needs, greenhouses are heated to a specific night temperature, which is far more important to plants than the daytime readings. A cool greenhouse is one in which the night temperatures are in the 50- to 55-degree range, though some of them run as low as 45 degrees. An intermediate greenhouse has night temperatures of 55 to 60 degrees. A warm greenhouse is one with night temperatures of 60 to 65 degrees, or even, for some very unusual tropical plants, as high as 70 degrees. The decision about the night temperature of the greenhouse has to be made by the gardener according to the type of plants wanted, and the heating budget. Even small greenhouses can be partitioned and

The Victory Garden greenhouse on a warm spring day

zone-heated, so that two or more environments can be provided, allowing the gardener the luxury of growing plants with widely varying needs.

Furnishings Most owners equip their greenhouses with waist-high benches to make it easy to maintain their plants. The benches, usually of wood, have slotted bottoms to insure good drainage and raised sides to hold soil in place. Unless you use redwood to construct your benches, make the wood rot-resistant with *green* No. 10 Cuprinol. The fumes from most other wood preservatives are deadly

to plant life. This particular form of Cuprinol contains copper naphthanate which is harmless to plants, yet deadly to wood-decaying fungi and bacteria.

In a small greenhouse most plants are grown in pots set on the bottom of a bench, but the bench may be filled with a fertile soil mixture to grow a crop suitable to that method of culture, such as snapdragons, chrysanthemums, and carnations. Benches allow gardeners to vary crops from season to season. Bench placement is optional: you may want an open area for a wrought iron table and chairs where you can picnic in splendor in the midst of a February blizzard. Plan to reserve some floor space without benches so that you can grow tall plants that need all the headroom you can provide. The greenhouse manufacturer will be pleased to advise you in the design of benches.

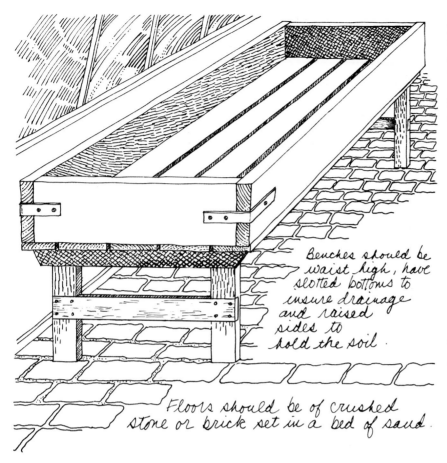

Benches should be waist high, have slotted bottoms to insure drainage and raised sides to hold the soil.

Floors should be of crushed stone or brick set in a bed of sand.

Bibliography Greenhouses can, but need not, be technically complicated pieces of equipment. If you have always grown plants indoors at a bright window, you will find running a greenhouse a wonderful, exciting experience because the added light and humidity make even difficult plants relatively easy to grow. The information on plant care given in this book is applicable to both windowsills and greenhouses. If you wish to read further on the subject of greenhouses, try these books. The first one deals primarily with the care of specific plants and when to do certain cultural procedures; Mr. Pierce's book is a thorough treatise on the subject of greenhouses themselves and how to get the most from them.

Crockett, James Underwood. *Greenhouse Gardening as a Hobby.* New York: Doubleday and Company, 1961.

Pierce, John H. *Greenhouse Grow How.* Seattle, Washington: Plants Alive Books, 1977.

Because the floor of a greenhouse is usually damp, provision must be made for drainage. You shouldn't simply pave the floor with concrete — concrete does not absorb water and it becomes extremely heat retentive during the summer. A concrete *path*, though not my choice, would be fine as long as a porous material such as pebbles were used under the benches. In the Victory Garden greenhouse we use a 6- to 8-inch bed of ¾-inch crushed rock; it drains well and needs only an occasional raking to smooth out the surface. In my home greenhouse I have a floor of used brick, which is porous, over a bed of sand and pebbles. It's handsome, well drained, and maintenance free, though more complicated and expensive to install than a simple pebble floor.

DEC

Aloe
Arabian Violet
Chinese Hibiscus
Christmas Cactus
Dieffenbachia
Fittonia
Flowering Maple
Gloxinia
Kalanchoe
Norfolk Island Pine
Poinsettia
Wandering Jew

Feature: Buying Houseplants

Gloxinias

DEC

Houseplants have been popular Christmas presents for years, and they're excellent gifts that bring joy for months after the holiday season has passed. The December feature lists plants according to the conditions they need to grow well, and it would pay to consult it before you set your money down. If you're not sure what kinds of conditions your friend can offer, buy a tolerant plant that will put up with nearly any conditions, such as a Norfolk Island pine or a poinsettia. If your friend has a little experience with plants, an orchid would make a splendid gift. All three listed in this book are relatively easy to care for and bring long-term satisfaction.

In spite of the preoccupation with the busy holiday period, houseplants need tending this month. This is the last opportunity to plant freesia corms; they'll come into flower in March. Zebra plants, which bloom in the fall, should be cut back to the second-lowest node on the stem and repotted about a month after the flowers fade.

If you're intending to buy a cut Christmas tree for the holiday, here are some pointers. First of all, try to buy a freshly cut tree. The way to test for this is to tug at a few needles. If they pull easily from the branch, the tree has been cut for some length of time, and it won't last as long indoors as a fresh tree. Before you set the tree up at home, cut off an inch or two of the base of the trunk to expose fresh cells that are efficient at drawing water up into the tree. When you set the tree up, make sure the bottom of the stem is in a couple of inches of water and keep adding more water as it's needed. This will keep the tree fresher longer.

By the way, if you love live greenery for the holidays but don't have the space for a large Christmas tree, try decorating a Norfolk Island pine, which has the shape and needlelike foliage of pine trees, and yet is small enough to fit into most rooms without crowding. Best of all, it lives on year after year.

Aloe *(Aloe)* The aloe has been grown in pots for centuries, not only for its good looks but because its succulent leaves contain a sticky fluid that offers quick relief from cuts and burns; it's said that the Roman legions carried aloe plants with them to treat wounds and there are many medications for the skin on the market today that include juices from this plant. A native of Cape Verde, the Canary Islands, and Madeira, the aloe, usually referred to as the true aloe (*A. vera* but more correctly as *A. barbadensis*), produces dagger-shaped leaves up to 2 feet long and lined with spines that look sharp but are soft and harmless.

The aloe is a very easy-to-grow houseplant. It prefers to have at least half days of sunlight, but it does fairly well

Aloe *(Aloe)*

291

in bright indirect light. The night temperatures should be in the 50s and the days at 70 or so for the plant to do its best. Aloe leaves are fleshy and thick and can hold moisture, so water these plants only after the soil has had a chance to dry out somewhat. I feed my plants only once yearly, in the fall, with a half-strength fertilizer. Aloe plants can be propagated at any time of year from the suckers that grow at the soil line. The soil should be well drained; I use equal parts potting soil and sharp sand with a dusting of ground limestone and bone meal. When you work with the plant, be careful not to scratch the leaves or break them off. They will continue to live if they're injured, but they will show their scars forever.

⬚   **Arabian Violet** *(Exacum)* The Arabian violet (*E. affine*) is a dainty, fragrant houseplant whose cheerful blue or white flowers are held above the mass of small leaves; I've usually grown the blue varieties because flowers of this color are so hard to come by. The plants are best-looking when they're young and no taller than 8 inches or so; as they

The flowers of the Arabian violet, slightly smaller than those of the African violet and borne continuously through the year

Allied Florists Association
of Greater Baltimore

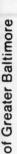

(For further information see your professional florist.)

CARE TIPS FOR CUT FLOWERS

1. Cut flower stems slantwise or straight accros with a sharp knife.
   Never use shears. Remove any foliage below the water line.

2. Place flower stems in water as hot as hand can stand and set in
   a cool place for an hour or two. Then arrange, using fresh cool
   water in your vase or container.

3. Place the flower arrangement in a cool location, away from heat
   and drafts. Keep them in a cool place overnight.

4. If you use special cut flower perservatives which prolong the life
   of flowers and arrest bacterial action in the water, just add
   water to the container as needed. If you dont't use preservatives,
   the following should be done every day: change water, scrub
   containers clean, cut the flower stems with a sharp knife.

These simple suggestions, methodically followed will help a great deal
toward keeping flowers lovely longer.

age they become straggly and unattractive. I was given a plant one July that was still in bloom the following spring, but it was past its prime. Arabian violets are actually biennials, but they're treated as annuals when they're grown indoors and discarded when their good looks have gone by.

These plants are at their best in bright indirect light, with night temperatures no cooler than 60 degrees. I pot them in a mix of 2 parts peat moss, 1 part soil, and 1 part either perlite or sand, and I keep this mix constantly moist throughout their lifetimes. Every other week I add some mild houseplant fertilizer to the water. When the plants begin to lose their looks, I take cuttings and throw the old plants away. This can be done at any time of the year, as their blooming period is related to their age, not to the season. Arabian violets can be started from seed, too, but seed-sown plants take longer to reach flowering size. Seeds sown in the spring will be ready to flower in the fall and winter.

Arabian Violet (*Exacum*)

Chinese Hibiscus *(Hibiscus)* I have two Chinese hibiscus plants (*H. rosa-sinensis*) in my collection. One is a red-flowered plant that I've had since 1968. The other, a double-flowered yellow variety, is one I brought to Massachusetts from a Texas nursery in the early 1950s; it has hardly missed a day of blossoming in all those years. I keep both plants pruned to about 3 feet tall, though if I let them they would probably grow to nearly twice that height; in the tropics, where they're standard fixtures in even the most simple of gardens, they can reach a height of 20 feet or more. Whether indoors or out, the larger the plant, the more flowers it bears. Hibiscus fanciers have produced varieties with blooms that are nearly 12 inches across, but most plants, like my own, have flowers about 5 inches in diameter. The flowers last for 1 day only, but oddly enough they last the same length of time whether left on the plant, cut and floated in water, or worn in the hair as is the custom among young Hawaiian girls. When nightfall comes, the flowers die, regardless.

Given proper conditions, Chinese hibiscus plants grow actively month after month and year after year; they don't have a resting period, and they don't ever die of old age. They want sunshine for at least 4 hours every day, constantly moist soil, and a monthly feeding with houseplant fertilizer. (If the foliage starts to yellow, the plant probably needs nitrogen. If you're using a low-nitrogen fertilizer, switch to one that's higher in this green-growth element.) They need warmth in order to maintain active growth, with temperatures in the middle 60s at night and 70 degrees or warmer during the day.

Chinese Hibiscus (*Hibiscus*)

The flowers of the Chinese hibiscus open in the morning and die at dusk

New plants are easily propagated from stem cuttings inserted in moist sand, although they are often slow to root; providing bottom heat of 65 to 70 degrees will speed up the rooting process. The best time to repot Chinese hibiscuses is in the early spring; use any commercial potting soil. Spring is also the best time to cut an overgrown plant back severely. Even if cut to within 4 inches of the soil level it will make fine new growth rapidly at that time of the year.

Christmas Cactus *(Schlumbergera)* Two similar, but slightly different species of *Schlumbergera* are commonly grown houseplants that are the basis for many questions sent to Crockett's Victory Garden. *Schlumbergera bridgesii,* the Christmas cactus, has smooth stem segments while *S. truncata,* the Thanksgiving or crab cactus, has hook-like appendages on each stem segment. But they have been hybridized so that varying stem shapes appear, as well as handsome 3-inch cerise, salmon, pink, violet, or multicolored flowers in the autumn. They are often confused with the Easter cactus, *Rhipsalidopsis gaertneri,* which also has seg-

294

mented stems, but bears red flowers in the spring. All are epiphytic cactuses that are native to the jungles of South America.

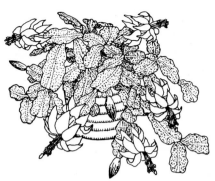

It is not particularly difficult to get the plants to blossom every winter, as long as they're given some special attention during their rest period, from early September until flower buds form. Their flowering is related to the length of the day and to night temperature. If the fall nights are in the 50- to 55-degree range, the buds will form regardless of how many hours of darkness the plants receive. But if the night temperatures are in the 60- to 65-degree range, the plants need 13 hours of uninterrupted darkness every night; either set the plants off in an unused room, or drape them with a dark cloth if they're in a lighted room. (A plant left outdoors until frost is likely to have had enough cool nights to have formed its buds by the time it's brought inside.) During the fall, while the buds are forming, stop fertilizing the plants and give them only enough water to keep the green stems from shriveling.

If you buy a plant in bloom, set it in a bright spot out of the sun; too much light will make the leaves turn yellow. Average household temperatures are fine. Keep the soil constantly moist and feed the plants every other week. The plants will stop blooming through the late winter or early spring, but continue to give them this care until the fall. Set the plants outside for the summer in a shady spot, and bring them inside before the first frost.

Christmas Cactus *(Schlumbergera)*

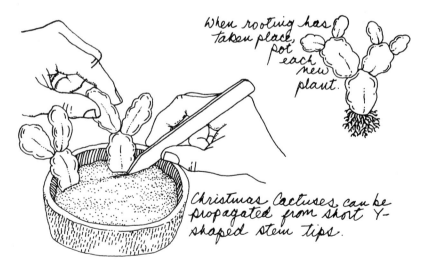

When rooting has taken place, pot each new plant.

Christmas Cactuses can be propagated from short Y-shaped stem tips.

Once the flower buds appear, the night temperatures and hours of darkness no longer matter. Set the plant where you can enjoy it and see the buds open. From the time the buds appear, keep the soil moist and feed the plant every other week.

These cactuses flower best when they're rather pot-bound, but if they become too crowded for space, they don't bloom well. So when you notice a loss of flower production, or if it's been several years since the plant was repotted, move it on to a larger pot in the spring before you set the plant out for the summer.

They are most easily propagated from a section of the stem tip. The cuttings can be started at any time of the year.

Dieffenbachia *(Dieffenbachia)* These natives of the tropical forests of Costa Rica and Colombia take their formal name from the German botanist Herr J. F. Dieffenbach, who ran the imperial gardens at Schönbrunn Castle in

Vienna in the nineteenth century. They take their two common names, dumbcane and mother-in-law's tongue, from the fact that their leaves contain calcium oxalate crystals, which if chewed cause temporary speechlessness. And pain, I hasten to add.

Dieffenbachias (dee-fen-*bak*-ia) have been popular houseplants for well over a century because they thrive in warm, sunless conditions. Ideally, dieffenbachias want bright indirect light (or about 400 foot-candles 14 to 16 hours daily if they must grow entirely with artificial light), day temperatures between 75 and 85 degrees, and nights no cooler than 65 degrees. This is warmer than most houses today so it's best to give the plant a cozy spot out of drafts. The plants should be allowed to dry out somewhat between thorough waterings.

For many years after dieffenbachias became popular houseplants, the only kinds available were native species whose ancestors came directly from the jungle. Now there are some fifty different species and varieties, including some exceptional hybrids and mutations. Of these, I recommend four in particular that make good houseplants. They vary primarily in the size and coloration of the leaves. The exotic dumbcane, *D. exotica*, is one of the best for the home gardener: it produces 8- to 10-inch firm dull green leaves spotted with white, and it stays small and manageable longer than some of the other varieties. The Bause dieffenbachia, *D. bausei*, is a hybrid with larger greenish yellow leaves dappled with green and white and edged with green. The handsome variety Rudolph Roehrs bears 10- to 12-inch gold-green leaves with white blotches and dark green edges and ribs, and the charming dumbcane, *D. amoena*, has 18-inch blue-green leaves faintly marked with white; it is particularly tolerant of dim light.

Dieffenbachias are at their best when they're young, because as they grow they lose their lower foliage and eventually wind up looking like tall, wobbly palm trees; most florists sell "mature" plants when they're about 2½ feet tall. I have no interest in them when they start aiming for the ceiling, so I usually cut the plants back to within 5 inches or so from the rim of the pot when they begin to look ungainly. If I want some new plants as well, there's a way to propagate them and rejuvenate the old growth at the same time. The first step is to air-layer the plant. This is a technique that involves encouraging the plant to produce roots high on the stem where the leaves are fresh and robust. It can take several months for the roots to form, but once they do the stem can be cut just below them, and the new, short plant given its own pot.

A single specimen of the charming dumbcane

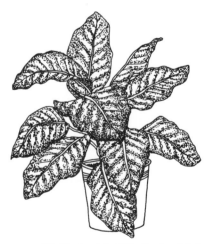

Dieffenbachia *(Dieffenbachia)*

297

2. Lay the stalk in a bed of moist sand. New plants will grow along its length.

1. After the air-layer has taken and the stalk cut to 4" to 6" from soil line, the extra length of stalk can be used for cane cuttings.

4 to 6"

3. When the new plants are about 2" tall, cut them free with a sharp knife and plant them individually.

cut here

Cross section of stalk

Once the air-layer has taken, there is still plenty of life left in the dieffenbachia stalk, and dozens of new plants can be propagated from it. If the stalk is cut down nearly to soil level, a new plant will grow from the old stump. Then only the length of stalk remains, and it too will produce offspring. (For complete instructions on air-layering and cane cuttings, see the April feature.) Dieffenbachias grow happily when potted in packaged general-purpose potting soil.

Fittonia (*Fittonia*)

■ **Fittonia** (*Fittonia*) Fittonias are creeping or trailing plants whose leaves are so intricately veined (or "nerved") that even a small plant or two can add texture and sparkle to a plant collection. There are two prominent varieties: *F. verschaffeltii* (known as the red-nerved fittonia) has deep green leaves and red veins; *F. verschaffeltii argyoneura*, whose leaves are bright green with silvery veins, is often referred to as a silver-nerved fittonia or a mosaic plant.

I would mislead you if I were to say fittonias are easy to grow. On the contrary, they require such warm, shadowless, humid conditions that they are best off in a terrarium. But if they're pampered a bit by misting the foliage with tepid water occasionally and given the light of a north window (or 150 foot-candles of artificial light 14 to 15 hours daily), set on a tray of pebbles and water so the soil is moist all the time, and kept in a spot where the temperatures are between 75 and 85 with nights no lower than the mid-60s, they'll do fine. They also need to be fed monthly with any houseplant fertilizer at half strength, waiting 3 or 4 months

after they've been bought or repotted before the feeding starts.

A mat of creeping silver-nerved fittonia

Fittonias (fit-*o*-nia) don't age particularly well, and as they approach their first birthday they can look straggly and out of shape. Before that ugly stage arrives I start new plants from stem cuttings, which root easily in sand. When the roots take hold I pot the new plants in African violet soil, available from any florist or garden center.

Flowering Maple *(Abutilon)* A century ago, these plants with the maplelike foliage were known as parlor maples. When the parlor went out of vogue, in name anyway, so did the plant. Now it's come back into fashion with the more up-to-date name of flowering maple. Of course, neither name is really accurate. The *Abutilon* (ab-*yew*-til-on) is not a maple at all, but a genus of about 90 species of small South American shrubs, sometimes semiclimbing.

If properly cared for, the flowering maple is rarely without blossoms. In grandmother's day, most varieties had bell-shaped blossoms of gold and crimson, but with the mod-

299

Flowering Maple *(Abutilon)*

ern hybrids there are several new colors, including shades of pink and red as well as yellow, orange, salmon, purple, and snowy white. The flowers on hybrid plants are mostly an inch or more long, often with the delicate texture of crepe paper.

As handsome as the flowers are, they are not the plants' only source of color; some varieties have bright variegated foliage that complements the blooms. Gold Dust has orange flowers and green leaves mottled with gold; Souvenir de Bonn has salmon flowers veined with crimson, and green leaves with creamy borders; *A. megapotamicum variegatum* has stunning yellow-and-red flowers and slender green leaves marked with ivory and yellow; *A. striatum aureamaculatum* has reddish orange flowers and green leaves with yellow blotches; and *A. striatum thompsonii* has orange-salmon flowers and green leaves with chartreuse mottling.

300

Their needs are relatively uncomplicated. They're happiest in bright reflected light. They are most content if the night temperatures are in the low 50s and the days some 20 degrees warmer. I plant them in any commercial potting soil or in a combination of 2 parts loam, 1 part peat moss, and 1 part coarse sand, and I keep this medium constantly moist. Once a month on my fertilizer tour I feed them with an ordinary houseplant fertilizer; this is particularly important with flowering maples as they drop their lower leaves if they're underfed. Flowering maples are very fast-growing plants that need frequent repotting — as often as every 4 months or so.

If these needs are met a flowering maple blossoms month after month, but it produces more flowers in the spring, summer, and fall than in the winter. As long as the flowering tapers off anyway at this time of the year, I take the opportunity either this month or next to do the pruning necessary to keep the plant healthy and within a height range of 18 to 30 inches. This usually means healthy new shoots by March. I've sometimes used these young flowering maples as bedding and window box plants; they are a welcome change from the usual petunia-and-geranium syndrome and blossom profusely outdoors.

Flowering maple cuttings root readily at any time. Sometimes I take cuttings late in the summer so they'll grow slowly through the winter and come into their prime the following spring and summer.

You can also propagate these plants from seed, and the seedlings, being of hybrid origin, sometimes yield delightful surprises. Cuttings from selected named varieties, however, assure a gardener that the plants are of known quality, far better than those ordinarily grown from seeds.

Gloxinia (*Sinningia*) In 1845, a Scottish gardener named John Fyfe discovered among his gloxinia seedlings, which normally had nodding slipper-shaped flowers, one whose blossoms were symmetrically bell-shaped and held erect. All of today's varieties, with their vivid colors and single or double flowers, are the descendants of that single, chance seedling.

Gloxinias are related to African violets, and when they're in flower they need the same growing conditions. Give them bright indirect light, night temperatures in the high 60s, and monthly feedings. Keep the soil barely moist all the time, but be gentle, as gloxinias are extremely sensitive to excess moisture. Don't let water get into the crowns of buds or onto new foliage, and when you bottom-water, make sure the pots don't sit in the water beyond the time

Gloxinia *(Sinningia)*

Norfolk Island Pine *(Araucaria)*

early October. These plants are not as extremely light-sensitive as poinsettias are, so having the plants in bloom in time for Christmas shouldn't be difficult at all.

🪴 **Norfolk Island Pine** *(Araucaria)* The Norfolk Island pine is one of my favorite houseplants. I like its shape, its needlelike foliage, and its capacity for survival. Though it's popular as a Christmas tree and most prominent on the market at this time of the year, it is a full-time foliage plant that will live year after year. When you buy a Norfolk Island pine (*A. heterophylla*), don't look for a bargain. These plants are such guaranteed sellers at Christmastime that they are sometimes grown too quickly in order to be ready

304

for the market; they look sparse when they're young, and they will never make up for their bad start. Pay a little more for a full, densely foliated plant that will be handsome all its life. Don't think that you have to buy a large plant, though. In normal household conditions, a Norfolk Island pine will put on 3 to 6 inches of height a year. (In the wild on tiny Norfolk Island in the South Pacific, they can grow as tall as 200 feet with trunks 10 feet in diameter.)

A Norfolk Island pine

Norfolk Island pines are very easy-to-please house-plants. They will grow in full sun or bright indirect light. They'll actually survive in quite dim light. Eventually old plants will lose some of their lower branches, and there is no way to get them back or encourage new ones to grow. They do best if the night temperatures are in the low 50s with daytime readings near 70, but they'll tolerate any temperature in the 45- to 85-degree range. Keep the soil constantly moist and feed the plants every 3 or 4 months. They can stay in the same pot for 3 years or so; when they're overcrowded, repot them in African violet soil.

Norfolk Island pines are unique among popular foliage plants in that they are not propagated vegetatively nowadays. If the tip of the plant is used for a stem cutting, a healthy new young tree will be born, but the parent will send up multiple branches from the point of the cut and its shape will be destroyed. Any cutting taken from the tip of a branch will grow sideways, as the branches do on the tree. There is no way around either of these eccentricities. The plants can be started from seed but it's a very slow proposition. My advice is to buy a healthy, small plant and leave propagation to the experts.

⊽ **Poinsettia** *(Euphorbia)* In 1825, Joel Roberts Poinsett was appointed United States Minister to Mexico. Four years later he found himself in political trouble and returned to his home in South Carolina, bringing with him cuttings of the beautiful Mexican wildflower that continues to bear his name to this day. But the plant that we know now is very different from its Mexican forebears, and different from the houseplants that were grown for Christmas color for the next 130 years. Throughout that entire period of time, poinsettias were short-lived plants. Keeping a Christmas plant good-looking until New Year's Eve required all a gardener's skill and attention. The colorful bracts lasted, but the foliage dropped and left the flowers stranded atop naked stems. Then, in 1963, a mutation was discovered that held its leaves; that plant was used in further plant breeding and its genetic characteristics were imparted to plants sold today. As a result of this chance find, it's not unusual for poinset-

Poinsettia *(Euphorbia)*

305

tias (*E. pulcherrima*) to bloom well into the summer, and retain their leaves the entire time.

A poinsettia should be given sun for at least half the day, and be set in a spot free of drafts. Give it night temperatures in the 50s or low 60s, with days 70 degrees or warmer. Let the soil dry out slightly between thorough waterings, and don't feed it at all.

Even with the longer life these plants now enjoy, they do eventually pass their prime. Many gardeners throw them away at this point, but there's no reason to do so. If they're cut back and repotted when the bracts fade in the summer, and then given careful attention through the fall while they're forming their buds, they'll bloom every winter for years to come.

A well-grown, compact poinsettia plant

In the wild, poinsettia plants form their buds over a 6-week period beginning with the autumnal equinox, when the nights become progressively longer, and then bloom in December. If indoor plants are given a controlled daily pattern of light and darkness, they will do the same. So starting around September 21 and continuing through the end of October, give them 9 to 10 hours of bright indirect or sunny light and 14 to 15 hours of darkness, with the night temperatures at about 65 degrees. I find that the best way to guarantee that the plants aren't forgotten is to set up a routine, covering them at 5 o'clock every afternoon and uncovering them at 7 or 8 the next morning. The plants are extraordinarily sensitive about this routine, and will refuse to form buds if light penetrates their darkness. So their night spot has to be absolutely light-tight. You might try putting them in the back of a closet, or in an unused but warm room, or under a completely opaque black cloth. With this attention, the buds will form through October and by the first of November the plants can be treated like normal members of the family again.

Wandering Jew *(Tradescantia)* Wandering Jews are old-time houseplants. In the days before florists raised and sold plants as a business, gardeners would pass cuttings along to their friends, who would continue the practice with their friends. The name wandering Jew was a reference to their reputation as travelers, like many of the Jews of Europe who moved from town to town, having no homeland to call their own.

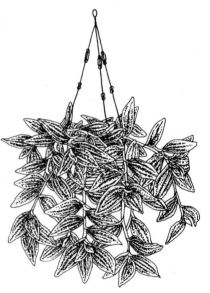

Wandering Jew *(Tradescantia)*

Many plants now carry this common name, including members of two different genera: *Tradescantia* and *Zebrina*. This shouldn't cause the home gardener any concern. All plants sold as wandering Jews, regardless of their botanical name, are easy-to-grow houseplants that require the same care. Give them bright indirect light; the variegated types will lose their pale markings if the light is too dim. The night temperatures should be in the 50s. Allow the soil to dry out moderately between thorough waterings, and feed the plants every other week with half-strength fertilizer.

Wandering Jews do not age well. As they near their first birthday they lose their foliage at the base. They can't be cut back satisfactorily, so when the plants begin to look straggly, take a few cuttings. They will be so eager to root that it isn't necessary to use a rooting medium. Just fill a 6-inch hanging pot with commercial potting soil, moisten it, and set four cuttings around the edge of the pot, with a fifth in the center. They will root and grow and present a fine cascade of foliage within a month or two.

*The markings on the leaves of the
wandering Jew vary noticeably,
even on the same plant*

Q: A friend of mine is a specialist in cactuses and
succulents. When I went to see him recently I asked him for
a plant that wouldn't die, even in my amateurish hands. He
suggested a haworthia, which is a plant I've never heard of.
Can you give me any advice?

A: In the late 1960s my wife, Margaret, and I attended an exhibition of succulent plants in California. As
luck would have it, Margaret won the door prize, a plant
called the pearly haworthia or pearl plant (*Haworthia mar-
garitifera*). Ever since we returned home, that plant has
been sitting on a windowsill above the kitchen sink. It's had
indifferent care, often going without water for a week or

more at a time. Yet it continues to thrive and occasionally sends up slender flower spikes bearing tiny white blossoms. I think your friend has given you a good suggestion.

Q: I notice my local florist sells forget-me-nots during the winter. I just love them. Could I grow them indoors?

A: I'm afraid not. The forget-me-not (*Myosotis sylvatica*) is a plant that needs temperatures so cool that they can't live indoors. But if you have a cool greenhouse, you'll have no trouble at all. I usually sow a few seeds every 6 weeks from August through January and have flowers from late fall until late spring. The plants grow to be only 10 or 12 inches tall, but they are tall enough to produce lovely cut flowers. Keep the soil moist under them all the time and feed them once a month with any houseplant fertilizer until the flower buds open. They're annuals, so when the flowering season is over the plants should be discarded.

Q: When my daughter was married, she carried stephanotis flowers in her bouquet. They were so beautiful that I'd like to try to grow them in my home. Is this at all possible?

A: Yes. All you need is a warm sunny windowsill. The stephanotis is a climbing vine and should be trained around some sort of support that will allow the vine to grow longer and longer without getting too tall. I have a plant whose runners are probably 20 feet long, but they're wound around and around a support only 3 feet tall. The stephanotis blossoms most freely from late spring until late fall, but it sends up a few flowers at other seasons, too. From March through midfall, keep the soil constantly moist and feed the plant every month with a houseplant fertilizer. For the rest of the year, let the soil dry out between waterings and don't feed the plant at all. You can propagate the stephanotis either from stem cuttings or from seeds.

BUYING HOUSE-PLANTS

Gardening is America's number-1 hobby, its participants far outnumbering those of all sports combined. As the nationwide interest in plants increases, more and more retail shops, including department and grocery stores as well as traditional florists and garden centers, are selling more and more houseplants. It is my belief that it's best to buy from professionals who truly understand plants and their needs. Such persons are plant lovers themselves or they wouldn't be in the business. Too many supermarkets tend to load up a counter in the produce department during a holiday season with a few plants, apparently cheap, but usually overpriced for the value they offer. These plants are treated as "merchandise" and are seldom given enough light to maintain their health for more than a few days. Moreover, few of these markets employ a person trained to provide such a basic need as correct watering. Ethylene gas given off by ripening fruit on nearby counters tends to shorten the beauty life of many flowers. Some few stores are putting money and thought into their plant sections, providing carefully selected plants with the environment and expert care that will keep them healthy, but such establishments are very much in the minority.

Beware of "bargains" in horticulture. Invariably your reputable local florist or garden center who has to operate responsibly in your community in order to stay in business offers you far better value than do organizations that sell plants only on an occasional basis.

In any event, look a plant over carefully before you put your money down. Buy pest-free plants with good color, healthy leaves, and a full shape. If they look poor in the shop, they are bound to look poorer after a few days in the dim light of your house or apartment. If you're buying a flowering plant, select one with as many buds as possible. If the flowers are already open, you've missed some of the beauty life of the plant.

By contrast, if you see a plant being sold at a very low price, be especially cautious. It may be that the seller is trying to clear away space for incoming plants, and the plant is perfectly healthy. This is sometimes true of flowering plants nearing the end of their cycle; you may as well buy them inexpensively, but do not expect them to perform as well as would younger plants. It's also true that some houseplants are sold inexpensively because they have been shortchanged in their youth. They may not have been given time in the greenhouse to develop the root systems they will need for vigorous growth. They may not have been acclimated to the dim light conditions they will meet in the home. They may have been grown too quickly, with great amounts of light and moisture and fertilizer, which added to their size at the expense of their strength. Let your eye and common sense be your judge.

All stores that market houseplants concentrate on those that are known to sell well. The small shop owner can't afford to buy obscure plants. So gardeners never see them, and the demand isn't created. But there are many plants that do well in the home that can be bought through the mail. Usually they are young plants that have been carefully packaged for shipment. You may be disappointed at their size, but in many cases this is the only way to start a collection. There are several companies that serve the mail-order need, and they often advertise in horticultural magazines.

When you select a houseplant, make sure it's one for which you can provide good growing conditions. Start with easy-to-care-for plants. If you have good luck, branch out into more complicated plants. There is no quicker way to kill your enthusiasm for gardening than by starting with plants that require special attention you may not be able to give them.

The most important criteria in a plant's needs are light and temperature. Most gardeners can follow directions, and keep plants properly moistened and fed. But you can't manufacture sunlight where none exists, or vary the temperature you find comfortable or economical in order to suit your plants. Some gardeners find that they can only meet certain plants' needs in a remote section of the house. They buy two sets of these plants, and rotate them, giving each set a week or two of good growing conditions alternated with a similar period in poorer conditions in a more prominent spot. This seems to work very well.

The following lists organize the houseplants included in this book according to the light and temperature they need for ideal growth.

	Sunlight		Bright Indirect Light	
Normal: Nights 50-65 Degrees F.	Aloe Amaryllis Bougainvillea Boxwood Burro's Tail Calamondin Orange Calla Lily Century Plant Chinese Hibiscus Copperleaf Echeveria Geranium Golden Trumpet Jade Plant Jerusalem Cherry Kalanchoe Lantana Marigold Marguerite Miniature Rose Moses-in-the-Cradle Natal Plum Norfolk Island Pine Ornamental Pepper Oxalis	Panda Plant Passionflower Petunia Pineapple Pittosporum Ponytail Plant Queen's Tears Rosemary Shrimp Plant Silk-Oak Sweet Olive Umbrella Plant Wax Begonia Wax Plant	Aloe Arabian Violet Artillery Plant Boston Fern Boxwood Browallia Burro's Tail Caladium Cast-Iron Plant Cattleya Orchid Chinese Evergreen Christmas Cactus Clivia English Ivy Flame Violet Flowering Maple Glory Bower Gold-Dust Plant Grape Ivy Hydrangea Impatiens Madagascar Periwinkle Maidenhair Fern Moses-in-the-Cradle Norfolk Island Pine	Orchid Cactus Peperomia Pittosporum Podocarpus Rabbit's-Foot Fern Rex Begonia Rieger Begonia Silk-Oak Spider Plant Staghorn Fern Star Jasmine Strawberry Begonia Striped Inch Plant Swedish Ivy Sweet Olive Sword Plant Umbrella Plant Urn Plant Wandering Jew Wax Begonia Wax Plant Zebra Plant
Cool: Nights below 50 Degrees F.	Cape Cowslip Chrysanthemum Cineraria Cyclamen Fatsia Freesia Gardenia Venus Flytrap		Azalea Calceolaria Camellia Cyclamen Easter Lily Euonymus Fatsia Fuchsia Piggyback Plant Primrose String-of-Beads	
Warm: Nights above 65 Degrees F.	Coffee Croton False Aralia Hawaiian Ti Poinsettia Purple Passion Vine Rubber Tree Sanseveria Schefflera Screw-Pine Weeping Fig		Aluminum Plant African Violet Asparagus Fern Cape Primrose Coleus Devil's Ivy Dieffenbachia Dracaena False Aralia Fittonia Flamingo Flower Gloxinia Lipstick Plant Monstera Moth Orchid	Palms Paphiopedilum Philodendron Prayer Plant Rubber Tree Sanseveria Schefflera Screw-Pine Spathiphyllum Weeping Fig

APPENDIX: ON THE NAMING OF PLANTS

Every week the Victory Garden's mailbox bulges with letters from gardeners who watch the show. They write asking for advice about the blight on their flowers and the bugs on their vegetables, and they write about their houseplants. The questions that have to do with outdoor gardening are as varied as the gardeners, but many of the houseplant questions have a common theme. "A friend has given me a plant with tall, stiff leaves. I think she called it a snake, but my gardening book doesn't list anything by that name and I don't know what to do for the plant. Help!" "I have just bought a plant that was labeled with a long name having something to do with Moses. I've lost the label and now I don't know how to care for the plant, or how to track it down." The writers of these letters are facing a problem that has dogged plant lovers for years: accurate identification.

Most gardeners know plants by their nicknames, or common names. At their best, the common names used today are colorful and amusing and oddly descriptive. Prayer plants, for instance, are so named because they raise their leaves upward in the darkness. The new leaves of piggyback plants sit perched on the older foliage. And the bracts of shrimp plants form curved blossom clusters that resemble shrimp.

At their worst, though, common names are baffling and contradictory. Jerusalem cherries are native to the Madeira Islands; they do not grow wild in or near Jerusalem; their bright orange berries look a little like cherries, but they are in no way related and they definitely are not for eating! There's a pretty, everblooming plant known as patient Lucy, impatiens, and busy Lizzie. A large vining plant native to Central America is called monstera, hurricane plant, Swiss cheese plant, ceriman, cut-leaf philodendron, and split-leaf philodendron. Some of these titles have obvious application to the plant, but the others are perplexing at best. A popular wide-leaved fern is known both as a bird's-nest fern and a spleenwort. It might be argued that there's a resemblance between the plant and a bird's nest, though I don't find it a flattering comparison, but the term spleenwort is lost on modern gardeners who are unfamiliar with the plant's former use in treating diseases of the liver and spleen.

Multiply the problem by the number of different languages spoken in the world, and it is clear why scholars centuries ago adopted Latin as the official language of horticulture. They, in fact, hybridized ancient Latin, adding new words as they were necessary, Latinizing them and treating them according to the rules of Latin grammar. This common language brought all the world's botanists into easy communication with each other, regardless of their own native tongues.

Scholars have always been intent on detail, so the earliest Latin descriptions were far more accurate than the more familiar common names. For instance, the plant we know as the carnation was referred to by one Renaissance botanist, in bastardized Latin that makes a linguist cringe, as "*Dianthus floribus solitariis, squamis calycinis subovatis brevissimus, corollis crenatis.*" This described the plant as a single-flowered carnation having a scalelike calyx (the green segments beneath the petals), a very short ovary, and shallow, rounded, toothlike edges on the flower petals. This description identified the plant without question, but there were difficulties. For one, the phrase was cumbersome. For another, it was not accepted as the *only* way to describe a carnation; other scholars used descriptions that were every bit as accurate, but different. And, as accurate as these Latin phrases were, they did not provide any help in understanding the organization of the plant world; they simply made it possible for botanists to converse intelligently about individual plants.

Descriptive Latin was the terminology of botany when Carolus Linnaeus was born in Sweden in 1707. (Following the custom among the scholars of the day, the Swedish family name had been dropped in favor of a Latin name, and thus it was that Carl Ingemarsson became Carolus Linnaeus.) His genius was his ability to see simplicity and order where others saw only workable but ponderous chaos. He is the man who rethought and rewrote the language of botany. His first contribution to his field was his proclamation of the theory of a sexual life in plants. This had been suggested earlier, but was not seriously entertained as the principle upon which the green world is organized. The significance of this theory may be lost to modern readers. Before it was accepted, plants were categorized according to their appearance or their habits of growth. These systems provided some insights, but missed the essential point: that plants are members of families with genetic similarities. His declaration concerning the sexuality of plants and, especially, his contention that many plants were simultaneously male and female raised many a prudish brow. He was attacked by learned

314

men in high places and was forced for two years to leave his post at the university. As one man wrote, "Who would have thought that bluebells, lilies and onions could be up to such immorality?"

Once his theory of plants' sexuality was accepted, Linnaeus devised a shorthand language that would accurately identify both individual types of plants *and* their place within each family, just as my name identifies me as a single individual, Jim, in the family Crockett. With some modifications, the Linnaean system is the one we use today, and it has beautifully stood the test of time. Each plant is given a two-word name, the first word being its genus and the second its species. By this system the laborious carnation description cited above was reduced to *Dianthus caryophyllus*. This places the carnation within the genus *Dianthus*, and separates it from other species within the genus. The system has proved to be very adaptable: for instance, if a particular variety of a species is to be identified, its name is written after the species name; varietal names are usually in the vernacular, not Latin. Thus we have *Episcia cupreata* "Chocolate Soldier" or *Dianthus caryophyllus* "Hercules." (In this book I've chosen not to use quotation marks to set off varietal names.)

The system for registering newly discovered plants and their names has not changed much since Linnaeus's time. Once the botanist is certain that he has, indeed, found a new plant, a dried specimen of the plant is carefully mounted and sent to an herbarium, which is a library of plant specimens. There are many herbariums worldwide, some dating back four centuries. Even in the oldest of them, the specimens are intact and readable. A detailed description of the plant accompanies the specimen, along with the Latin name, which the botanist has the privilege of coining. Then the name is registered with an international body of taxonomists who meet at regular intervals to validate the plants new to science. In the United States, new plants can also be registered for patent so that, for a specified length of time, the plants cannot be commercially propagated by anyone other than the patent-holder or his agents, who pay a royalty for each plant they grow. Perhaps the most common of patented plants are roses. New varieties are almost always patented as a protection for the originator against exploitation by competitors. Among houseplants, new varieties of African violets are high on the list of patented plants.

There is a rule in botany that a plant must be known by its oldest name, that is, by the name that accompanies the oldest herbarium specimen of the plant. Because plants are scattered in herbariums around the world without complete cross-indexing, it is common for a plant to undergo a name change when a researcher turns up an older herbarium specimen under a different name. Name changes in botany are always going further into the past of the plant. During the months between the writing of the drafts of this book and the checking of the first sets of galleys, a new volume of *Hortus*, the dictionary of plant names, listed name changes for several of the plants covered in this book. This process is bound to continue through the years. During my own lifetime the familiar garden shrub called Japanese quince has undergone three changes in name. I first learned to call it *Cydonia japonica;* before that it was *Pyrus cydonia* and *Pyrus japonica;* the Romans called it *Mala cydonia.* After *Cydonia japonica* it became *Chaenomeles lagenaria;* now it's called *Chaenomeles speciosa.* As to its next name change, your guess is as good as mine!

Both botanical names and common ones are here to stay and we shouldn't be afraid to use either of them. If you want to be sure of getting the exact plant you want, ask for it by its scientific name; if that approach seems too formal, use the plant's common name. Remember that many plants have identical scientific and common names — calendula, camellia, petunia, anemone, hydrangea, bougainvillea, monstera, podocarpus, caladium, coleus, gardenia, lantana, fuchsia, peperomia, euonymus, fatsia, freesia, narcissus, browallia, chrysanthemum, dracaena, sanseveria, begonia, clivia, cyclamen, pittosporum, spathiphyllum, aloe, fittonia, hibiscus, kalanchoe, and, of course, philodendron! There, you already have a head start toward learning the Latin names of all the plants you see!

INDEX

Boldface page numbers indicate the main entry for a subject.